Gender Studies in Wales
Astudiaethau Rhywedd yng Nghymru

The aim of this series is to fill a current gap in knowledge. As a number of historians, sociologists and literary critics have for some time been pointing out, there is a dearth of published research on the characteristics and effects of gender difference in Wales, both as it affected lives in the past and as it continues to shape present-day experience. Socially constructed concepts of masculine and feminine difference influence every aspect of individuals' lives; experiences in employment, in education, in culture and politics, as well as in personal relationships, are all shaped by them. Ethnic identities are also gendered; a country's history affects its concepts of gender difference so that what is seen as appropriately 'masculine' or 'feminine' varies within different cultures. What is needed in the Welsh context is more detailed research on the ways in which gender difference has operated and continues to operate within Welsh societies. Accordingly, this interdisciplinary and bilingual series of volumes on Gender Studies in Wales, authored by academics who are leaders in their particular fields of study, is designed to explore the diverse aspects of male and female identities in Wales, past and present. The series is bilingual, in the sense that some of its intended volumes will be in Welsh and some in English.

OUR CHANGING LAND

Revisting Gender, Class and Identity in
Contemporary Wales

Edited by

Dawn Mannay

UNIVERSITY OF WALES PRESS
CARDIFF
2016

www.uwp.co.uk

British Library Cataloguing-in-Publication Data
A catalogue record for this book is available from the British Library.

ISBN   9781783168842
e-ISBN   9781783168859

Typeset by Mark Heslington Ltd, Scarborough, North Yorkshire
Printed by CPI Antony Rowe, Chippenham, Wiltshire

Contents

List of Illustrations, Figures and Tables

List of Illustrations

List of Figures

List of Tables

List of Contributors

JANE AARON is Emeritus Professor of English at the University of South Wales. Her publications include the monographs *Pur fel y Dur: Y Gymraes yn Llên Menywod y Bedwaredd Ganrif ar Bymtheg* (Cardiff: University of Wales Press, 1998), which won the Ellis Griffith prize in 1999, *Nineteenth-century Women's Writing in Wales* (Cardiff: University of Wales Press, 2007), which won the Roland Mathias Award in 2009, and *Welsh Gothic* (Cardiff: University of Wales Press, 2013). She co-edited the essay collections *Our Sisters' Land: The Changing Identities of Women in Wales* (Cardiff: University of Wales Press, 1994), *Postcolonial Wales* (Cardiff: University of Wales Press, 2005) and *Gendering Border Studies* (Cardiff: University of Wales Press, 2010), and is also co-editor of the series Gender Studies in Wales and Writers of Wales, both published by the University of Wales Press, and editor of Honno Press's reprint series of Welsh Women's Classics, for which she has edited five volumes.

DAVE ADAMSON is Emeritus Professor of the University of South Wales and was CEO of the Centre for Regeneration Excellence Wales (CREW). Professor Adamson was awarded the OBE for his contribution to regeneration in Wales and his research has shaped policy in Wales at local and national level in this field. Dave's doctoral thesis and subsequent book centred on the historical emergence of Welsh nationalism and his post-doctoral work analysed social class and political change in Wales. More recently, Dave's work has focused on poverty and social exclusion and the identification of innovative strategies for eradicating poverty. His most recent publication is Adamson and Lang *Toward a New Settlement: A Deep Place Approach to Equitable and Sustainable Places* (Merthyr Tydfil: CREW, 2014). He is currently working in Australia on poverty and social housing issues.

NATHAN BOND is a Welsh artist based in the Victoria Park area of Cardiff. Nathan studied art and design at Glan Hafren College and then undertook studies in computer animation at Glamorgan University. Nathan's approach is particularly influenced by the early work of Hanna-Barbera and Walt Disney and he works in the fields of illustration, character design and graphic art. Nathan created the *Dr Who* image to represent Hugh Mackay's chapter, 'The Transformation of the Media in Wales: Technology and Democracy'.

PAUL CHANEY is Professor of Policy and Politics at Cardiff University's School of Social Sciences. His books include *Women, Politics and Constitutional Change* (Cardiff: University of Wales Press, 2007; co-authored with Fiona Mackay and Laura McAllister), *Equality and Public Policy* (Cardiff: University of Wales Press, 2011) and *Public Policy-making and the Devolved State* (Cardiff: University of Wales Press, forthcoming). He was co-editor of *Contemporary Wales: An Annual Review of Economic, Political and Social Research*. He has published widely in leading academic journals. His research interests include: equality and human rights; territorial politics; public policy-making and devolution.

RICHARD COWELL completed undergraduate and postgraduate studies at the Department of Geography, Cambridge University. Since arriving at Cardiff University's School of Planning and Geography, Richard has held appointments as a research fellow, and is presently a Reader (from 2011). Richard's research interests cover theoretical and political aspects of the relationship between public policy and sustainable development, with particular reference to land use planning, public participation and renewable energy. His current work focuses on the relationship between devolution in the British state and the delivery of renewable energy; spatial planning and renewable energy; and community benefits from wind energy development.

JAMIE FEENEY AKA SAPIEN is a hip hop artist, producer and youth worker from Cardiff. He is part of a rap duo called Juxtaposition alongside an artist called S.C.O Double T. Sapien is passionate about making music that challenges social issues and tackles controversial topics. He classes himself as a conscious rapper but feels he is not restricted by his personal views as he thrives to make music that people from all walks of life can relate to. Sapien produced the instrumental for *Politricks*, as well as writing and delivering the lyrics. He feels that the song touches upon important subjects that need to be addressed as they affect people in Wales.

NON GERAINT recently graduated from Cardiff University with a First Class Honours degree in BA Education (BPS). Her third-year dissertation looked at young teenagers' use of and attitudes towards the Welsh language, focusing specifically on pupils at a bilingual school in mid Wales. Her research interests include Welsh language and culture, within education and wider society. She is currently studying for a Primary PGCE at Cardiff Metropolitan University, and is hoping to further pursue her research career after gaining experience working within the field of education.

TASHA HARVEY is a 21-year-old singer songwriter from Tremorfa in Cardiff. She is currently studying commercial music at Bath Spa University. She started writing songs and taught herself to play the guitar about three years ago. As well as writing and performing as a solo artist she is also in a band called Beyond the Blue and they play jazz and indie styles of music. Her musical influences include Tracy Chapman. She wrote this song *Beautiful* about two years ago, to help with anti-bullying work and she recorded this new version of the track to represent the theme on education, and the issues that young people face in educational institutions.

IAN HOMER has been a photographer for the past eighteen years and in that time he has worked for a range of editorial clients from national press to specialist professional journals; Ian has also undertaken public relations, corporate identity and conference work for universities, NGOs and commercial companies. In 2001, Ian helped found PhotoMission (*photomission.com*), an international organization for Christian photographers. Ian has travelled overseas and undertaken work in Africa and India as well as Europe. Latterly, he has been working on diversifying into documentary film. Ian is based in south Wales and he worked with Ministry of Life and the young people in their workshops to develop bespoke images and select images from his existing catalogue to represent each of the chapters in this collection.

KAOS features three rappers: Tempo (Tejan Sesay, 17), Potential (Quasim Falzon, 19) and Biztrumentals (Abel Getahun, 16). Abel also made the instrumental for the *Hybrid Identity* track, which features the singer Chantelle Barani. Quasim was born in London and his mother was also born in the UK. Tejan is originally from Sierra Leone and Abel is from Eritrea, they came to Wales when they were primary school age. Quasim and Tejan are doing a BTEC course with Ministry of Life, and Tejan and Abel are also studying at St David's College. They all live in Cardiff and have all been attending Ministry of Life music workshop sessions for a couple of years. Chantelle is 17, she was born in Wales and she is currently studying at Cardiff and Vale College for an NVQ in Health and Beauty. Chantelle knows KAOS from attending Ministry of Life music sessions and she was invited to feature on the *Hybrid Identity* track.

CAROLINE LLOYD is Professor at the School of Social Sciences, Cardiff University. Her research focuses on the relationships between product markets, labour markets, work organization and skill. She has published widely on issues related to the political economy of skill and the causes and consequences of low-wage work, including co-editing with G. Mason and K. Mayhew, *Low-Wage Work in the United Kingdom* (New York: Russell Sage Foundation, 2008). Her current research is a comparative study of work organization in the service sector, to be published by The Open University Press as *Skills in the Age of Overqualification: Comparing Service Sector Work in Europe*.

HUGH MACKAY was responsible for the Faculty of Social Sciences in Wales, then in Wales, Ireland and Scotland, at The Open University (OU). He holds honorary positions at the OU and at Humboldt University, Berlin. At the OU he was chair of the module 'Contemporary Wales' (D172), which introduces the economy, culture, society and politics of Wales. He was a core member of the module teams that produced 'Understanding Media', 'Culture, Media and Identities', 'Introducing the Social Sciences' and 'Investigating the Information Society'. His research interests focus empirically on new media technologies, and in particular on how users and producers shape technologies. He is working with a group of researchers at universities across Wales with *Cyfrwng* Media Wales, strengthening the network of researchers on the Welsh media and connecting *Cyfrwng* more with the concerns of the Welsh Government and the National Assembly for Wales regarding the 'democratic deficit' in Wales.

DAWN MANNAY is Lecturer in Social Science at Cardiff University and also held the posts of Associate Lecturer at The Open University and Visiting Lecturer at the University of Newport, as well acting as a trustee for the Women Making a Difference programme. Her research interests revolve around class, education, gender, geography, generation, national identity, violence and inequality; and she employs participatory, visual, creative and narrative methods in her work with communities. Dawn is currently the principal investigator on a Welsh Government-funded project exploring the educational experiences and aspirations of looked-after children in Wales. She is also the co-convener of the British Sociological Association's Visual Sociology Study Group and she has facilitated a number of international workshops on the use of visual and creative methods. Dawn has recently published *Visual, Narrative and Creative Research Methods: Application, Reflection and Ethics* (Abingdon: Routledge, 2016).

MINISTRY OF LIFE, run by Tim Buckley, Jonathan Gunter (Joff), Michael Ivins (Zippy) and Tom Ivins, are a south Wales-based community organization who run creative and musical workshops, youth clubs and events for young people. Ministry of Life have delivered youth work to disadvantaged and marginalized young people for six years. During this time they have organized community events, youth workshops and youth clubs, accreditations and artistic outputs. For example, Ministry of Life designed and delivered an anti-social behaviour diversionary event during Halloween 2012 in which vandalism was reported by south Wales police to have been significantly reduced. They have employed their existing community and youth networks to draw on music and art to disseminate a message of community cohesion and tolerance in south Wales, by raising awareness of issues of racism and urban railway hazards. Ministry of Life organized the music- and art-based productions for this volume through workshops with young people and the local photographer Ian Homer.

MELANIE MORGAN was a mature student and mother when she did her first degree in the social sciences; and she is currently a final-year doctoral student studying at Cardiff University's School of Social Sciences. Melanie previously held an assistant editorial role for the international transdisciplinary social science journal *Subjectivity*. Her research interests revolve around social class, higher education, gender and psychosocial research methods. Melanie's current research explores the subjectivities of working-class mothers in higher education in the geographical area of south Wales.

MAGNUS OBOH-LEONARD is a self-taught videographer with five years of experience running the visual company TAB Media, a professional video company based in Cardiff. TAB Media have worked with local up-and-coming artists and professional artists, as well as established organizations including the Prince's Trust and Save the Children. Magnus produced the videos for the tracks by Jamie Feeney aka Sapien, KAOS and Tasha Harvey.

ALISON PARKEN is Senior Research Fellow in the School of Social Sciences, Cardiff University and project director for 'Women Adding Value to the Economy' (WAVE). The project was funded by the European Social Fund through the Welsh Government and key partners from the University of South Wales, The Women's Workshop @ BAWSO and Cardiff University. Alison's research contributes towards building an evidence base for promoting socio-economic equality through policy-making and organizational practice. Most recently she has been working with collaborating employers to examine how gender inequalities in occupational segregation sustain gender pay gaps, and to innovate improvements in workforce planning and development through the WAVE project. Her research interests include gender employment and pay within labour markets, knowledge economies, employment and workplaces. She has advised several EU member states on adopting gender mainstreaming in policy-making, and works with international partners to development methods for undertaking mainstreaming equality on an intersectional basis.

KAREN PARKHILL is Lecturer in Human Geography at the University of York. Previously she was based in SENRGy at Bangor University and prior to this Karen was a research fellow with the Understanding Risk Group within the School of Psychology at Cardiff University. Karen's research interests are broadly around exploring public thoughts and ideas about environmental and technological risk issues. These include: energy technologies such as civil nuclear power, renewables or coal with carbon capture and storage; climate change; geoengineering; as well as issues related to transitioning to low(er) carbon ways of living. The interaction of place, space and context underpins and flows throughout all of these interests as does a continued interest in using and developing innovative qualitative research methods. Karen is a fellow of the Royal Geographical Society with the Institute of British Geographers (RGS-IBG), and is chair of their Energy Geographies Research Group (EnGRG).

JANE SALISBURY was previously the course director for the PGCE (PCET) programmes at Cardiff University, and prior to her doctorate, she was a schoolteacher of Sociology and English. She co-edited, with Sheila Riddel, *Gender Policy and Educational Change: Shifting Agendas in UK and Europe* (London: Routledge, 2000), which resulted from research on Wales conducted in 1996 for the Equal Opportunities Commission on educational reforms and their impact on gender equality in schools. Jane's research interests are in qualitative methods, post-16 education and training, gender, classroom interaction and the occupational socialization of teachers. She was the principal ethnographer in the Economic and Social Research Council (ESRC) and Teaching and Learning Research Programme (TLRP) funded research project 'Learning and working in further education colleges in Wales', which focused on a hitherto under-researched sector of education in Wales. Recent research undertaken with collaborators from the University of South Wales has resulted in an edited volume, *Academic Working Life: Experience Practice and Change* (London: Bloomsbury, 2013).

MICHAEL R. M. WARD is a sociological researcher and Associate Lecturer at The Open University and tutor at Cardiff University. His work centres on the performance of working-class masculinities within and beyond educational institutions and he is the author of *From Labouring to Learning, Working-class Masculinities, Education and De-industrialization* (London: Palgrave MacMillan, 2015). He is also the editor of *Gender Identity and Research Relationships* (Bingley: Emerald, forthcoming), which is volume 14 in the Studies in Qualitative Methods book series, and joint editor of *Higher Education and Social Inequalities: Getting in, Getting on and Getting out* (Abingdon: Routledge, forthcoming). He has taught sociology at both further and higher education institutions to students of all ages, and is also co-convenor of the BSA Education Study Group and editorial board member for Sociological Research Online.

Acknowledgements

In editing this collection, *Our Changing Land: Revisiting Gender, Class and Identity in Contemporary Wales*, there are many people who should be thanked and acknowledged, too many perhaps to fit in an acknowledgements section so I apologize in advance to those not named individually. As much of my initial engagement with questions of gender, class and place in the Welsh context began with my doctoral research project, 'Mothers and Daughters on the Margins: Gender, Generation and Education', funded by the Economic and Social Research Council (PTA031200600088), I would like to acknowledge all the participants who made this study possible. Also my thanks go to Professor John Fitz, Professor Emma Renold and Professor Bella Dicks for supervising my doctoral research project; and Gill Boden and Clare O'Connell who were my mentors.

In terms of drawing on my doctoral work to revisit classic studies of Welsh life, I am indebted to Dr Sara Delamont who introduced me to Diana Leonard's seminal paper 'Keeping close and spoiling in a south Wales town'. Diana Leonard died aged sixty-eight on 27 November 2010, and a special issue of *Gender and Education, Thinking Education Feminisms: Engagements with the Work of Diana Leonard* was edited by Professor Miriam David and Professor Debbie Epstein to pay tribute to and to encourage serious engagement with her work. The special edition also aimed to counter the tendency in much academic work, of all kinds, to reinvent the wheel, with little or no reference to earlier scholarship and theory. I was privileged to be able to contribute an article to this special issue, '"Keeping close and spoiling" revisited: exploring the significance of "home" for family relationships and educational trajectories in a marginalised estate in urban south Wales', and the development of this article fostered an appreciation of the importance of remembering, valuing and revisiting classic Welsh studies and publications.

I am grateful to Professor Paul Chaney for his invaluable help and guidance in putting together the initial proposal for this book, and for his ongoing support and encouragement, without which producing this edited collection would have been impossible. I would also like to acknowledge Professor Teresa Rees and Dr Sandra Betts Borland who were unable to contribute a chapter to this collection but were nevertheless hugely supportive of the project. I am also grateful to a wide range of authors and inspiring speakers and although I cannot name them all individually, much of their work is cited in the book. I have also learned a lot working with my colleagues in Cardiff University and my co-conveners in the *Families Identity and Gender Research Network*, and my Welsh-language lessons with many patient tutors. I should also mention the inspirational courses I attended much earlier in my academic career at Cardiff University's Centre for Lifelong Learning and the Women Making a Different Project, where I was first introduced to the book *Our Sisters' Land: The Changing Identities of Women in Wales* (Cardiff: University of Wales Press, 1994), which was the guiding muse for this collection; and Dr Hugh Mackay for writing The Open University module 'Understanding Contemporary Wales', which I really enjoyed studying and later teaching.

It is also important, of course, to thank all of the individual contributors for engaging with the project and offering a set of diverse and thoughtful 'revistings', drawing on their depth of knowledge and expertise. Many of the contributors are friends and colleagues and those who I do not know personally, I feel I have come to know through the editing process. I have a deep respect for the research and scholarship of all the authors in this collection and I selected them based on my reading of their work; therefore, I was privileged that they accepted the invitation to be part of *Our Changing Land*. I have learned a lot in editing this collection about facets of Welsh life, its politics, literature, language and the identities of place and people in Wales. The contributors' enthusiasm for the collection and their carefully crafted responses to revisiting classic Welsh work has been inspiring. Overall, the contributors' commitment has engendered an exciting set of chapters, which has exceeded my aims, hopes and vision of the collection – *diolch yn fawr i chi*.

The chapters in the collection have been enhanced by the creative contributions led by community organization Ministry of Life, Tim Buckley, Jonathan Gunter (Joff), Michael Ivins (Zippy) and Tom Ivins, who ran workshops with the young Welsh artists, KAOS (featuring

Chantelle), Tasha Harvey and Jamie Feeney aka Sapien, to create, produce and record the musical contributions for the three key themes of the collection. Ministry of Life also organized workshops with young people to represent each chapter visually with support from the local photographer Ian Homer and the Welsh artist Nathan Bond. I am grateful to all of these key contributors and would also like to thank all of the young people who contributed to the workshops, and the individuals who modelled for the bespoke photographs, particularly Tim, Toyah, Taya, Paula the cleaner at Eastmoors Youth Centre, the school pupils from Willows High School and their teacher Rebecca Kay, and Jayne Tariq, at Splott Play Centre, for providing permissions for the photographs, and JFM Exotics in Cardiff for hosting the image for chapter 7. Thanks also go to Magnus Oboh-Leonard, at TAB Media, for producing the videos for KAOS, Tasha Harvey and Jamie Feeney aka Sapien.

I would also like to thank the proposal reviewers for their comments and suggestions; and the commissioning team at University of Wales Press for their support, particularly Llion Wigley, Siân Chapman, Robin Grossman and Sarah Lewis, who worked with me patiently to attend all the essential administrative tasks that were necessary to move forward. I should also acknowledge Sarah Roberts at Cardiff University's planning division for assisting me in applying for the university-managed University of Wales Press-fund to support scholarly publications and related activities in the fields of Welsh culture, history and literature. This funding was essential in publishing this collection and supporting the arts and music-based productions.

I would also like to thank all my great friends for being there and although I am unable to name everyone, I must mention my friend, and cousin, Janine, who has been waiting to read this book and supporting me from New Zealand with chants of *Cymru am byth*! Last but certainly not least, with much love, I would like to thank my very big immediate and extended family – *diolch i chi*. Particularly my partner in life and for life, David, whose experience as an Englishman, who has embraced Wales as his home, has made me rethink the casual xenophobia, which is unnecessary to sustain a Welsh identity if we are to be an inclusive nation that celebrates and values diversity and difference. Also our wonderful children, who are no longer children, Toyah, Jordon and Travis, and their partners Tim, Sherelle and Jamie for talking through ideas with me about the book, listening to my concerns in the process and for stepping in as models for photographs when required. I am also grateful to our granddaughters Taya and Tilleah, who have brought a lot of fun and laughter into our lives and will continue to do so; and thanks again go to Taya who was given her parents' permission to feature in the cover photograph and represent *Our Changing Land* and its future.

1

Introduction

DAWN MANNAY

Starting places

In common with most introductory sections, this chapter provides the reader with an insight into the rationale for bringing this edited collection together. It sets out the aims and scope of the volume, as well as providing an overview of the following chapters and the ways in which they connect to the core themes of Welshness and everyday life in contemporary Wales. In this way, it forms a starting place, an opening and a beginning but no commencement is entirely novel – for the present is always embedded in the past; and at the same time oriented to the future. As Berger (1972, p. 370) contends:

> The present tense of the verb to be refers only to the present: but neverthe-less with the first person singular in front of it, it absorbs the past, which is inseparable from it. 'I am' includes all that has made me so. It is more than a statement of immediate fact: it is already biographical.

Throughout *Our Changing Land: Revisiting Gender, Class and Identity in Contemporary Wales*, there is an emphasis on this temporal position-ing as all of the chapters are reflective, contemporary and forward thinking. As Steedman (1986, p. 6) argues, 'specifity of place and poli-tics has to be reckoned with in making an account of anybody's life, and their use of their own past'; and this premise holds for studies of the collective, and the nation, as well as understandings of individual biog-raphies and futures.

Definitions of Welshness are never static and each generation passes their memories on to the next: such memories are 'conditioned by the times in which they lived' (Beddoe, 2000, p. 3) and they shadow our immediate experience. Consequently, it is important to revisit: and here there are two key, iconic sources that provide the contextualization for the present volume; the edited collection *Our Sisters' Land: The Changing Identities of Women in Wales* (1994), edited by Jane Aaron, Teresa Rees, Sandra Betts and Moira Vincentelli, and early editions of the journal *Contemporary Wales*, previously edited by Paul Chaney and Elin Royles, and published by the University of Wales Press.

Our Sisters' Land

Our Sisters' Land: The Changing Identities of Women in Wales argued for a focus on Welsh women because of their increasing importance to the world of paid work, while retaining their roles and responsibilities in the home. The book demonstrated the ways in which women's lives were characterized by diversity. At the time of its publication, the text addressed an important lacuna for the changing identity of Welsh women as they managed the balance between private and public lives, which had been relatively uncharted. For this reason, the text was groundbreaking in bringing together a collection of interdisciplinary research papers on the changing identity of women in Wales.

The text was introduced to me as a student on the inspirational Women Making a Difference programme run by the contemporary Welsh champion of gender equality, Paula Manley. As part of this programme, I took the course Women into Public Life, where Jan Stephens, of Cardiff University, guided students to a body of inspirational work by Deirdre Beddoe, Jane Pilcher and Teresa Rees; and centralized in this reading list was *Our Sisters' Land*. As a Welsh-language learner, Welsh-language sources still remain a closed book for me – a body of work that with greater proficiency I hope to one day explore. However, *Our Sisters' Land* allowed an entry point into a richer understanding of the 'particularities of women's experience in one minority culture' (Aaron et al., 1994, p. xv): the culture of Wales.

Our Sisters' Land was concerned with addressing the absence of minority voices, drawing on the Welsh proverb, *nid byd, byd heb wybodaeth*, a world without knowledge is no world; the book aimed to address the doubly under-represented world of Welsh women 'within the dominant English and male-oriented culture' (Aaron and Rees, 1994, p. 2), which subsumed their existence. Despite shifts in the visibility of women in public life, in the early 1990s women still could be defined by the concept of 'muted groups' (Delamont and Duffin, 1978, p. 11) in relation to the dominant group of men in social structure; and Welsh women were in a double bind as residents in a colonized nation within nations, in terms of language, law and social policy. A position that demanded a decolonizing methodology (Smith, 1999) to bring twenty-first-century Welsh women 'out of the shadows', as Beddoe (2000) had for twentieth-century Welsh women in her book, which made visible their hidden histories.

The journey for visibility was travelled in twenty-one chapters in the edited collection *Our Sisters' Land*. Each chapter was written by a woman in Wales, and the themes of the book were broad and diverse with attention given to home and community; education, training and work; culture and governance; women in rural Wales, material culture, religion, sexuality and the politics of identity. The book established the ways in which women's lives in Wales were changing and evolving, setting these changes in written testimony, which hoped to increase an understanding of these shifts and 'mitigate against the possibility of any future erosion of women's hard won emancipation' (Aaron and Rees, 1994, p. 14). Setting the evolving worlds of Welsh women on record was a major achievement of this collection; however, how far we can avoid slipping back in terms of the ideologies of feminism will be explored in this new collection. In contemporary Wales, it remains important to centralize the voices of women; but, to engender positive change, it is also important to acknowledge the voices of Welsh men.

Contemporary Wales

The pattern of family life and public life has continued to shift since the seminal publication of *Our Sisters' Land* and it has become important to revisit and re-examine the lives of both men and women in Wales. For this reason, *Our Changing Land* engages with issues emerging from earlier work in the journal *Contemporary Wales*, allowing for a reflection on gender in a wider sense. Drawing from the work of leading writers and emerging academics, in Welsh history, social policy, education, sociology, psychology and geography, and revisiting two seminal sources allows this edited collection to examine what is distinctive about Wales and Welshness in an interdisciplinary manner, which allows room for multiple voices and narratives of authors in Wales, regardless of their gender.

Contemporary Wales was published annually by the University of Wales Press between 1987 and 2014, and the journal was at the forefront of research into economic, political and social sciences relating to Wales. Its interdisciplinary content featured research on Wales and attracted leading Welsh authors from a wide range of academic fields. It incorporated both academic and practitioner-based articles, annual economic and legal reviews, and book reviews. The journal worked across a range of subject areas including the social sciences, history, law, media and languages and offered academic articles and reviews relating to politics, policy, economics and current affairs.

Previously edited by Paul Chaney, of Cardiff University, and Elin Royles, of Aberystwyth University, *Contemporary Wales* was arguably the leading journal of modern Welsh public life for almost three decades. The current collection will revisit carefully selected articles published around the early 1990s, with four authors revisiting their original work and four authors revisiting papers in relation to their own contemporary Welsh research. Importantly, the original authors of papers in the journal are both men and women – as are those revisiting the classic articles – providing the multiple insights needed to explore the postcolonial landscape of a devolved and evolving Wales, which forms the geographical, cultural and psychological site that *Our Changing Land* sets out to revisit, exploring the changes and continuities in the Welsh nation across this temporal space.

Our Changing Land

The last two decades have seen big changes within a small nation, and the distinctiveness of Wales, in terms of its political life and culture, has grown considerably. Nevertheless, beneath the imagery of the definitive nation, Wales remains a complex and divided land (Mackay, 2010), and this collection will explore the themes of continuity, change, unity and division that actively contribute to the making of contemporary Wales. The collection will explore what it means to be Welsh in postcolonial Wales, in a politically devolved and continuingly evolving nation.

Drawing from the work of leading writers and emerging academics, in Welsh history, social policy, education, sociology, psychology and geography, this edited collection examines what is distinctive about Wales and Welshness in an interdisciplinary yet comprehensive manner. Core themes and issues will be explored throughout the book, which presents twelve chapters in three distinct yet overlapping thematic sections, 'Wales, Welshness, Language and Identity', 'Education, Labour Markets and Gender in Wales' and 'Welsh Public Life, Social Policy, Class and Inequality'.

Wales, Welshness, language and identity

Nation is a powerful concept for drawing distinctions that act to 'other' places and people, consecutively constructing, imagining and maintaining a sense of Wales and Welshness (Clarke, 2009). In Wales, rugby illustrates a symbolic, internal source of unified Welsh expression, which powerfully unites a nation divided by gender, language, race and class (Mackay, 2010). However, a sporting game, no matter how beautiful, cannot engender a sense of national identity in isolation, and there are other processes that must be considered, such as nationalism and the Welsh language, literary and cultural imagery, and historical, geographical, gendered ideologies.

This first section of the book explores these themes by returning to previous identity positioning, in earlier Welsh texts, from the standpoint of the present. The section begins with a chapter from Jane Aaron, editor of *Our Sisters' Land*, who revisits her seminal chapter 'Finding a voice in two tongues: gender and colonization'. The original chapter charted the ways in which the pressures that circumscribed Welsh women's lives were not engendered solely from Welsh culture itself, but from the tensions between Wales and England.

'Finding a voice in two tongues: gender and colonization' returned to the Victorian era by exploring the moral imperative to adopt an English middle-class model of femininity put forward in the English 1847 Report of the Commissions of Inquiry, which was central in placing Welsh women, and the Welsh language, as inferior, dirty and immoral (Aaron, 1994). The branding of the Welsh woman as lawless and licentious in regard to their sexual conduct and the consequent moral imperative of purity rendered these 'colonised others' voiceless (Smith, 1999), culturally and linguistically. The chapter moved from this starting point to explore the journey of 'finding a voice' through literature, poetry and in social and political movements including Welsh

Women's Aid, Greenham Common and Cymdeithas yr Iaith Gymraeg – the Welsh Language Society.

Aaron's writing was rich and evocative: it painted a history of Wales that I had not seen before and made a lasting impression. My reading of the chapter was re-evoked as I encountered the legacies of this history and its pervasive influence over the communities that I work with in Wales. In this new chapter, 'Devolved voices: Welsh women's writing post 1999', Aaron focuses on the work of contemporary Welsh women writers post-devolution, exploring how women's greater representation in constitutional government, through the Welsh Government, has affected women writers' lives and their sense of Welsh identity. The chapter examines the pervasiveness of the divisive elements of class, ethnic, linguistic and sexual difference in Welsh life, and revisits the traditional role of the 'Welsh Mam' in relation to discourses of feminism and nationalism through the literary activism of 'finding a voice in two tongues'.

The theme of 'finding a voice in two tongues' is carried forward in the following chapter by the emerging author Non Geraint, who I was privileged to supervise in her undergraduate degree research dissertation. As Sapir contends, 'common speech serves as a peculiarly potent symbol of the social solidarity of those who speak the language' (cited in Davies, 2010, p. 162): language then can be a powerful expression of collective identity and belonging. However, the Act of Union 1536 banned Welsh from official use and the 1847 Report into the State of Education in Wales further marginalized the language by forbidding its use in schools (Davies, 2010). Consequently, Welsh declined and distinctions developed between regions leading to the linguistic tensions.

Children and young people are imperative in nation building, and Heini Gruffudd's (1997) article 'Young people's use of Welsh: the influence of home and community', published in *Contemporary Wales*, explored these linguistic tensions by documenting young people's relationship with the Welsh language. Gruffudd reported an equal balance between English and Welsh language when young people spoke about school and education; however, in conversations around popular culture, music and visual entertainment, English became the dominant mode of communication. English was also seen as transitionally fashionable among young people, where adopting the English language engendered a level of kudos in youth subcultures – an association that was seen to negatively impact on their everyday use of

Welsh. Gruffudd (1997, p. 217) argued that Welsh media and youth provision needed to create new opportunities for Welsh young people to have 'their own means of cultural expression and identity'.

Geraint's chapter, 'Only inside the classroom? Young people's use of the Welsh language in the school, the community and the peer group' revisits Gruffudd's article. The chapter explores the continuities and changes in the use of Welsh and attitudes towards the language amongst bilingual and monolingual children, in relation to their subjective feelings of national identity. Drawing on findings from a research study conducted with children aged 12 to 13 in a dual-stream bilingual school in mid Wales the chapter argues that at this age, Welsh-speaking children have a stronger sense of Welsh identity, based on their stronger negative attitudes towards the 'British' label and its association with England. However, the chapter also provides evidence that suggests that children view the Welsh language as an important commodity and advantage for future employment rather than as the language of social life, with Welsh-speaking children often assimilating to English due to peer influences. Geraint contends that government initiatives to create a 'bilingual nation' through education may limit the language to the educational and occupational domain rather than creating a bilingual nation more widely.

Following on from Geraint's chapter, the focus on identity shifts from the Welsh language to issues of gender and class. My own contribution to the collection is 'Who should do the dishes now? Revisiting gender and housework in contemporary urban south Wales'. This chapter revisits Jane Pilcher's (1994) important chapter from *Our Sisters' Land* – 'Who should do the dishes? Three generations of Welsh women talking about men and housework'. Pilcher's chapter was based on research with grandmothers, daughters and granddaughters that examined the legacy of the myth of the 'Welsh Mam' (Beddoe, 1989; Mannay, 2013) in maintaining acceptable feminine identities. Despite intergeneration shifts in relation to ideologies of egalitarianism in women's talk, Pilcher found that the actual domestic arrangements acted to counter this rhetoric of gender equality.

Two decades on from the original study, my chapter looks again at the cultural legacy of the ideology 'Welsh Mam' on women's everyday lives, and explores this question in contemporary south Wales by drawing upon data generated in a study of mothers and daughters residing in a Welsh, marginalized, urban housing area. The chapter argues that in contemporary Wales, the domestic sphere remains a site of inequality, where women are negotiating the impossibility of being both in full-time employment and meeting the ideological tenets of the 'Welsh Mam'. Furthermore, the work of women and the accompanying expectations have moved from being peripheral to becoming central, and the chapter suggests that this places women in a psychological impasse where they identify themselves as 'lazy' when they cannot simultaneously fulfil these roles to the unreachable standards of the new respectable working-class femininity.

In the final chapter of the section, Michael Ward shifts the discussion focus from working-class femininities to the complexities of working-class masculinities. While the work on men, masculinities and gender identities has exploded across the social sciences since the late 1980s, very little of this work has looked at masculinities and what it means to be a young man in a Welsh context. This chapter revisits a seminal paper, 'Boys from nowhere', published at the end of the millennium in *Contemporary Wales* by Jonathan Scourfield and Mark Drakeford, which argued that to understand Wales there was a need to understand its inhabitants, both those with and without power. They suggested that by analysing Welsh men it would be possible to critically explore the social process of the construction, production and reproduction of masculinities within the nation. However, research has been slow to develop in this area, arguably because of the diversity of masculinities within the nation, in terms of linguistic divisions, social-class dynamics and the north/south/urban/rural divide.

To gain a nuanced understanding of Welsh men, Ward suggests that research must appreciate the separate historical and geographical contexts, within the social construction of gender and specific localities. In this chapter, '"Placing young men": the performance of young working-class masculinities in the south Wales valleys', Ward draws on an ethnographic study with a group of young working-class men in a post-industrial community to explore how young masculinities are performed across a variety of educational and leisure spaces, and to illustrate the ways in which social, economic and cultural processes impact on the formation of self. Ward argues that expectations and transitions to adulthood are continually framed through geographically and historically shaped class and gender codes.

Education, labour markets and gender in Wales

Between 1945 and 1980 the income differential between individuals in Wales narrowed; however, since 1980 the gap between rich and poor has widened (Evans, 2010). This section argues that the increase in social polarization makes it increasingly difficult for marginalized working-class individuals in Wales to succeed in the labour market. However, the workplace is preceded by the education system and social mobility is intrinsically linked with Bourdieu's (1984) concepts of social and cultural capital so that those born into poverty do not have the resources and connections that are inherited by middle-class children. Furthermore, according to the historian Deidre Beddoe (2000), the lives of Welsh women have been shaped by nonconformity, religion, industrialization and a virulent strain of patriarchy, which have meant that in Wales, more than other parts of Britain, women have been denied access to the public sphere, which has arguably engendered a legacy of gendered inequalities.

In this section, gendered patterns of social mobility in the Welsh education system are revisited by Melanie Morgan, who draws on her own psychosocial study to make comparisons with the earlier work of Pam Garland, who explored the journeys of mature students in her chapter in *Our Sisters' Land*, 'Educating Rhian: experiences of mature women students'. Garland interviewed thirty north Wales mothers about their experiences as mature students in university and found that their journeys were characterized by difficulties. These mature student mothers 'muddled, struggled and juggled their way through both university life and home life, in order to meet the competing demands made upon them' (Garland, 1994, p. 120), and Garland argued that basic support from both the university and the family could have significantly improved the experiences of the participants in her study. In her chapter, 'Re-educating Rhian: experiences of working-class mature student mothers', Morgan reflects on Garland's chapter in relation to her four-year, Economic and Social Research Council-funded study that applied psychosocial interviews to explore the subjectivities of Welsh working-class mothers in higher education. Morgan's chapter focuses specifically on the mechanisms and strategies this group of women employed in constructing, negotiating and managing identity/subjectivity within university: and their motivations for pursuing academic success despite the emotional and practical conflicts of doing so.

The focus then shifts to the experiences of teachers in further education as Jane Salisbury revisits her own chapter, 'Chasing credentials: women further-education teachers and in-service training', again from *Our Sisters' Land*. Her original chapter was based on research with six women on a part-time In-service Certificate in Education at a university in Wales. Similar to the women in Garland's study, Salisbury's participants spoke about 'surviving the course' (Salisbury, 1994, p. 156); however, they all displayed a positive commitment to their work as teachers and felt that the training engendered a more professional identity and improved self-image.

In her new chapter, 'Private lives used for public work: women further education teachers in Wales', Salisbury draws on data from the 'Learning and working in further education colleges' study to provide a contemporary lens on this educational sector. The ethnographic study followed the learning journeys of twenty-seven teachers and forty-five students who were core participants over two years. The empirical material in this particular chapter focuses on six women teachers who had been employed as further education teachers from between four and fifteen years teaching a range of vocational courses and A-level subjects. Each of the women was passionate about scaffolding and supporting their diversely motivated students to secure qualifications. As in the earlier study, all of them were also striving for self-improvement and were engaged in various types of continuing professional development, acknowledging that they were too 'chasing credentials'.

In relation to the workplace, Caroline Lloyd revisits her article in *Contemporary Wales* titled 'Tailor-made Occupations: a Study of Gender and Skill in the Welsh Clothing Industry' through a discussion of the widespread loss of female manufacturing jobs in modern Wales. The original article highlighted the gender segregation of jobs in the clothing industry and the impact of product market and technological change on skills and the gendered division of labour. Since this early publication, Lloyd's research has explored the political economy of skill, workplace industrial relations and the relationship between product markets, labour markets, work organization and skills.

This body of research has examined low waged work internationally, with a particular focus on Europe, but in this edited collection she returns her focus to the Welsh context. In her chapter, 'From low-wage manufacturing industries to the low-wage service sector: the changing nature of women's employment in Wales', Lloyd revisits the issues raised in her earlier article through a discussion of the widespread loss of female manufacturing jobs in Wales, the failure of the UK to assist in the restructuring and renewal of traditional industries and the expansion of low-wage jobs in the service sector for both men and women.

In the closing chapter of this section, Alison Parken revisits Teresa Rees's seminal chapter 'Women in paid work in Wales' and reflects on how successful policy has been in closing gender pay gaps at the structural level in contemporary Wales. Teresa Rees was recently awarded a DBE for her body of work developing gender mainstreaming approaches to policy development, implementation and evaluation; and in her chapter she argued that the prevalence of post-feminist and equal opportunities discourses were in stark contrast to the realities of women's everyday lives in Wales. Rees explored the role of the 'greedy institutions', the home and the workplace, which placed unreasonable demands on women in the workforce as well as the gendered assumptions that deny women access to senior positions in the workplace.

Reflecting on the available evidence, Rees (1994, p. 104) argued that decisions were made for women based largely on their gender and that the majority of women could not access the competition for top jobs, 'irrespective of their desires or capabilities'. As project director for 'Women adding value to the economy', a European Social Fund project part funded through the Welsh Government, Parken is perfectly placed to revisit this work and examine the present picture for women in paid work in Wales. In her chapter, 'Changes and continuities: women in paid work in Wales 1994–2014', Parken examines Welsh data and equalities policy reviews, and secondary data analysis of gender segregation in occupations and working patterns in Wales. The chapter argues that despite shifts in policy that recognize the gendering of labour markets, and the unequal division of labour, many women are finding it increasingly hard to 'make work pay' given their over-concentration in low-skilled, low-paid, part-time work.

Welsh public life, social policy, class and inequality

Since the creation of the National Assembly in 1999 successive admin-istrations have governed in a distinctly 'Welsh way', differentiating provision and policy from that adopted in London as promised in First Minister Rhodri Morgan's 2003,'clear red water' speech. In the same way that Welsh Labour drew on nationalism, socialism and connections with *y werin* to align the party with an ideology of 'Welshness', arguably the Welsh Government has been committed to communitarian and collective policies that embrace bilingualism, civic nationalism and connect the political system with the people of Wales. This section explores post-devolution Wales in relation to the themes of public life, social policy, class and inequality.

In the opening chapter, Dave Adamson revisits his earlier work from the 1990s into the changing class structure evident in Wales, including the discussions in his *Contemporary Wales* article 'Still living on the edge', which focused on the ways in which a marginalized working class had come to characterize areas of Wales dominated by poverty and social exclusion. Adamson's work was concerned with understanding the 'fracturing' of a traditional working class in Wales and to map the patterns of poverty and social exclusion that resulted from the rapid process of economic decline, which was especially evident in the south Wales valleys.

In his chapter, 'Class, poverty and politics in devolved Wales', Adamson explores how devolved policy-making has responded to poverty and the consequences of poverty in Welsh society. Reflecting on his earlier work, Adamson had hoped that with the correct policies and full political commitment to change, the tide of rising poverty would be turned; however, despite nearly fifteen years of regeneration policies in Wales, his new chapter demonstrates that little has changed for the poor. This chapter suggests that in the quest to eradicate poverty, policy has only achieved an ameliorative role, and it remains inadequate to tackle the fundamental causes of poverty in Wales.

Paul Chaney also focuses on issues of equality by revisiting his substantive work on the place of women in public life in Wales, drawing specifically from work in his co-edited book *New Governance: New Democracy* (2001). His new chapter, 'Women and policy-making: devolution, civil society and political representation', offers a critical perspective on how issues of gender equality have evolved, drawing on a series of studies conducted over the past fifteen years as well as secondary data sources including Assembly proceedings, policy documents and government reports. The chapter also reflects on his more recent research based on seventy-five interviewees undertaken in 2013–14 with managers of a purposive sample of third-sector organizations. Importantly, these were not solely with 'women's organizations', rather, further to the ethos of mainstreaming, they relate to a broad range of NGOs, considering views on gender equality from across the sector.

Chaney problemitizes discourses of gender parity in public life and argues that the overemphasis on the number of women elected to the Assembly has created the false impression that devolution has transformed gender relations in Wales, when this is far from the case. The chapter illustrates the variability across policy areas and issues, where some have seen greater progress whilst others have registered little change. Issues of permanency are also explored as interviewees discussed sustainability, fearing that the gains made to date are vulnerable to reversal, notably in the face of current austerity and spending cuts. Overall, the chapter contends that whilst the past fifteen years have seen some progress, this progress has fallen short of achieving gender parity and eliminating inequality.

In the following chapter, Hugh Mackay turns the lens of inquiry on the media in Wales, revisiting the article, 'Wales and its media', published in *Contemporary Wales* (Mackay and Powell, 1996). The article argued that the Welsh print press mediascape was characterized by fragmentation and the dominance of the London press; in terms of newer technologies, these were seen as central to enhancing consumer choice but also fragmenting the experience of media consumption. In this way, the internet and cable television were positioned as meeting minority interests but antithetical to the Welsh media's goals in relation to the construction of nationhood. The monolithic ideology of nationhood was envisaged to be replaced with more hybrid forms and representations of nation, Welshness and individuality, within the emerging global village.

There have been two striking changes in the intervening period between the publication of 'Wales and its media' and Mackay's new chapter, 'The transformation of the media in Wales: technology and democracy'. One is the arrival of the National Assembly for Wales and Welsh Government, which Mackay argues has given rise to concerns about the communications environment in Wales, and the need for Assembly members and the government to communicate its message to the people of Wales. The other notable change is the phenomenal growth of the internet, which was still in its infancy as a communication technology in 1997. The chapter provides a review and update of the original summary of media technologies in Wales, discussing both changes and continuities in the Welsh mediascape.

Lastly, Karen Parkhill and Richard Cowell revisit Merylyn McKenzie Hedger's 1994 article 'Wind energy: the debate in Wales', published in *Contemporary Wales*, which explored the support for and opposition against the introduction of wind farms in rural Wales. On the one hand, supporters evoked discourses of clean energy, sustainability and additional income for farmers, as well as bringing employment to economically depressed areas. On the other hand, the opposition regarded wind farms as effectively an 'industrialisation of the hills involving some long term and irreversible effects' (McKenzie Hedger, 1994, p. 122), which would threaten the natural beauty of Wales.

In relation to the intensity of the dispute, McKenzie Hedger (1994) was doubtful about any short-term resolution but advised that any developments should be systematically reviewed before any rapid expansion. Continuing with the theme of inequalities in the chapter 'Wind energy: revisiting the debate in Wales', Parkhill and Cowell draw upon the latest scientific evidence, national policies and planning case studies to explore the ways in which battle lines continue to be drawn with consequential winners and losers in relation to sustainability, carbon reduction and maintaining the identity of the Welsh rural idyll.

Visions of Wales in photography and verse

In *Our Sisters' Land* there was recognition of Welsh art and culture through the inclusion of poetry and a series of illustrations especially commissioned from the photographer Mary Giles. Again, this collection sets out to engage with the discourse of the Welsh bard. However, to extend the concept in relation to contemporary Wales, original rap poetry and songs were written, produced and recorded by the young Welsh artists KAOS (featuring Chantelle), Tasha Harvey and Jamie Feeney aka Sapien, for each of the three themes of the book. The lyrics of the songs are presented to introduce each of the themes and here you will find web links to the audio and video recordings hosted on the Ministry of Life website.

These bespoke musical reflections on contemporary Welsh life were created in collaboration with the community organization Ministry of Life, who ran workshops with young artists to create, produce and record these materials. Ministry of Life also organized workshops with young people to explore the key arguments in each of the chapters in the collection and discuss how these could be represented visually.

Working with the local photographer, Ian Homer, Ministry of Life and the young people in their workshops developed bespoke illustrations and selected images from the photographer's existing catalogue to represent each of the chapters in this collection. In addition to the photographs, an original piece of artwork was commissioned from the Welsh artist Nathan Bond to represent Hugh Mackay's chapter. These images are presented throughout the book, alongside the chapters that they represent, and the messages that these artistic productions convey will be discussed in the concluding chapter.

Conclusion

The following chapters in *Our Changing Land: Revisiting Gender, Class and Identity in Contemporary Wales* are all structured around the central theme of revisiting seminal writings about Wales and Welsh life from the 1990s, reflexively exploring the changes and continuities in the nation across this temporal space. The last two decades have seen big changes within a small nation, and the chapters shift across these temporal spaces, the political landscape of post-devolution and the geographical areas that constitute Wales.

The concluding chapter will revisit the aims set out in this introduction and reflect on the key points from the intervening chapters, linking these findings to the overarching themes spanning the chapters. It will summarize what the collection tells us about the role of men and women in Wales and Wales itself as a nation, an economy, and in relation to questions of equality and identity. The chapter will reflect on the changes and continuities presented in relation to the original chapters presented in *Our Sisters' Land* and the seminal papers revisited from *Contemporary Wales*. It will reflect also on the musical and photographic contributions and explore what can be learnt from the voices of young people living in Wales. As well as looking back, the chapter will also look forward to the next two decades of changing identities, gender relations and discourses of class, suggesting future academic research and emerging agendas from the volume, and considering the future of *Our Changing Land*.

References

Aaron, J., 'Finding a voice in two tongues: gender and colonization', in J. Aaron, T. Rees, S. Betts and M. Vincentelli (eds), *Our Sisters' Land: The Changing Identities of Women in Wales* (Cardiff: University of Wales Press, 1994), pp. 183–98.

—— and Rees, T., 'Introduction', in J. Aaron, T. Rees, S. Betts and M. Vincentelli (eds), *Our Sisters' Land: The Changing Identities of Women in Wales* (Cardiff: University of Wales Press, 1994), pp. 1–16.

——, ——, Betts, S. and Vincentelli, M. (eds), *Our Sisters' Land: The Changing Identities of Women in Wales* (Cardiff: University of Wales Press, 1994).

Adamson, D., 'Still Living on the Edge', *Contemporary Wales*, 21 (2008), 47–66.

Beddoe, D., *Back to Home and Duty: Women between the Wars, 1919–39* (London: Rivers Oram Press/Pandora List, 1989).

——, *Out of the Shadows: A History of Women in Twentieth-century Wales* (Cardiff: University of Wales Press, 2000).

Berger, J., *About Looking: Writers and Readers* (London: Penguin, 1972).

Bourdieu, P., *Distinction: A Social Critique of the Judgement of Taste* (Oxford: Routledge, 1984).

Chaney, P., Hall, T. and Pithouse, A. (eds), *New Governance: New Democracy?* (Cardiff: University of Wales Press, 2001).

Clarke, J., 'Making national identities: Britishness in question', in S. Bromley, J. Clarke, S., Hinchcliffe and S. Taylor (eds), *Exploring Social Lives* (Milton Keynes: The Open University, 2009), pp. 203–46.

Davies, C. A., 'Nationalism and the Welsh language', in H. Mackay (ed.), *Understanding Contemporary Wales* (Cardiff: University of Wales Press and The Open University, 2010), pp. 159–96.

Delamont, S. and Duffin, L. (eds), *The Nineteenth Century Woman* (London: Routledge, 1978).

Evans, N., 'Class', in H. Mackay (ed.), *Understanding Contemporary Wales* (Cardiff: University of Wales Press and The Open University, 2010), pp. 125–58.

Garland, P., 'Educating Rhian: experiences of mature women students', in J. Aaron, T. Rees, S. Betts and M. Vincentelli (eds), *Our Sisters' Land: The Changing Identities of Women in Wales* (Cardiff: University of Wales Press, 1994), pp. 107–21.

Gruffudd, H., 'Young People's Use of Welsh: The Influence of Home and Community', *Contemporary Wales*, 10 (1997), 200–18.

Lloyd, C., 'Tailor-Made Occupations: A Study of Gender and Skill in the Welsh Clothing Industry', *Contemporary Wales*, 5 (1992), 115–29.

Mackay, H., 'Rugby – an introduction to contemporary Wales', in H. Mackay (ed.), *Understanding Contemporary Wales* (Cardiff: University of Wales Press and The Open University, 2010), pp. 1–24.

—— and Powell, A., 'Wales and its Media', *Contemporary Wales*, 9 (1996), 8–39.

McKenzie Hedger, M., 'Wind Energy: The Debate in Wales', *Contemporary Wales*, 7 (1994), 117–34.

Mannay, D., 'Keeping Close and Spoiling: Exploring the Significance of "Home" for Family Relationships and Educational Trajectories in a Marginalised Estate in Urban South Wales', *Gender and Education*, 25/1 (2013), 91–107.

Pilcher, J., 'Who should do the dishes? Three generations of Welsh women talking about men and housework', in J. Aaron, T. Rees, S. Betts and M. Vincentelli (eds), *Our Sisters' Land: The Changing Identities of Women in Wales* (Cardiff: University of Wales Press, 1994), pp. 31–47.

Rees, T., 'Women in paid work in Wales', in J. Aaron, T. Rees, S. Betts and M. Vincentelli (eds), *Our Sisters' Land: The Changing Identities of Women in Wales* (Cardiff: University of Wales Press, 1994), pp. 89–106.

Salisbury, J., 'Chasing credentials: women further-education teachers in-service training', in J. Aaron, T. Rees, S. Betts and M. Vincentelli (eds), *Our Sisters' Land: The Changing Identities of Women in Wales* (Cardiff: University of Wales Press, 1994), pp. 140–60.

Scourfield, J. and Drakeford, M., 'Boys from Nowhere: Finding Welsh Men and Putting them in their Place', *Contemporary Wales*, 12 (1999), 3–17.

Smith, L. T., *Decolonizing Methodologies: Research and Indigenous Peoples* (London: Zed Books, 1999).

Steedman, C., *Landscape for a Good Woman: A Story of Two Women* (London: Virago, 1986).

I

Wales, Welshness, Language and Identity

Hybrid Identity by KAOS

Chorus
Hybrid Identity this is what it meant
   to me
Wales is home but Africa's in my
   soul
And even though these streets ain't
   paved with gold
Wales is home but Africa's in my
   soul

Tempo
If I told you I was great you would
   say that I'm stupid
So I'll be on my way to take the
   place where you sit
Cos it's the only day your heads will
   play this music
If you lay in the same bed as I did to
   do this
Or you came with the same legs as I
   fit my shoes in
Or you're scraping the same bread
   that my countries using
Then maybe you'd at least get some
   empathy in you
That courtesy to seem stressed
   when I'm put in this mood,
   (mood)

But that's impossible cos the
   possibility's just about as
   possible as my fertility
Yeah, so try being African in Wales
   with this accent (Ello)
See how far you can get whenever
   you rap son
Cos for now I'm just too upset to
   answer these questions
And plus I really do suggest you
   cancel these sessions
I don't need the attention, Zip I see
   your discretion
It's like a tree without leaves it
   needs an identity

Potential
I'm mixed race, a descendant of
   many nationalities
It's a shame people have tried to
   use that to embarrass me
I've been told I'm not African just
   because I'm mixed
Nah forget that, that's ludicrous
Say I'm confused because I don't
   originate from one nation
I didn't realise being African had
   certain stipulations

It's strange how I never wanted acceptance
But the jokes harnessed an uncontrollable resentment
The colour of my skin I started to question
A mindset I've put into permanent detention
I got to be true to myself
I'm at Cardiff City games saying I'm proud to be Welsh
But I'm from London, Harlesden
But that's a minor like Carlton
Cos I left there when I was 7 or 6
So let me sum up all this
Africa's in my bloodline, Wales is where I live
I'm a hybrid identity my experience is a bliss

Bizstrumentals

I remember the time when I was half my age
Walking through the street with a smile on my face
Then a couple of grownups had to ruin my day

Cos they started throwing pennies towards my way
After sinister laughs they told me their reason
Cos I wasn't from Wales I'm not from their region
Man that really hurt me when I was eight
But I've grown up now and here to say
That it ain't all bad when you're with the right people
I mean the ones that ask and don't judge you when they see you
Cos at the end of the day we're all from one race
But some people don't see and put you in a place
So if you ever find yourself in that predicament
Talk to the person who sees you as singular
Tell them why being hybrid is so great
By opening their minds and showing them our way.

Music and media webcontent is hosted on the following websites:
www.molgroup.org.uk/ourchangingland and
https://www.youtube.com/watch?v=lECT5lxl7os.

Millennium Centre Poem, Gwyneth Lewis – by Ian Homer

2

Devolved Voices: Welsh Women's Writing Post 1999

JANE AARON

Introduction

On the face of it, devolution in the United Kingdom has been good for women writers, poets in particular. In her forward to Alice Entwistle's *In Her Own Words: Women Talking Poetry and Wales* (2014), Gillian Clarke comments 'At the time of writing, my three colleague Poets Laureate are women. They voice the world with a new music' (Entwistle, 2014, p. 6). She is referring to Carol Ann Duffy who in 2009 became not only the first woman Poet Laureate of Britain's Royal household, but also its first Scottish and first openly LGB laureate too; to Liz Lochhead who in 2011 became the first female Scots Makar, the national poet of Scotland, a post created in 2004; and to Paula Meehan who since 2013 has been Ireland's Professor of Poetry, jointly representing both devolved Northern Ireland and the Republic. Earlier, from 2001–4 Nuala Ní Dhomhnaill was the first woman to hold that Irish laureateship, first established in 1998. In 2008 Clarke herself became the third National Poet of Wales, a post created in 2005 and first held by a woman, Gwyneth Lewis. 'It's time the girls had a go on the golden lyre', says Anne Stevenson in her 'Ode on the Changes to be Reckoned with in the New Scotland' (Stevenson, 2007, p. 50), and since 1999 women throughout the Isles have indeed taken up the opportunity to avail themselves of their national instruments and become the poetic representatives of their respective nations.

    Given that the role of the bard used to be considered a particularly unsuitable job for a female, the fact that women have recently risen to such prominence within bardic ranks constitutes no less than a quiet revolution. Recollecting her upbringing in Cardiff in the middle decades of the twentieth century, Gillian Clarke remembers that in those years 'Formal education offered only poetry by men, and all of them English ... As a Welsh girl I had no poet-heroines to follow' (Entwistle, 2014, p. 6). But now, with Gwyneth Lewis's bilingual lines emblazoned on the forehead of the Millennium Centre in Cardiff's docklands, the largest poem in the world, no budding female poet in Wales can complain of a lack of models to emulate. Within Welsh-language culture too women's readiness to have a go on the golden harp has also been made manifest. The Welsh-language equivalent to the Poet Laureate role is today for the first time held by a woman: Christine James from the Rhondda, who was not reared in a Welsh-speaking home, became the first female National Eisteddfod Archdruid in 2013. Twice since 1999 the eisteddfod chair – awarded for an *awdl* in the strict *cynghanedd* metres and always previously throughout the long centuries of eisteddfod history a men-only prize – has been bestowed upon a woman: Mererid Hopwood became the first female chaired bard in 2001 and Hilma Lloyd Edwards the second in 2008. Post-devolution, Welsh women it would appear have indeed found their voices in two tongues, their 'new music' heard and publically acclaimed as never before.

Nor have Welsh women fiction writers been far behind their poetic sisters in terms of winning national and indeed international laurels post 1999. Since that year ten women have won the National Eisteddfod prose medal, and seven have won its Daniel Owen novel prize, giving women well over 50 per cent of Wales's main awards for the writing of Welsh-language fiction. Some of those winners have gone on to receive acclaim across Wales's borders, in translation. Angharad Price's *O! Tyn y Gorchudd* (2002), which won the prose medal in 2002 and also the Welsh Book of the Year Award in 2003, was subsequently translated into English by Lloyd Jones and published as *The Life of Rebecca Jones* by two presses, Gomer in Wales and Quercus in London. Hailed as 'a Book of the Year 2012' by both *The Irish Times* and *The Independent*, it has been translated into five languages. In 2005, Caryl Lewis's *Martha, Jac a Sianco* (2004) won the Welsh-language Book of the Year award; in 2012 its translation by Gwen Thomas was selected as representative of the whole of UK fiction, past and present, by Ann Morgan in her 'Reading the World' project, in which she chose one novel to represent the cultures of each of the 196 independent countries across the globe. In 2006 Fflur Dafydd won the eisteddfod prose medal with *Atyniad*, a novel on a Bardsey Island visitors' community, and her English-language reworking of the same theme, *Twenty Thousand Saints* (2008), won the Oxfam Hay Emerging Writer of the Year Award in 2009. In 2006 Rachel Trezise, who had already won an Orange Futures Award for her first novel, *In and Out of the Goldfish Bowl* (2000), and been acclaimed in *Harpers & Queen* magazine in 2003 as 'the New Face of Literature', became the first winner of the £60,000 international Dylan Thomas Prize with her short-story collection, *Fresh Apples* (2005); her work has also since been translated into several languages.

Such data suggests that the change in the public prominence of Welsh women writers, post 1999, is comparable to the transformation in Welsh women's political representation since that date. In 1996, Ann Clwyd was the sole Welsh representative of her sex in Westminster, but when the Assembly members took their seats in Cardiff Bay in 1999 twenty-four out of their sixty members were women, and women members have to date featured prominently in the Assembly's cabinets. In 2011, women made up 40 per cent of the members of the Welsh National Assembly, compared to 35 per cent of the Scottish Parliament members, 19 per cent in Northern Ireland and 22 per cent in the House of Commons. In 2006, 52 per cent of Assembly members were women, a world record. After a century in which Wales had lagged behind in terms of gender equality in political representation, it abruptly became one of the more enlightened territories on the globe in that respect; a similar transformation can be said to have occurred in terms of the gender of its more prominent literary representatives also. 'Arguably perhaps nowhere else in the UK can women writing poetry enjoy the sense of critical mass which Wales and Wales-based publishers today make available', suggests Alice Entwistle in her recent study *Poetry, Geography, Gender: Women Rewriting Contemporary Wales* (2013, p. xviii). The fact that of all the feminist presses established in England, Scotland, Ireland and Wales during the 1970s and 1980s, the only one still in existence is the flourishing Welsh women's press, Honno, is also telling. The arguments put forward in 1994 in *Our Sisters' Land* – that the cumulative effect of the grass-roots political and feminist movements of the 1960s and 1970s would, once Wales had gained some independence, allow for a blossoming of female confidence and creativity – may thus be said to have been endorsed. Devolution gave Wales a more distinct presence and a greater capacity for self-determination, and the self which it determined to show the world from its newly expanded platform was a modern, liberated one, a 'cool Cymru' in which gender equality featured large.

Yet, as Paul Chaney argues in this book and elsewhere (Chaney, 2011), greater equality in political spheres does not necessarily translate into the transformation of gender roles in everyday life. Is the same true in the literary field as well? Are these prominent women writers but the decorative icing on a mass which has remained immured under suppressive patriarchal systems? How far are the current breakthroughs sustainable? In some ways, women's literary successes can give rise to greater optimism than their political equivalent. For one thing, they have been achieved without the need for any such arguably artificial means as 'twinning' or 'zipping' and have not consequently been greeted with much opposition. All the arts institutions had to do was to open their minds to the possibility that 'well, perhaps after all these centuries the times might be ripe for a female Archdruid' and the prize-worthy talent was there, evident enough even on the institutions' own terms. In terms of future sustainability also, the paramount importance of role models in fostering the necessary self-belief and aspiring dedication of embryo artists is more direct and personal in the creative world than the political one, making it more difficult to reverse these major changes in gender representation. Many of the writers referred to in this chapter also by now have public roles as professors and lecturers in the literature and creative writing departments of the universities of Wales or as editors of Welsh literary journals, positions that enable them to further and consolidate the careers of other promising women writers, as well as their own. Yet it is of course the case that should women's time remain absorbed by the double burden of childcare and poorly paid work, should class and ethnic inequalities in education and social expectation continue to erode women's confidence, and fears as to the continuing decline of the minority language silence potential Welsh-language writers, then the current luminosity of Welsh female creativity could indeed in retrospect appear but a bright flash in the pan.

In the attempt to contribute to an exploration of the extent to which contemporary Wales does indeed constitute a 'changing land' for women, this chapter will focus on the manner in which post-devolution women writers represent and criticize those social systems which affect and can distort women's lives. 'Give me a gaze / that sees deep into systems' Gwyneth Lewis requests in *Zero Gravity* (1998, p. 24): women poets and novelists alike, writing in both Welsh and English, have endeavoured during these past fifteen years to probe Welsh ways of life and represent them, figuratively or realistically, so that their depths may be grasped. Systems of gender, class, sexual, ethnic and linguistic difference, and the institutions through which they function, feature prominently in their texts. Through focusing on both the recent twenty-first-century works of women who made their reputations as poets or novelists before 1999 and the testimonies of a new generation of younger women writers, this chapter aims to investigate their contribution to our understanding of the way we live now.

Representing changing gender roles in contemporary Wales

Not surprisingly perhaps, on the evidence of these texts at any rate, three thousand years or so of patriarchy have not been dismantled once and for all by the twentieth century's first and second waves of feminism. Women may have the vote, sexual discrimination at work may – on paper at least – have become illegal, but still in Lleucu Roberts's 2014 story 'Ddynes' (Woman) a contemporary farmer's unthinking sexism reduces his hard-working wife to virtually slave status. 'Simon isn't often wrong' (*Dyw Seimon ddim yn amal yn rong*; Roberts, 2014, p. 70), thinks his wife, as she accepts that, because of her sex, she is unfit to drive a Land Rover or use a computer, while at the same time working every hour of the day to keep their small-holding afloat. But to the reader it is apparent that Simon, though not portrayed as a monster, is often very wrong indeed, and has darkened his own life as well as stunting his wife's through not recognizing her as his equal. 'Woman' to Simon is a term of derision, as in his comment 'Can't you hold your beer, woman? Where the fuck's the coffee?' (*'Ti ffili dal dy gwrw, ddynes? Lle ffyc ma'r coffi?'*, p. 77), delivered at a moment when his wife is just relaxing into getting to know their prospective new daughter-in-law after an elaborate meal, carefully cooked and served by the 'woman' alone, of course. At least his comment has the effect of alienating the younger generation, who are clearly not planning to live their own marriage on such terms. But his wife's only response is to castigate herself for having momentarily taken her ease.

Similarly in Tessa Hadley's 2004 story 'The Enemy', complex emotions besiege a 'respectable middle-aged PA living in suburban Cardiff' when she welcomes into her home the 'enemy' of her younger years, an ageing 1960s socialist activist whose rich Welsh valleys voice had dominated the left-wing groups in which she herself as a student had learned her politics. Within those groups 'the girls really did get asked to make the tea: and really did make it' (Hadley, 2004, pp. 148

and 150). Keith Reid, the activist, had ended up partnered to Caro's, the narrator's, 'softer-seeming, prettier' sister, who for twenty years put up with 'his infidelities, his drinking, his disappearances, his contempts' before finally leaving him (pp. 154–5). For all her clear-headed recognition of his failings, Caro is still evidently in thrall to 'that sheer imperturbable male certainty' Keith continues to exude, and she with her 'smiles and reassurances' continues to bolster (pp. 153 and 161). The longevity of 'thrilled abjection' as a constituent of sexual attraction for women, persisting after its recognition and theoretical condemnation, is what is at stake in this subtle story, as the apparently independent-minded Caro grooms herself in preparation for becoming the servant partner of Keith's later years, even keeping 'Keith's mother's recipes for Welsh cakes and bara brith' (pp. 153 and 164).

Embedded within both these tales, however, is a realization on the part of the apparently complicit but conflicted narrator of the injustices of the outmoded mindset which neither she nor her partner/enemy has yet shed. In many other texts, a younger generation of writers, who could be said to be participants in the twenty-first-century 'third wave' of feminism, are roused to open, often ribald, protest at such attitudes. In Rhian Edwards's poem 'Girl Meats Boy' (2013), for example, the speaker takes a ghoulish revenge on her former abusive lover, cooking up his carcass for her own delectation:

> I ripped and gutted, as he did me,
> and reduced this man to crumbs.
>
> ....
>
> I cured his heart, I syruped it sweet [...]
> My menyou [*sic*] done, I throned to dine
>
> ....
>
> This woman, she made
> a meal of you. (Edwards, 2012, pp. 61–2)

'Girl Meats Boy' won both the judges' and audience's John Tripp award for performed poetry in 2011–12, and the collection in which it appeared, *Clueless Dogs*, was in 2013 the all-round prize-winner for the Welsh Book of the Year, as well as winner in the poetry section, evincing contemporary audiences' enthusiasm for the use of humour to explode historical suppression. Similarly in Bethan Gwanas's prize-winning popular fictions a series of assertive heroines take their revenge on patriarchy: in her *Gwrach y Gwyllt* (Witch of the Wild), for example, another female avenger, a time-travelling witch, also makes a meal of her former tormentor, turning him into 'the best stew I ever had' (*'y stiw gorau ges i rioed*'; Gwanas, 2003, p. 160).

Gwanas's witches enjoy lesbian sex (pp. 138–9), and lesbianism generally features with some frequency in twenty-first-century Welsh women's writing. Though none of the lesbian fictions of Pembrokeshire-born Sarah Waters are to date located in Wales or include Welsh characters (Waters, 1998, 1999, 2002), Stevie Davies's temporally multi-layered novel *Impassioned Clay* (2000) very positively portrays as one of its central protagonists a seventeenth-century Welsh lesbian, and Lleucu Roberts in her collection *Saith Oes Efa* (The Seven Ages of Eve) has a tale, 'Chiwia' ('Colours', in north-Walian dialect), in which the narrator blissfully celebrates her lesbian marriage, though her ultra-respectable mother, the 'Grey Woman' who dares not venture beyond 'her grey prejudices like a net about her' (*ei rhagfarnau llwyd fel rhwyd amdani*, p. 53), has refused to attend the ceremony. By the close of Fflur Dafydd's *Atyniad* (Attraction), the most stable transformation brought about in the lives of sundry characters, who find themselves charmed and changed by one summer on Bardsey Island, is a lesbian relationship between a married woman and her former work-colleague. The most extensive exploration of lesbianism within a Welsh context remains, however, Erica Wooff's *Mud Puppy* (2002), in which homosexual culture features as a taken-for-granted facet of Welsh life in contemporary Newport. Taken for granted by those in the know, that is: it remains a hidden underworld for some of the novel's characters. In a telling scene, the chief protagonist Daryl is taken aback to realize that her closest childhood friend, Louise, though a *Guardian* reader, has never guessed at Daryl's sexuality. 'It's just such a surprise', says Louise when Daryl finally comes out to her, to which Daryl replies

'Oh, come on, it's all over the place these days. TV, film, books, you name it.'

'Not in Newport,' Louise says firmly.

'Please,' I say. 'Newport's got its fair share, all right. I had two of them cruising me in Commercial Street last Saturday morning.' (Wooff, 2002, p. 98)

Post-devolution Welsh women writers also represent the female body and its physicality, as well as its sexuality, with greater freedom and detail than hitherto: Mair Rees, in her recent extensive study of the body and its symbolism in Welsh-language women's fiction since 1948, finds 'female experiences of the body moving from the shadowy margins to the centre of the stage' (*'profiadau benywaidd o gorfforiad yn symud o'r cyrion cysgodol i ganol y llwyfan'*; Rees, 2014, p. 198) in the work of contemporary novelists like Sonia Edwards, Meleri Wyn James and Caryl Lewis. One theme dominates the representation of reproduction and motherhood in the current fictions of both of Wales's languages, however, and that is the struggle to rear offspring in single-parent families without an adequate childcare system. The insecurities of modern-day heterosexual relations and the expectation that women of child-bearing age should work as well as rear their young have left the younger generation more burdened in this respect than their mothers were. In *Rara Avis* (2005), in which a troubled child struggles to conceal and live around her widowed mother's slide into chronic depression, Manon Rhys looked back movingly to a south Wales valleys upbringing in the 1950s. The distress of her protagonist is compounded by the fact that she stands out as unusual amongst her peers by virtue of her fatherlessness; the single-parented state is, however, a common one in volumes depicting the contemporary valleys.

In Catrin Dafydd's *Random Deaths and Custard* (2007), a Rhondda valleys teenager, who is herself suffering from the emotional effects of her parents' separation and the shock of encountering her mother's new partner, refers, nearly in passing, to a school friend's rape by her stepfather (p. 24), as if virtually inured to such trauma. The second wave of the feminist movement has been criticized for not having paid sufficient heed to the question of childcare, and the inadequacy of the existing system, which for some offers but a stark choice between children being taken into state care or suffering some insecurity in the home, is frequently fictionalized.

Rachel Trezise's autobiographically based *In and Out of the Goldfish Bowl* (2000) remains the most extensive exploration of that theme: its protagonist Rebecca is sexually abused by her stepfather, an unemployed collier himself thrown on the scrapheap by the collapse of the south Wales mining industry, while her mother struggles with a series of cleaning jobs in a single-handed effort to keep herself and her household fed. Knowing as she does that her mother was the victim of domestic violence from both the stepfather and her children's biological father, Rebecca cannot bear to sully her further by telling her of the rape, but as a result she becomes enclosed in a 'goldfish-bowl' of trauma, which cuts her off from others. By the close of the novel, however, she has come to recognize that '[t]he sad reality is, that I've grown up in a very ordinary manner, not knowing that some of my best friends have lived identical lives' (p. 120). Her trauma, she now realizes, was political as much as personal, the outcome of an inadequate social system, the depths of which she has now grasped. In telling her tale she hopes to provide a way out for others from a similar isolation: the sharing of her past has 'dissolved' it, 'it isn't mine any more. And what a relief it is, to give an unwanted gift to someone who needs it much more than I' (p. 121).

It is a representative of the older, pre-Thatcherite generation who has inspired Rebecca with the strength of mind to survive and see into the system which oppresses her: her grandmother, she says, 'gave me the person who is writing this sentence. She gave me treasured stories and examples and standards to live by, reasons to fight my way to where I want to be. She ... handed out to me her gift-wrapped strength' (p. 118). Though the Welsh Mam, that secure rock of earlier Welsh industrial fictions, emerges as well nigh broken by the combined effects of resistant patriarchy and late capitalism in these more contemporary texts, the Welsh Gran, as critics have suggested, appears to have taken over the salt of the earth imago formerly attributed to Mam, as if only the older generation could retain the steely grit of the old survival systems under the onslaughts of recent social change (see Aaron, 2004, pp. 94–6; Gramich, 2007, pp. 183–4). The grandmothers' futures are also ill-omened, however, according to the testimony of recent writers. In Stevie Davies's *The Eyrie* (2007), an ageing Amazon, a veteran of the Spanish Civil War, befriended by a survivor of 1960s Welsh-language activism, chooses suicide when threatened by a stroke, rather than a moribund existence in an old people's home. 'I'd rather be shot through the head like a horse', says Dora on a visit to Carmarthen's Home for the Aged, in which another of her friends has just been incarcerated by financially motivated relatives (Davies, 2007, p. 174).

But suicide is just as tempting an option for those members of the younger generation who have fallen prey to the endemic drug culture of the post-industrial areas. In Lucy Gough's verse play for radio *The Raft*, first broadcast in 2002, the prison system is condemned as whole-heartedly as the care of the elderly was in *The Eyrie*, and exposed as not fit for purpose in its dealings with such inmates as Mags, an addict of eighteen convicted of shoplifting. As Mags and her resistant Soul struggle between them, trying to resolve the question of whether she should opt for life or death, an accompanying Chorus of three Fates, willing her demise, rhythmically chant, 'Society the wrecker / feeds us our prey' (Gough, 2006, pp. 86, 92 and 96). Mags eventually survives her drug withdrawal symptoms but only through focusing on a photograph of her infant son from whose actual presence she is debarred by 'society the wrecker', as depicted here, with its prison system, its lack of prospects for the young, and the tempting 'raft' of its drug culture.

Gough's use of a classical chorus to deepen the tragic significance of a drug addict's struggle with suicide is echoed in many other women's texts of the post-devolution period which extend the reach of their subject through incorporating intertextual devices. The most startlingly innovative of these is perhaps Angharad Tomos's *Wrth fy Nagrau i* (2007), in which the narrator, as a patient in the mental health ward of a north Walian hospital, suffering from severe postnatal depression, finds all about her in the neighbouring beds an array of disturbed female figures sprung alive from the classics of Welsh-language literature. From Heledd, maddened by the seventh-century slaughter of her tribe in the 'Elegy on Cynddylan' (ninth century) to Bet, the twentieth-century minister's wife who has a mental breakdown in Kate Roberts's *Tywyll Heno* (1960), these characters suffer alongside the narrator the humiliations of the ward life, not least of which is the fact that while the majority of the patients are Welsh-speaking none of the doctors and managers are, and few of the nurses. It is through her negotiations with the literary figures, and the exchanges through which they grow to understand the historically disparate systems of concealment and induced guilt which effectively broke each one of them, that the narrator finds healing, and not through the hospital's drugs. At the same time the mismatch between the literary worlds of the characters and the detailed realities of their existence in the here and now of the twenty-first-century mental health ward makes for much humour, to leaven the text's in-depth exploration of a topic of traumatic relevance to many women: one in five mothers suffer some degree of postnatal depression or psychosis.

The twenty-first-century National Health System, for all its inadequacies and gross underfunding, can at least be said to have had the virtue of inspiring two major classics of Welsh women's writing, *Wrth fy Nagrau i* and the equally intertextual *A Hospital Odyssey* (2010) by Gwyneth Lewis. Homer, rather than the Welsh classics is the major inspiration behind Lewis's epic poem, of course, though characters from Welsh mythology also figure on its pages, as they accompany its speaker Maris on a nightmare journey through the bowels of the NHS system in search of the stem cells which 'can undo the mistakes of time' and heal her husband, threatened by cancer (Lewis, 2010, p. 139). A surreal humour again punctuates the grimness of the journey, as Maris encounters such figures as the 'Mother of Cancer' who fulminates against humans' under-appreciation of her son's 'super-success' as 'the Olympic elite / of life forms'. 'Does any one ever thank me / for the way I wake up people', she complains, 'How I remind you of the simple joys?' (pp. 102–3). Through her ultimate acceptance of the interdependency of all living systems, Maris finally achieves her goal. Adopting a musical metaphor to describe the healing process, she suggests that a stem cell operates by 'striking a tuning fork, the chord / that leads to others'. All matter here becomes 'a coherent song // for many voices' to which poetry also contributes, participating in 'the transfer of energy // from one state to another – this poem from me / to you' in a 'continued exchange' which 'must be our purpose' (pp. 146–7).

The manner in which entry into the hospital system underlines the shared vulnerability of all animal matter is also central to two recent publications by another Welsh-based poet, Ann Drysdale from Newport, who records a similar journey with, in Drysdale's case, a sadder ending. The title of the first of these two prose and poetry journal accounts, *Three-three, two-two, five-six*, denotes her husband's number in the NHS system; Drysdale represents the NHS as a dehumanizing culture arousing 'great expectations' which it does not have 'the staffing levels or cash resources to fulfil' (Drysdale, 2009, p. 59; 2007, p. 59). In one scene she describes herself lying awake on the floor beside her husband's hospital bed, puzzling over the curious familiarity of the 'thin wailing' she hears around her throughout the night: 'The old lady calling over and over again on the one note – Dad! Dad! Dad! The old man with a lower, sadder register – Nurse! Nurse! Nurse!' Her earlier experience as a hill-farmer helps her find the key to these cries: 'They were animal. This was the desolation of the cow-byre when the calves had been taken away. The confusion of the sheepfold ... when the ewes have been separated from their lambs ... each one alone in an agony of puzzlement and loss' (Drysdale, 2007, pp. 52–3). But the hospital is short-staffed, without the resources to go round 'mothering-up the scared and bewildered' as she would have done in her 'other life'.

Of course the systems that these writers try to penetrate – the gender system, the post-industrial social system, the NHS and prison systems and the system of living matter itself – each affect men and masculine bodies as much as women and female bodies. What is striking, however, is the degree to which contemporary women writers are taking upon themselves the role of systems analysts and heroic explorers. Since 1999, Welsh women poets in particular have imaginatively immersed themselves in the furthest reaches of geographical, spatial or scientific exploration. Often using the extended poem series form, they focus on such traditionally male experiences as that of the nineteenth-century polar explorer or twentieth-century space adventurer, recreating and appropriating for women as much as for men the expansion of mind and knowledge that comes with the penetration of such newfound worlds. When Sheenagh Pugh, for example, in the series 'The Arctic Chart' from her 1999 collection *Stonelight*, enters into the experience of the mid-nineteenth-century navigators who left their names on the Arctic chart as they sought for the North-west Passage, and attributes to them an apprehension of the existence, behind the 'drifting distorted' ice mountains, of an 'immense mind, unexplored, / unbounded', the voyager's sense of expanded consciousness becomes that of the reader as well (Pugh, 1999, p. 10). Similarly, as we have seen, Gwyneth Lewis in the series *Zero Gravity*, as she records her cousin's mission to repair the Hubble's space telescope, appropriates from him 'a gaze / that sees deep into systems through clouds of debris / to the heart's lone pulsar'. Following the gaze of the explorer out into unchartered territory brings with it in both cases a sense of increased awe at 'the sheer luminosity/ that plays all around us' (1998, p. 24). The appropriation of masculine experience in such poems carries a particular message to women readers, telling them that where the imagination can go you can follow if you will: no routes to greater awareness are limited by gender.

Representing ethnic and linguistic difference post devolution

Recent technological advances in global communication have also highlighted the imperative need for greater understanding of systems of ethnic difference and in this field too women writers feature prominently. Since Wales became for the first time a nation with a border marking out the fact that those living to the west of that line, under the governance of the Welsh Government, have a distinct civic identity, ethnic difference within Wales has been more extensively explored in literature than hitherto. In Trezise's short story 'Jigsaws' from the collection *Fresh Apples* which won her the 2006 Dylan Thomas Prize, a valley girl is shocked when her father intervenes to prevent her growing friendship with the son of the local Italian cafe owner on the grounds that 'they're not like us' (Trezise, 2005, p. 150). Initially she acqui-esces, and marries her father's choice of suitor, only to realize subsequently that neither she nor her generation share the patriarch's narrow values and cannot live as a community within them: the ethnic hybridity of the community in which she was reared is part and parcel of its meaning and history. Another contingent from the 'jigsaw' of the valleys' ethnic diversity is remembered in Catherine Fisher's series 'Estuary poems', from her 1999 collection *Altered States*, which explores the slow integration of south Wales's Irish population, describ-ing the Irish settlers who fled the famine arriving at Newport as ballast in the holds of returning coal ships, only to be dumped unceremoni-ously on the estuary's mudflats:

> Under the stars they come ashore all night,
> wading chest high through the lights of Weston ...
> See them flounder, waist-deep, long skirts dragging ...
> till the bank is firm and the land forms,
> and they sit on the saltmarsh and slither into their shoes.
> Cheaper than ballast, dumped in the dark.
> Never uprooted from the memory's mud.

That laborious arrival prefigures the long process of getting acclima-tized to the new environment, 'learning a new country, new weather, / resettling', with the memory of the former home and identity slowly, generation by generation, 'receding into legend, and all the while / unnoticed, this is home' (Fisher, 1999, pp. 49 and 53).

The long-established mixed-race population of the Cardiff docklands area found representation in Trezza Azzopardi's *The Hiding Place* (2000), in which a Maltese-Welsh narrator records a 1960s childhood, darkened by her father's economic and social insecurities: his only route to survival as an immigrant in Cardiff was through virtually enslaving himself within a mafiaesque under-economy. Such is his chagrin at not having a son that the family must hide from his drunken violence his youngest daughter Dolores, the narrator, tucked in a chest as a baby and thrust into a rabbit hutch in childhood. But when Dolores returns to Cardiff Bay in adulthood, she finds the area transformed, 'busy, set and full of purpose', the dark alleyways in which she and her mother formerly crouched and hid from abuse now cleared and planted with young saplings: 'something,' she realizes, 'was being unearthed' (Azzopardi, 2000, pp. 200–1). The fullest literary exploration to date of such hybrid ethnic identities in Wales, however, is perhaps Charlotte

Williams's *Sugar and Slate* (2002), intertwining as it does the histories of Williams's Afro-Caribbean father's people and those of her Welsh mother from the slate-quarrying communities of north Wales. At the close of this autobiographical volume, Williams opts for Welshness out of the array of possible ethnicities available to her precisely because Wales is so diverse, 'as mixed up as I was', she says: 'I like it because it is fragmented, because there is a loud bawling row raging, because its inner pain is coming to terms with its differences and its divisions, because it realises it can't hold on to the myth of sameness, past or present' (Williams, 2002, pp. 169 and 191).

One of those characteristic Welsh 'differences and divisions' is, of course, linguistic difference. In 2007 Menna Elfyn in her poem 'Caerdydd Amlieithog' (Multilingual Cardiff) celebrates the linguistic diversity of Wales's capital: 'This is the city of *cariad* and *karaoke* ... of *babushka* and *banjos* ... of *cwtsho* and *caboodle*', she says, happily comparing 'Wales's *lingua franca*' to 'the rainbow on the back of a trout in the river' (*Dyma ddinas y cariad a'r* karaoke, / *Tir melys* babushka *a* banjos ... *Dinas cwtsho a caboodle* ... *Mae* lingua franca *Cymru / Fel enfys ar gefn brithyll mewn afon*'; Elfyn, 2007a, p. 27). During the 2000s, the results of the 2001 Census, which showed that between 1991 and 2001 the percentage of Welsh-language speakers had risen for the first time since records began, allowed for hope that Wales might indeed be set on a journey to full bilingualism. One outcome of the new optimism may be the unprecedented number of both English- and Welsh-language texts in both poetry and prose published during the 2000s which celebrate and encourage the Welsh-language learner.

Gwyneth Lewis, in her 1999 sequence *Y Llofrudd Iaith* (parts of which have been translated in the first section of *Keeping Mum*, 2003), had anticipated the death of the Welsh language, portraying it as a murdered old crone, and suggesting as one of her possible murderers a disenchanted Welsh learner, who had repeatedly been repulsed and refused entrance to the crone's family. As the Welsh learner confesses to the detective investigating the case, 'my Welsh is terrible. *Fe wrthodai'n lân / fy nerbyn* ('She completely refused to accept me'; Lewis, 1999, p. 40), and in his anger and frustration, 'just to get a reaction', he assaulted her. But in the 2000s many Welsh-speaking writers, with the clear intention of doing all they could to encourage Welsh learners, on the contrary welcomed them warmly into the community of Welsh speakers. Menna Elfyn, for one, has devoted poetry collections to Welsh learners, encouraging them in through 'wide open doors' and comparing their struggles positively to those of the poet, equally 'doting on words, tripping over letters' (*'Ffoli ar eiriau, / Baglu dros lythrennau'*; Elfyn, *Er Dy Fod*, 2007a, pp. 17 and 46). Catrin Dafydd's popular fictions *Random Deaths and Custard* (2007) and its sequel *Random Births and Love Hearts* (2015) are also written specifically for those students from English-speaking homes with whom she attended Welsh-medium schools in the south Wales valleys. The difficulties of her factory-worker heroine, Samantha Jones, in attempting to keep up her Welsh-speaking skills after she has left school, aided only by an ailing Welsh-speaking grandmother and the television series *Pobol y Cwm*, are portrayed with empathy and humour.

As the 2011 Census made only too dismally clear, the real threat to the Welsh language came not from the post-industrial areas but from the continuing economic decline of the rural Welsh-language heartlands of the north and west, as farmer after farmer was forced to give up the struggle for survival. One text which was hailed as capturing both the former vitality of the rural Welsh lifestyle and its current vulnerability was Angharad Price's *O! Tyn y Gorchudd* (2002), translated under the title as *The Life of Rebecca Jones* (2010). Its narrator Rebecca presents herself as embedded within her family – farmers in the Maesglasau valley for a thousand years – and within the history of that valley and its Welsh-speaking community. When on the novel's final page it is disclosed that the historical Rebecca Jones in fact died in childhood in 1916, the sense of sudden loss seems to encompass much more than her figure alone. Momentarily it is as if the continuation of Welsh-language culture in the twentieth century has abruptly been exposed as a mirage, a dream that never was; it all ended back during those corrosive First World War years. The reader flounders in a strange vacuum, before recognizing that only one voice has in fact been lost in this instance, and the relief makes the actual reality of twentieth-century Welsh rural culture as it has been represented throughout the rest of the text by contrast all the more precious, as well as all the more vulnerable. In this context, the Welsh title of the novel – '*O! Tyn y Gorchudd*' (Oh! Pull aside the Veil') – seems to refer not only to the physical blindness of the narrator's brothers but also to the psychological blindness of those who remain unaware of the value of their linguistic culture and its peril. It is no doubt because it manages thus at one and the same time to celebrate in lyric prose the longevity and value of a minority culture and to arouse dread at its disintegration that this novel has struck a chord with many thousands of readers, in a number of languages.

Rural Welsh-speaking communities in decline are also the key concern of Caryl Lewis in her *Martha, Jac and Sianco* (2004), in which a woman experiences herself as entombed alive on the failing farm in which she was reared. Though Martha has to sell off Graig-ddu's dairy stock, because she has secretly buried on its land her stillborn infant, the result of an unreported rape, she cannot bring herself to leave the farm. Omens of doom proliferate: a raven knocks frenziedly on the farm's windows, an *aderyn y drycin* (storm bird, foretelling death), but still Martha stays on, even after her mentally damaged brother steals the poison she had intended for the bird and uses it to put out of his misery their older brother, a stroke victim, before taking the rest of it himself, leaving the sister alone at last, like a 'ghost of light in the darkness' of her home ('*fel ysbryd gole yn y tywyllwch*') (Lewis, 2004, p. 190). Agrarian communities disintegrating economically are also the subject of the title story in Glenda Beagan's short-story collection *The Great Master of Ecstasy* (2009). The Vaughans of Maes Derwen have traditionally acted as the guardians of their border mountains area, walking its boundaries and 'noticing and blessing all the plants and animals in the old way and stopping in special places like Ffynnon Wna and Craig Rwlff to repeat the rhymes' (Beagan, 2009, p. 53). Hidden in the chimney breast of their farm is a human skull which 'represents the Guardian' (p. 54), and in each generation of the family one of its members has been blessed or cursed with shamanic gifts, marking them out as the reincarnated Guardian for that generation. But the last two gifted members, Olwen and her son Kieran, flee the responsibility as too complex and conflicted a burden for them to carry without the traditional community support, and both die in England with the farm left to perish or fall into strangers' hands.

'A gaze that sees deep into systems'

The imperative at least to keep on record the history of Wales's rural communities and their ways of life has constituted the *modus vivendi* of the Abergwesyn poet, Ruth Bidgood. '[F]orgotten in a wrinkle / of a small country's mountains' the often derelict hamlets she describes in her 2012 collection *Above the Forest* yet 'hold encircled the life, / through millennia after millennia, of a world'. 'Tectonic plates had shiggled and slid, / continents parted and joined, ice ages come and gone' to make up the particular singularity of her Abergwesyn view, lit by 'A long-dying sun burning on towards doom' (2012, p. 53). Similar shifts in perspective from the micro to macrocosmic feature in Anne Cluysenaar's sequence 'Through Time' from her 2011 collection *Migrations*. As the poet climbs Sarn Helen in the Brecon Beacons she notices at her feet, on 'these temporary hills', 'a whiteness – / little-finger-tip inner half / of a hatched shell' and considers that out of it had come 'a mode of life / older than ours' (Cluysenaar, 2011, pp. 36–7). As in the 'new nature poetry' of the 1980s and 1990s, associated in particular with Gillian Clarke, such lines point to the paradoxical fragility as well as antiquity of the systems they contemplate. In her poetry diary *Touching Distances* (2014), Cluysenaar records a 'rare event', the eclipse on the solstice that occurred in December 2010, and comments, 'When we're next slung between sun and moon / creatures that live with us now will be gone' (Cluysenaar, 2014, p. 17).

Inevitably, in the twenty-first century, the threat of global warming deepens that sense of precariousness, adding an extra urgency to the need to see 'deep into systems'. In *A Recipe for Water* (2009), Gillian Clarke compares the slipping of Greenland's glaciers to the slipping of a slag-heap in Aberfan forty years previously, both the consequence of 'the century of waste' (Clarke, 2009, p. 34). The increasing precariousness of 'the fit between ... plant and bird and human, fish and mammal' intensifies for Wendy Mulford, too, in her 2007 poem 'Alltud' (Exile), which depicts the human 'creatures of stardust' as 'intent on meaning / learning' (Mulford, 2007, p. 154).

> Whatever we're made of, it wants to know
> how it came to be what it is. In us,
> for a while at least, the stuff of stars
> gets a glimpse of its own precarious life

says Cluysenaar in her poem 'Hunting the Higgs' (2014, p. 77), with full assurance that the energies of the mind are accessible and vital to all prescient beings, whatever their gender.

As I write, news of the recent silencing of Anne Cluysenaar's voice adds, of course, additional grievous weight to her lines. But that body of Welsh women's writing to which Cluysenaar so richly contributed is itself at the moment in fuller voice than it has been during any previous epoch in Welsh history. Never before has an Archdruid written of the eisteddfodol 'hwyl' coming upon her as she prepared the family dinner ('*Fe es i hwyl eisteddfodol / wrth roi cinio i'r teulu ar gân*'), or of unpremeditated alliterative patterns and half-rhyme schemes interfering with the preparation of a cooked breakfast (*'Bu'r wyau'n cytseinio â'i gilydd, / y cig moch yn lled-odli â'r tost'*; James, 2013, p. 43). Never before have women in Wales in such numbers experimented with innovative poetic forms: traditionally female poets have been perceived as conservative in their choice of form, and lacking in the confidence to experiment metrically, but poets like Zoe Skoulding and Nerys Williams are today pioneering the new 'language' poetry in Wales with collections such as *Sound Archive* (Williams, 2011) and *The Museum of Disappearing Sounds* (Skoulding, 2013). Both Skoulding and Nerys Williams were early inspired by their involvement in the 1990s independent music scene in Wales (see Entwistle, 2014, pp. 168 and 200); the figures they name as sources of inspiration – Owain Wright of Rheinallt H. Rowlands, or David R. Edwards of Datblygu – were male to a man, but it is the women poets themselves and writers like them who stand fair to influence a new generation. Since 1999, Welsh women authors have come a long way in a short time; the energy of the new work, in all its various genres, and the drive within it to understand and deconstruct the systems which have hitherto suppressed female creativity, does give rise to the hope that this revolution will not quickly be overthrown. Within the 'changing land' of present-day Wales, gender equality in the literary field at any rate is no longer a distant prospect.

References

Aaron, J., 'Valleys' Women Writing', in A. von Rothkirch and D. Williams (eds), *Beyond the Difference: Welsh Literature in Comparative Contexts. Essays for M. Wynn Thomas at Sixty* (Cardiff: University of Wales Press, 2004), pp. 84–96.

Azzopardi, T., *The Hiding Place* (London: Picador, 2000).

Beagan, G., *The Great Master of Ecstasy* (Bridgend: Seren, 2009).

Bidgood, R., *Time Being* (Bridgend: Seren, 2009).

——, *Above the Forests* (Blaenau Ffestiniog: Cinnamon Press, 2012).

Chaney, P., *Equality and Public Policy: Exploring the Impact of Devolution in the UK* (Cardiff: University of Wales Press, 2011).

Clarke, G., *A Recipe for Water* (Manchester: Carcanet, 2009).

Cluysenaar, A., *Migrations* (Blaenau Ffestiniog: Cinnamon Press, 2011).

——, *Touching Distances: Diary Poems* (Blaenau Ffestiniog: Cinnamon Press, 2014).

Dafydd, C., *Random Deaths and Custard* (Llandysul: Gwasg Gomer, 2007).

——, *Random Births and Love Hearts* (Llandysul: Gwasg Gomer, 2015).

Dafydd, Ff., *Atyniad* (Talybont: Y Lolfa, 2006).

——, *Twenty Thousand Saints* (Talybont: Alcemi Books, 2008).

Davies, S., *Impassioned Clay* (London: The Women's Press, 2000).

——, *The Eyrie* (London: Wiedenfeld & Nicolson, 2007).

Drysdale, A., *Three-three, two-two, five-six* (Blaenau Ffestiniog: Cinnamon Press, 2007).

——, *Discussing Wittgenstein* (Blaenau Ffestiniog: Cinnamon Press, 2009).

Edwards, R., *Clueless Dogs* (Bridgend: Seren, 2012).

Elfyn, M., *Er Dy Fod* (Llandysul: Gwasg Gomer, 2007a).

——, *Perffaith Nam/Perfect Blemish* (Tarset: Bloodaxe, 2007b).

Entwistle, A., *Poetry, Geography, Gender: Women Rewriting Contemporary Wales* (Cardiff: University of Wales Press, 2013).

——, *In Her Own Words: Women Talking Poetry and Wales* (Bridgend: Seren, 2014).

Fisher, C., *Altered States* (Bridgend: Seren Books, 1999).

Gough, L., *By a Thread & The Raft* (London: Methuen, 2006).

Gramich, K., *Twentieth-Century Women's Writing in Wales: Land, Gender, Belonging* (Cardiff: University of Wales Press, 2007).

Gwanas, B., *Gwrach y Gwyllt* (Llandysul: Gwasg Gomer, 2003).

Hadley, Tessa, 'The Enemy', in J. Williams (ed.), *Wales Half Welsh* (London: Bloomsbury, 2004), pp. 147–64.

James, C., *Rhwng y Llinellau* (Abertawe: Cyhoeddiadau Barddas, 2013).

Lewis, C., *Martha, Jac a Sianco* (Talybont: Y Lolfa, 2004).

——, *Martha, Jack and Shanco*, trans. Gwen Davies (Cardigan: Parthian, 2007).

Lewis, G., *Zero Gravity* (Newcastle upon Tyne: Bloodaxe, 1998).

——, *Y Llofrudd Iaith* (Abertawe: Cyhoeddiadau Barddas, 1999).

——, *Keeping Mum* (Tarset: Bloodaxe, 2003).

——, *A Hospital Odyssey* (Tarset: Bloodaxe, 2010).

Mulford, W., 'Alltud', *Scintilla*, 11 (2007), 153–61.

Morgan, A., *Reading the World: Confessions of a Literary Explorer* (London: Harvill Secker, 2015).

Price, A., *O! Tyn y Gorchudd / The Life of Rebecca Jones*, trans. Lloyd Jones (Llandysul: Gwasg Gomer, 2010).

Pugh, S., *Stonelight* (Bridgend: Seren, 1999).

Rees, M., *Y Llawes Goch a'r Faneg Wen: Y Corff Benywaidd a'i Symbolaeth mewn Ffuglen Gymraeg gan Fenywod* (Caerdydd: University of Wales Press, 2014).

Rees-Jones, D., *Consorting with Angels: Essays on Modern Women Poets* (Tarset: Bloodaxe, 2005).

Rhys, M., *Rara Avis* (Llandysul: Gwasg Gomer, 2005).

Roberts, Ll., *Saith Oes Efa* (Talybont: Y Lolfa, 2014).

Roberts, S., *Tywyll Heno* (Denbigh: Gwasg Gee, 1960).

Skoulding, Z., *The Museum of Disappearing Sounds* (Bridgend: Seren, 2013).

Stevenson, A., *Stone Milk* (Tarset: Bloodaxe, 2007).

Tomos, A., *Wrth fy Nagrau i* (Llanrwst: Gwasg Carreg Gwalch, 2007).

Trezise, R., *In and Out of the Goldfish Bowl* (Cardiff: Parthian, 2000).

——, *Fresh Apples* (Cardigan: Parthian, 2005).

Waters, S., *Tipping the Velvet* (London: Virago, 1998).

——, *Affinity* (London: Virago, 1999).

——, *Fingersmith* (London: Virago, 2002).

Williams, C., *Sugar and Slate* (Aberystwyth: Planet, 2002).

Williams, N., *Sound Archive* (Bridgend: Seren, 2011).

Wooff, E., *Mud Puppy* (London: The Women's Press, 2002).

School Students and Popular Literature – by Ian Homer

3

Only Inside the Classroom? Young People's Use of the Welsh Language in the School, Community and Peer Group

NON GERAINT

Introduction

This chapter revisits Heini Gruffudd's (1997) article 'Young people's use of Welsh: the influence of home and community', an article published in *Contemporary Wales* at a time when the numbers of Welsh-speaking children and Welsh-medium schools were continuing to increase steadily, particularly in the less traditional Welsh-speaking areas of south Wales. The study explored the linguistic patterns of young people attending bilingual and monolingual Welsh-medium schools in southern parts of the country, and the reasons as to why the English language tended to replace the Welsh language in the social sphere.

The research inferred that young people's home-language patterns had the most influential effect on their language use in other domains, and suggested a complex pattern of language use dependent on various factors such as family background, age, location, people spoken to and subject discussed. Finding evidence of English domination and preference amongst the participants in the study, Gruffudd then suggested ways in which the threatened language could progress and develop as the preferred chosen language amongst young people in Wales.

In a research study conducted for my undergraduate dissertation, I similarly studied young people's use of the Welsh language and its association with their subjective feelings of identity with the Welsh nation. The study found that participants' use of Welsh and attitudes to the language were highly influenced by their family's views and linguistic backgrounds, and Welsh-medium pupils demonstrated stronger negative attitudes towards the 'British' label and its association with England, suggesting that speaking the language may result in a stronger sense of belonging.

However, the language did not overtly appear to be used as a personal identity marker or as influential in friendship-group formation, particularly in the school setting where Welsh-speaking pupils conveyed that they assimilated to speaking the dominant English language amongst peers. Similarly, participants' comments implied that the language was viewed as a commodity rather than as the language of social spheres, suggesting that the Welsh Government's initiatives to create a 'bilingual nation' through education may have limited the language to the educational and occupational domain rather than creating a bilingual nation socially.

This chapter will discuss the findings of my research in relation to the earlier article by Gruffudd, looking particularly at the ways in which views and attitudes towards the Welsh language have evolved or demonstrated continuity. Almost two decades on from Gruffudd's original publication, this chapter revisits young people's use of Welsh in a devolved and contemporary Welsh locale.

Background

The political and linguistic history of Wales is characterized by struggle and conflict, with the Welsh nation arising primarily from the affiliation of Celtic tribes in order to defend territory from Roman, and later Anglo-Saxon and Norman invasions. Wales lost its independence as a principality in 1283, when it was occupied by the English following an invasion led by Edward I (Jenkins, 2007). The strong feeling of Welsh national identity was formed over centuries as the Welsh battled against absorption into bordering cultures. The language and culture of the Welsh was maintained extensively through oral transmission of poetry, stories and musical traditions, whilst the introduction of publishing and literacy further allowed the Welsh language to be preserved.

In 1536, the Act of Union erased the distinction between English and Welsh law, resulting in Wales existing effectively as an area within England. English was thus the only official language of the courts, with some beginning to see the Welsh language as a source of shame. Further oppression was experienced in consecutive centuries, particularly through a report of enquiry by the parliament in Westminster in 1847 into the state of education in Wales, referred to as *Brad y Llyfrau Gleision* (The Treachery of the Blue Books) (Roberts, 1998). The report proclaimed the Welsh language as the core of immorality and the prevalent social problems in Wales. The subsequent prohibition of Welsh in schools in the late nineteenth century had a potentially devastating effect on attitudes towards the language and its role in the community (Davies, 2010). The Industrial Revolution came to Wales in the same period, bringing an influx of international workers, languages and cultures, which led to increased anglicization of daily life (May, 2008).

Although Welsh continued to exist as the dominant language of the majority of the population throughout the nineteenth century, the percentage of Welsh-speakers then declined, leading to a total of 18.7 per cent of the population by the 1991 census (ONS, 2002). The acknowledgement of the steady decline, as well as the influx of international people and languages, led to strong feelings of nationalism at the beginning of the twentieth century, contributing to the establishment of the Welsh Nationalist Party in 1925 (May, 2008). The language was a key source of inspiration for nationalist visions in Wales and since then, many factors such as the establishment of S4C (Welsh-language television channel) and Radio Cymru, as well as the Welsh Language Act in 1993, contributed to the language's increasing status. The demand for Welsh-medium education similarly increased in the second half of the twentieth century, and continues to grow, resulting in the most significant increase in Welsh-speaking ability amongst children and young people (ONS, 2011).

The literature suggests that Wales has managed to keep its cultural distinctiveness as a stateless nation within Britain largely due to its distinctive language. However, there are differences in the significance people place on the language and its role in determining Welsh national identity. Balsom's (1985) three Wales model was formed in an attempt to demonstrate the internal variations in experiences and perceptions in Wales, and the country is still often divided into these distinct areas in contemporary discussions despite the impact of globalization and assimilation (Day, 2010). The model distinguishes between three areas in Wales: *Y Fro Gymraeg* (the Welsh heartland), Welsh Wales and British Wales. These distinct categories were created based on how inhabitants of these areas identified themselves: as 'Welsh', 'British' or 'something else', as well as Welsh-speaking ability.

Gruffudd's (1997) study involved young people aged 16–17 from five distinct areas in south Wales, encapsulating all three of Balsom's categories. Each area, therefore, varied in their traditional Welsh-speaking tendencies. Gwendraeth Valley, for example, was considered an area in the Welsh heartland – one of the most Welsh-speaking parts of Wales, whilst Swansea was considered an anglicized area based on the lower numbers of Welsh speakers. As Gruffudd noted, a dearth of research existed regarding the use of the language amongst the young people at the centre of the changing landscape within Welsh education, and he claimed that the struggle for language domination in this particular area meant it had a great significance for the future of the language. Consequently, Gruffudd's research sought to decipher young people's language habits in order to better understand how to take positive steps forward in terms of the future of the Welsh language.

Significant correlations were found between young people's home-language patterns and language patterns outside the home, with parental use of the language being more influential than parental ability. Furthermore, an apparent shift had occurred in the Welsh heartland, with considerably fewer siblings speaking Welsh together compared to the high proportion of parents who claimed a high-level of Welsh-language use at home. However, in other areas, the figures regarding sibling Welsh-language use and parental Welsh-language use were very close, suggesting a positive effect in more anglicized areas in terms of language maintenance. Given this strong home influence, Gruffudd suggested a need for a determined attempt to encourage parents to use Welsh as the main language at home, regardless of their initial abilities in the language. The apparent decline in Welsh-speaking tendencies in the heartland required special attention according to Gruffudd, particularly from agencies concerned with the economy, due to the inextricable association between economic and linguistic prosperity.

Strong variations were found regarding language use amongst friends, based on the linguistic nature of the contrasting communities. Living in the Welsh heartland seemed to have the most positive influence on young people choosing to speak Welsh and young people in the study tended to speak Welsh to older people and younger children, but less so amongst themselves. English was clearly the dominant language in all social domains, and Gruffudd claimed that this could possibly reflect Fishman's (1991) earlier observations regarding the fact that the Welsh language may be a reflection of past values rather than the modern lives of the young. However, certain individuals in those communities who were particularly committed to speaking Welsh appeared to have a strong influence on others, suggesting the need to make individuals aware of the critical roles that they could play.

Welsh was positioned as not as 'fashionable' as English during school age. Consequently, Gruffudd acknowledged the need to introduce Welsh as a natural language of social and sporting activities, and suggested that the Welsh media should do careful market research in order to understand how to attract young people. Securing a strong Welsh rock scene was also stated as paramount in allowing young Welsh people to have their own means of identity and cultural expression, as popular music was a topic young people would rather discuss in English.

Shortly after Gruffudd's article was published, Wales became a devolved nation, and the Welsh Government has displayed a strong commitment to the Welsh language, arguably in an attempt to strengthen Welsh national identity. In 2003, their Welsh-language strategic framework 'Iaith Pawb: A National Action Plan for a Bilingual Wales' demonstrated the aim of creating a completely bilingual nation (Welsh Assembly Government, 2003). Subsequently in April 2010, the publication of their Welsh-medium education strategy delineated their intentions of increasing the provision of Welsh-medium education. But how have these initiatives affected young people who are faced with important decisions regarding language use in their daily lives? How do young people currently involved in Welsh-medium education relate to the language and how does it pertain to their sense of selves?

Despite the evidence for English domination and declining use in social arenas, Gruffudd stated that, on the whole, young people's attitudes towards the language were remarkably positive. The participants' support for the language was strong and widespread, and young people used Welsh willingly where the conditions were favourable and practical. This finding was later supported by an across-Wales survey conducted by the Welsh Language Board (2008), where 80 per cent of the participants believed the language to be 'something to be proud of', and would welcome the opportunity to speak more Welsh. In my research, I wanted to discover whether young people's views towards the language continued to be as positive and explore the experiences of those living in a bilingual area in which Welsh and English speakers are clearly separated on a daily basis.

Similar questions have been posed: for example, Coupland et al. (2005) examined subjective orientations to language to understand how young people's ethno-linguistic subjectivities may be affected by regional and linguistic differences. As secondary education is currently viewed as imperative for language revitalization, Coupland et al. studied secondary school students' affiliations in various sociolinguistic communities across Wales. Like Gruffudd, they discovered positive attitudes amongst young people in Wales regarding the revitalization of the language, particularly in their 'Gwynedd' cohort. However, they identified groups of young people in cohorts in Pembrokeshire, Powys and the Vale with moderate levels of affiliation with the nation as well as low levels of cultural engagement and use of Welsh in daily interaction. In their sample, the Welsh language was largely perceived to have low vitality and low priority in pupils' day-to-day lives.

More recently, Hodges (2009) studied young people's language use in the specific area of the Rhymney Valley, where Welsh-medium education has experienced a particularly successful surge during the past thirty years. Individuals who continued to use the language outside the school arena were those whose workplaces required them to do so, suggesting that formal frameworks are required to sustain the use of the minority language.

Furthermore, Scourfield et al. (2006) studied children (aged 8–11) across various locations in Wales to represent the diverse geographical areas identified by Balsom. They found that all children believed non-Welsh speakers to be just as Welsh as Welsh speakers, suggesting an inclusive vision of Welsh identity. However, they also found that first-language Welsh speakers had a stronger awareness of the difference between Welsh people and British people, which indicates that language does play a part in the way children perceive their national identity.

A body of research has been conducted on Welsh-language use and attitudes amongst young people, but the internal diversity in Wales requires further research and clarification. My research aimed to contribute to the existing literature, by exploring the views of young people in a geographical area that is often neglected in language research. It therefore varies from previous research in its qualitative focus on one particular group of young people from a contrasting area on the Welsh/English border.

Research context

The research was conducted in a comprehensive secondary school in north Powys, an area located close to the border between Wales and

England. It is considered an anglicized area based on its demographic characteristics, and little research has been conducted on the area in comparison to the more well-known areas in the Welsh heartland or the Welsh valleys.

The school is positioned in a small, rural town with around 1,200 inhabitants, and has a large catchment area. At the time of the study – 2012 – the school had a total of 875 pupils from the ages of 11–18 years, and was chosen partly due to its status as a dual-stream secondary school, consisting of both an English-medium (EM) and Welsh-medium (WM) stream. Approximately 16 per cent of the school's pupils' first language is Welsh and therefore a minority of pupils receive their education through the medium of Welsh. In this way, the school can be seen as a microcosm of Wales, which currently has a similar minority percentage of 19 per cent of the overall population claiming to be Welsh speakers (ONS, 2011).

The dual-stream nature of the school meant that it was possible to conduct research with fluent Welsh speakers as well as those who had limited knowledge of the language, allowing for consideration of their possibly differing views and the ways they related to the language and to each other. It was also believed that the similar composition might reflect the wider language relations that exist in Wales, although clearly it was not intended to be generalized to the population based on the small sample, the specific age group of the participants and the unique area and location of the school. The study aimed to demonstrate how young people in this minority language context negotiate their identities and relate to the language.

As a previous pupil in the school, my personal experience in the WM stream had motivated me to explore how language may be influential in identity processes as pupils are growing up. However, as the research was conducted in a familiar environment, issues regarding my position as an 'insider' must be considered (Mannay, 2010). Researching in a familiar territory can result in a more nuanced understanding of the identities and experiences of the participants, whilst the participants themselves may simultaneously be more inclined to share their personal lives (Atkinson et al., 2003).

Conversely, as an 'insider' researcher I may have been blinded by my own preconceptions (Vrasidas, 2001). I had felt a strong sense of separation between the WM stream and EM stream during my school years, and this may have led to an encouragement of responses that indicated this relationship from the participants, at the expense of other prominent findings. However, a focus-group method, which aimed to be fairly informal and unstructured, allowed the participants to discuss their views and opinions with minimal influence.

Methodology

The focus groups involved two mixed gender groups of year 8 pupils from the school (aged 12–13). A purposive sampling method was employed, as participants were chosen partly on the basis of the language in which they received their education, with one group of pupils from the WM stream and the other group from the EM stream. It was decided that five to six participants for each group would allow for a range of views to be expressed whilst engendering the opportunity for everyone to express their thoughts (Morgan et al., 2002). The sample included two participants who were currently involved in an immersion programme in which they were taught some subjects through the medium of Welsh, with the aim of being fluent by the end of the year when they would be able to choose which stream to join. This variety allowed for an exploration of differences in linguistic or national affiliations based on varying linguistic experiences.

Focus groups were conducted during school hours in a private room at the school, with no other pupils or teachers present during recording. The questions employed in the facilitation of the discussions consisted of topics regarding pupils' opinions of the Welsh language; Welsh lessons; nationalities; Wales and Britain as nations; their local area and the future. The fairly unstructured nature of the focus groups also allowed students to raise the issues that they deemed important, and provided opportunities to explore what was most salient to them in their daily lives. The discussions were recorded and subsequently transcribed verbatim, before being analysed thematically.

The thematic analysis explored the contention argued by socio-linguistic theorists such as Sachdev and Bourhis (2005) that language can be the most salient aspect of identity and is influential in group-formation. In identifying themes, I was interested in the participants' most salient identifications as well as their general views and attitudes towards the language and the nation. Concepts from Tajfel and Turner's (1986) Social Identity approach (SIT) and the closely related Ethno-linguistic Identity theory (ELIT; Giles and Johnson, 1987) were drawn upon to analyse the data. These models are designed to study inter-group relations, and they provide effective means for studying the role of language in identity constructions.

'Welsh not British'

Pupils illustrated a strong identification with Wales, with participants in both groups identifying themselves as Welsh with no hesitation when asked about their nationalities. This links to previous work by Evans (2007), where participants in north-east Wales easily defined their nationalities as Welsh, and appeared surprised when probed as to the reasoning behind this, as if it was a clear and unquestionable answer. Identification with Wales in the present study was mainly through the discussions around Britain, and the negative attitudes held towards Britishness. Both groups identified themselves as Welsh; however, participants in the EM group struggled to find reasons as to why they stated that they were Welsh rather than British, whilst the WM group offered a clearer rationale:

Ceri: Like, what is British?

Cai: … like what in the flag, what's in it that's Welsh?

Carwyn: Like there's a red cross for England and then blue for Scotland really on the banner, there's nothing to represent us really!

Catrin: I'd say that British was more England, if you say British then you're saying English.

These quotes demonstrate the WM students' understanding of Britain as usually referring to England, leading to a lack of identification with Britain as a nation. Their annoyance at the fact that they believe that Wales is not represented in the flag illustrates the wider belief that Wales is often not acknowledged as a separate nation within discourses of Britain (Clarke, 2010). A similar observation can be made about the following statement that arose in discussions about the 2012 London Olympics in the WM focus group:

Catrin: Ye, that was just really annoying, say if like someone like Chris Hoy won the Gold medal, he's a Scotsman, and then God Save the Queen comes on and that just, uuh, makes me angry!

This illustrates the anger felt towards Britain's marginalized nations being suppressed in the British label, and being overpowered by

England's 'superiority' (Clarke, 2010). This was followed by further belligerent language around the queen and symbols of Britishness/ Englishness. For example, in a discussion with the WM group regarding the national symbols, in mentioning the Welsh dragon and the 'cool flag', the flag was used as a form of comparison with England, whose flag was referred to as 'boring' as it only consisted of two colours. Resonant with Scourfield et al.'s (2006) research, students automatically used the neighbouring country of England to position themselves as Welsh, clearly marking the boundaries with the English as the 'other'. This links with the Social Identity perspective, which suggests individuals divide the world into 'them' and 'us' categories, before forming social comparisons between these perceived categories (Tajfel and Turner, 1986).

These observations echo those discovered in Carrington and Short's (1996) study, in which Scottish children demonstrated very negative attitudes towards the English and Britain, as well as Henry, Mayer and Kloep's (2007) study in south Wales in which teenagers became defensive and aggressive regarding their Welsh national identity when discussing England. Drawing on the Social Identity perspective, discussing the English, as a collective category, in a negative and discriminatory way could be seen as a way for the students to maintain their positive self-esteem in a British context in which they may feel relationally inferior (Tajfel and Turner, 1986).

As Sachdev and Bourhis (2005) argue, studies have shown that individuals who identify most with their category memberships engage in more discriminatory behaviour, in order to derive a more positive social identity. This was more evident in Welsh-speakers accounts, which suggests that speaking the Welsh language may result in an increased national identification and an augmented need to differentiate from the English out-group, a finding that attests Sachdev and Bourhis' (1991) claim that language is a salient aspect of identity.

A further observation regarding their views towards Wales's status within Britain was that of those who had an opinion on the matter, they were unanimous in their belief that Wales should have its own political independence. As expected at this young age, a few of the pupils had no interest in the topic, but those who did demonstrated strong awareness of the socio-political context.

Sion: ... people are saying that England is Great Britain, so it either has to turn to just Great Britain, or into Wales, England and Scotland, not just England being in charge of Great Britain.

Ceri: Ye it's so unfair, we should be allowed to do stuff ourselves; it's like calling us thick!

Catrin: It would be better for Wales to be independent.

Cai: Ye definitely.

These quotes could be seen as evidence of the students' motivation to achieve positive distinctiveness as part of their national social group (Tajfel and Turner, 1986), as well as their belief that the Welsh nation is being suppressed and overpowered (Clarke, 2010). Again, these views were presented most strongly in the WM group, and by Sion who is currently in the Welsh immersion programme, which suggests that the language is associated with a stronger national identity. However, although the discussion thus far suggests that this is the case, the participants in both groups agreed that speaking the language was not an important criterion for 'being Welsh'.

Ceri: No I think like, just believing in like Wales.

Catrin: Ye doesn't matter if you don't speak Welsh or not you're still …

Ceri: If you feel you're Welsh, then you are.

Similarly, the EM group expressed this attitude towards nationality:

Interviewer: Ok, so would you say that because they speak Welsh that they're more Welsh than you?

Shane: No.

Sarah: Well some of them speak Welsh in lessons but they don't like to speak it outside, so I wouldn't say that any of them were more Welsh than any of us.

These discussions demonstrate a belief amongst both groups of participants that speaking Welsh is not necessary for a Welsh national identity. This mirrors Scourfield et al.'s (2006) finding that the children across Wales stated that non-Welsh speakers were 'just as Welsh as Welsh-speakers' (p. 70), as well as Henry, Mayer and Kloep's (2007) study, where speaking Welsh was not seen as a condition for being Welsh. This suggests that being 'Welsh' is a subjective choice based on how an individual feels and how they want to categorize themselves, symptomatic of an inclusive, civic vision of Welsh nationality (Kellas, 1991). The comment articulated by Sarah that the Welsh speakers do not speak the language outside lessons provides an interesting insight into attitudes towards the language and its use amongst the students, and this will be returned to later in the chapter in the discussion around language use.

Although an inclusive vision of Wales was demonstrated on the whole within the sample, there was some evidence to suggest that one WM student may have thought differently regarding the relationship between language and national identity.

> Ceri: If you speak Welsh, you're a little bit more Welsh, but ... you can't really say that.

This comment suggests that although Ceri had originally stated that it does not matter whether you speak Welsh or not, she believed that speaking Welsh may result in a deeper level of national identity. Of all the participants in the sample, Ceri seemed the most strongly attached to the language, and showed evidence of the language being a source of identity conflict in her daily life. The fact that she suggested that making this statement would be considered controversial demonstrates awareness of the politically contentious nature of the issue, and the 'racist' connotations of the statement (Davies, 2010).

A similar observation was encountered in Scourfield et al.'s (2006) study, where only one participant, whose first language was Welsh, stated that she was not sure whether non-Welsh speakers could really be Welsh. However, this was the only suggestion in the present research regarding beliefs of a stronger national identity based on language, and on the whole, speaking the language was not perceived by the participants, at least not overtly, as strongly related to nationality. It may be that the language merely has a symbolic function (de Vos, 1975), but this symbolic use did not seem to cause an identity tension for the non-Welsh speakers as Scourfield et al. (2006) had suggested, and they did not perceive themselves to belong any less to the nation. These findings cannot be easily compared to Gruffudd's study: however, the following section resonates with Gruffudd's focus on the participants' stated use of the language in their daily lives.

Language use amongst friends

Friendship groups in the school setting were not primarily based around language, with the pupils forming friendship groups based on hobbies and interests, despite being segregated according to language during most lessons. Pupils commented that they 'all mixed' during break times and lunch hours and participants in both groups initially conveyed harmonious language relations. This would suggest that in this setting, language does not emerge as the most salient aspect of identity and group-formation as Sachdev and Bourhis (2005) suggested. This diverges from Gruffudd's research where a 'clear rift' was mentioned between pupils at a school in the Welsh heartland based on cultural differences (1997, p. 213). It may be that in the present study, the desire to fit in with the dominant majority overrides the desire to speak the Welsh language as a form of social identity. Comments made by participants in the WM group suggested that some found it difficult to speak the language due to social pressures, and that often non-Welsh speakers thought the language was 'funny' (Craig).

Ceri: Ye they get annoyed when you speak Welsh, they're like 'speak English please'!

Cai: Ye.

Ceri: So you feel like you have to change to English sometimes, even when you're just speaking to your Welsh friends!

Catrin: Ye, ye but it's difficult in a bilingual school to like speak Welsh.

As these extracts demonstrate, although the participants previously stated that the language relations were positive in the school, comments by non-Welsh-speaking pupils are influential in the Welsh speakers language choice. As Ceri stated, even in conversations with other Welsh-speaking students they often find they switch to speaking English to avoid any confrontation. As the Ethnolinguistic Identity Theory (ELIT) (Giles and Johnson, 1987) would suggest, if the language was an important aspect of the in-group identity of the Welsh speakers, they would in fact increase their distinctiveness by speaking the language, rather than switch to fit in with the majority, demonstrating language divergence. This supports Gruffudd's finding that the presence of EM education combined with anglicized homes has an adverse effect on the use of Welsh (1997, p. 206).

The point that this is not the case for these children can be explained by ELIT's concept of perceived vitality. Demographically, the Welsh language is a minority language in Wales, the local area and this particular school context, and it does not have a high status socially and historically. The children may, therefore, perceive the vitality of the language to be particularly low. For example, Owen stated how his

English cousins always 'took the mick' out of him for speaking Welsh. In this situation, ELIT suggests that members of the in-group may adopt strategies in order to achieve a more positive social identity, and in this particular situation they adopt a linguistic assimilation strategy (Giles and Johnson, 1987).

This strategy can also be seen in Gruffudd's study in a situation where Welsh is inferior to English. It was stated by an individual in his study that despite the fact that Welsh was the chosen language amongst her and her close friends at a younger age, that in a minority situation, English had started to replace Welsh in the college she attended due to the presence of non-Welsh-speaking individuals. This finding is also supported by Coupland et al.'s (2005) research where most sub-groups in their study perceived Welsh as having low vitality and thus was not a significant part of their daily social interactions.

A further comment made by the WM group in the present study was that they often felt pressure from teachers to speak Welsh, and therefore this can be seen as a source of identity conflict, where they are pressured to choose between 'keeping the language alive' (Catrin) and gaining social approval. The fact that some of the participants found this situation difficult suggests that they do identify quite strongly with the language. Comments made by the two girls from Welsh-speaking homes in the WM group suggested that this was the case, as can be seen in Ceri's response to the question regarding whether she would prefer to move to a Welsh-medium school.

> Ceri: I don't know, because like, it'd be difficult because you'd want to stay here with your English friends and you'd probably like, not fit in, but like you'd feel more at home.

Ceri's belief that she would probably feel more 'at home' in a Welsh-medium school suggests that she might feel uncomfortable and 'outnumbered' (Ceri) being in the minority group in the school. Catrin agreed, and further stated that she would like to move to north Wales as 'everyone speaks Welsh there'. This can be related to the fact that Welsh is not seen as fashionable amongst children of this age (Gruffudd, 1997) and therefore being in the Welsh-speaking minority is difficult for children who are more comfortable speaking Welsh.

It could also be seen as evidence that they believe they are more similar to people who speak the same language as them. This supports the findings of Giles, Taylor and Bourhis (1977) that members of the same ethnolinguistic group, in Wales, believed that they were more similar to individuals who spoke their native tongue than people who shared the same geographical origins. This is further supported by the following extract.

Ceri: Ye the Urdd is good, we make loads of friends, and good friends also, people like us.

Interviewer: From other schools?

Ceri: Ye, like they like, and Cwmni [Welsh-language theatre group] they're Welsh like us, but the things that they like too, like Eisteddfods and ... they're just like us.

Ceri and Catrin demonstrated that they felt a high degree of similarity to children who speak Welsh, which influenced their search for friendships and social groups outside the school setting. However, these views were only communicated by a minority of the WM focus group, and tended to be influenced by family background, suggesting that family linguistic practices play an important part in the relationship between language and identity. This supports Gruffudd's finding that Welsh-language use at home strongly influences use and attitudes outside the home, which will be discussed in the following section.

Language attitudes and the future

Although the language was not perceived as important to one's own Welshness, as discussed earlier in the chapter, it was clear from the discussions that the participants held positive views regarding the role of the Welsh language in maintaining Welsh national culture and the importance of this for the nation. The EM students communicated that they thoroughly enjoyed Welsh lessons and believed it was important for them to learn it at school, with no feelings of resentment or insignificance of learning Welsh as a second language, which might be expected considering the social and historical context in which the English language dominates. This echoes Gruffudd's study where participants in all geographical and linguistically differing areas held consistent positive views towards the language (Gruffudd, 1997, p. 217). As the following quote demonstrates, the group were unanimous in their belief that it would be sad if the language died, and that it's 'good that people speak Welsh' (Sam).

Sarah: 'Cause it's the traditional language of Wales and lots of minority languages have just been forgotten about because they weren't used very much, and umm ...

Sophia: Ye it's like a different culture, and it's important to keep cultures.

These views were similarly expressed by the WM group.

Ceri: Ye, if the Welsh language died, I think Wales would basically be the same as England, and Welsh would die also, like Wales.

These beliefs demonstrate the importance of the language as a marker of national difference and the most prominent factor in what makes Wales distinctive to England. Language is an important element of cultural identity and Sarah's statement demonstrates an awareness of the influence of dominant languages regarding the death of minority languages. So the language can be seen as a significant factor for national collective identity, but not to their individual sense of self, which is to be expected amongst non-Welsh speakers. These findings position the Welsh language as a symbol of a unique national identity, regardless of the fact that the majority of the nation does not speak it (de Vos, 1975).

However, despite the expression of these positive sentiments, both groups were in consensus that fewer people would speak the language in the future and that it would eventually cease to exist as a living language. Even Ceri, who made it clear that the language was an important element of her identity, stated that the Welsh language would eventually be 'like Latin', where some people might choose to learn it but no one would speak it. She may be making this statement in the knowledge that Welsh is not used as a social language in the school setting, and in the awareness that they assimilate to English as the dominant language.

When questioned about the reasoning behind the language's mortality, Sophia articulated that it is due to the fact that other languages are likely to be more useful than Welsh and therefore people are more likely to want to learn more widely used languages instead. Thus a combination of practical and ideological visions of language was discussed (Heller, 1999).

Sophia: I guess it's good for when you get a job when you're older, they look out for that as well as skills, like for a job they like you to have good variety, in other languages.

EM student Sophia's statements suggests that learning the Welsh language may be advantageous in terms of future employment within

Wales, but is no more beneficial than learning any other language and in fact, other languages are likely to be more useful considering the fact that the Welsh language is limited to employment within the Welsh context. Sion similarly expressed the view of the language as a commodity.

Sion: 'Cause if you live in Wales, it helps you with your jobs.

Sion perceives that learning the Welsh language may be beneficial in employment and economical terms rather than viewing it simply as a source of identity. Heller (1999) stated that this shift in language perception has similarly occurred in Quebec regarding the French language, with young people in Quebec using the language as a way of increasing future prospects rather than being fundamental to their perceptions of self. This might suggest that government initiatives to increase the proportion of Welsh speakers through WM educational provision may lead to the association of the language with education and work rather than leading to a bilingual nation socially.

However, it could be argued that, considering the historical background of the perceptions of the Welsh language, the fact that speaking the language is deemed as an advantage in the job market should be celebrated rather than viewed negatively (Scourfield et al., 2006). As Hodges's (2009) demonstrated, formal frameworks such as the workplace and schools are required in order to sustain language use and ensure that individuals who would not otherwise have the opportunity to speak the language continue to do so.

In the sample of students in this study, attitudes towards the language were significantly influenced by parental attitudes and family linguistic background. For example, Sion and Sarah, who were part of the immersion scheme, had extremely positive views regarding learning the language themselves, and suggested that they shared the same beliefs and values as their parents. Although their parents were English and did not speak Welsh themselves, they were very supportive of the language and eager for them to learn and become embraced in Welsh culture.

Sarah: I think my great, great granddad was Welsh, but umm, my mum and dad they don't speak Welsh, my mum comes from Sussex and my dad from London, but my mum is learning Welsh a bit.

Interviewer: So did they want you to come to the *trochi* (immersion scheme)?

Sarah: I wanted to, but they wanted me to as well.

59

As this excerpt demonstrates, Sarah's eagerness towards learning the language seemed to be reciprocated by the family. As Sarah had mentioned a distant ancestral connection to the Welsh nation, it may suggest that ancestral lineage may influence individuals' national identification and motivations and desire to become part of the culture. This contrasts to the views of other participants, such as Sophia from the EM group, who were more pessimistic and less interested in Welsh cultural life, particularly regarding the transmission of the language to their own children:

> Interviewer: So in the future so you think you'd want your kids to speak Welsh or ...?
>
> Sophia: No.
>
> Interviewer: How come?
>
> Sophia: Because English is a very popular language around the world, I think, and umm, ye it's just not important to me.
>
> Sarah: I would, because I've had lots of fun learning Welsh and I think that it would be really good fun to help them and teach them.

The views expressed by Sophia were shared with Cai from the WM group who stated that he was not sure whether he wanted his children to go to a Welsh-speaking school. Both participants conveyed that their parents were not particularly interested in the language, which seemed to influence their views regarding the future, which can be compared to Sarah's contrasting opinion. Scourfield et al. (2006) correspondingly found that parental influence was a key factor in determining whether children were pro- or anti-Welsh. This suggests that home influences continue to be as strong as those found in Gruffudd's study regarding language use, and should not be forgotten as an arena that would benefit from language preservation initiatives.

Conclusion

This research has involved the discussion of various aspects of the Welsh language and its relevance to young people's lives and identities. Despite the relatively small sample, it provides an insight into the ways the language is used and viewed by young people in a setting in which little research has been conducted. The study suggests that in relation to Gruffudd's initial research over two decades ago, many of the same issues are apparent. The home continues to provide a strong influence regarding use and attitudes towards the language despite the powerful effect of peer attitudes and actions, suggesting a need for a continued attempt to encourage positive linguistic attitudes by parents. The fact that the pupils in the Welsh stream displayed a seemingly stronger negative attitude towards the 'British' label suggests that speaking the language may result in a stronger sense of belonging with the Welsh nation, and this is a topic that could be studied further.

A clear finding from the study was that English dominated as the language of social relationships in the school setting, and Welsh-speaking pupils noted that they assimilated to speaking English as the dominant language due to peer influences. As Gruffudd had suggested in his previous research, English tends to be more fashionable during school age and therefore Welsh-medium education provides the only arena in which young people must continue to use the language. Therefore, a stronger attempt is still needed, especially in anglicized areas, to provide young people with social opportunities to speak the language, as well as the opportunities provided within education and the workplace.

Similar to Gruffudd, the positive sentiments towards the language in general, by Welsh and non-Welsh speakers, were very encouraging, and suggest a good platform for the future growth of the language. However, the pupils did display a strong belief that the language was likely to cease to exist in the future, perhaps in the knowledge that the language had a low status as a social language with peers. It is therefore crucial that the Welsh language is developed as a social language, and that this is a Welsh Government priority if Welsh is to survive as an active, thriving and vibrant language.

References

Atkinson, P., Coffey, A. and Delamont, S., *Key Themes in Qualitative Research* (Walnut Creek, CA: Alta Mira Press, 2003).

Baker, C., *Attitudes and Language* (Clevedon: Multilingual Matters, 1992).

Balsom, D., 'The three-Wales model', in J. Osmond (ed.), *The National Question Again* (Llandysul: Gomer, 1985).

Carrington, B. and Short, G., 'Who Counts; Who Cares? Scottish Children's Notions of National Identity', *Educational Studies*, 22/2 (1996), 203–24.

Clarke, J., 'Making national identities: Britishness in question', in S. Bromley, J. Clarke, S. Hinchcliffe and S. Taylor (eds), *Exploring Social Lives* (Milton Keynes: The Open University), pp. 203–46.

Coupland, N., Bishop, H., Williams, A., Evans, B. and Garrett, P., 'Affiliation, Engagement, Language Use and Vitality: Secondary School Students' Subjective Orientations to Welsh and Welshness', *International Journal of Bilingual Education and Bilingualism*, 8/1 (2005), 1–24.

Davies, C. A., 'Nationalism and the Welsh language', in H. Mackay (ed.), *Understanding Contemporary Wales* (Cardiff: University of Wales Press and The Open University, 2010), pp. 159–96.

Day, G., 'Place and belonging', in H. Mackay (ed.), *Understanding Contemporary Wales* (Cardiff: University of Wales Press and The Open University, 2010), pp. 26–57.

Evans, D., '"How Far across the Border do you Have to be, to be Considered Welsh?" National Identification at a Regional Level', *Contemporary Wales*, 20/1 (2007), 123–43.

Fishman, J. A., *Reversing Language Shift* (Clevedon: Multilingual Matters, 1991).

Giles, H., Taylor, D. M. and Bourhis, R. Y., 'Dimensions of Welsh Identity', *European Journal of Social Psychology*, 7/2 (1977), 165–74.

—— and Johnson, P., 'Ethnolinguistic Identity Theory: A social psychological approach to language maintenance', *International Journal of the Sociology of Language*, 68 (1987), 69–99.

Gruffudd, H., 'Young People's Use of Welsh: The Influence of Home and Community', *Contemporary Wales*, 10 (1997), 200–18.

Heller, M., *Linguistic Minorities and Modernity: A Sociolinguistic Ethnography* (Longman: Harlow, 1999).

Henry, L. B., Mayer, P. and Kloep, M., 'Belonging or Opposing? A Grounded Theory Approach to Young People's Cultural Identity in a Majority/Minority Societal Context Identity', *An International Journal of Theory and Research*, 7/3 (2007), 181–204.

Hodges, R., 'Welsh Language Use among Young People in the Rhymney Valley', *Contemporary Wales*, 22/1 (2009), 16–35.

James, A. and Prout, A. (eds), *Constructing and Reconstructing Childhood: Contemporary Issues in the Sociological Study of Childhood* (London: Falmer Press, 1997).

Jenkins, G. H., *A Concise History of Wales* (Cambridge: Cambridge University Press, 2007).

Kellas, J. G., *The Politics of Nationalism and Ethnicity* (Houndmills: Macmillan, 1991).

Mannay, D., 'Making the Familiar Strange: Can Visual Research Methods Render the Familiar Setting more Perceptible?', *Qualitative Research*, 10/1 (2010), 91–111.

May, S., *Language and Minority Rights: Ethnicity, Nationalism and the Politics of Language* (New York: Routledge, 2008).

Morgan, M., Gibbs, S., Maxwell, K. and Britten, N., 'Hearing Children's Voices: Methodological Issues in Conducting Focus Groups with Children Aged 7–11 Years', *Qualitative Research*, 2/5 (2002), 5–20.

Office for National Statistics, *Labour Force Survey of 2001* (London: HMSO, 2002).

——, *Census Data* (Newport: Office of National Statistics, 2011), *www.ons.gov. uk/ons/guide-method/census/2011/index.html* (accessed 10 December 2012).

Roberts, G. T., *The Language of the Blue Books: The Perfect Instrument of Empire* (Cardiff: University of Wales Press, 1998).

Sachdev, I. and Bourhis, R. Y., 'Power and Status Differentials in Minority and Majority Group Relations', *European Journal of Social Psychology*, 21/1 (1991), 1–24.

—— and ——, 'Multilingual Communication', in J. Harwood and H. Giles (eds), *Intergroup Communication: Multiple Perspectives* (New York: Peter Lang Publishing, 2005).

Scourfield, J., Dicks, B., Drakeford, M. and Davies, A., *Children, Place and Identity: Nation and Locality in Middle Childhood* (London: Routledge, 2006).

Tajfel, H. and Turner, J. C., 'The social identity theory of inter-group behavior', in S. Worchel and L. W. Austin (eds), *Psychology of Intergroup Relations* (Chicago: Nelson-Hall, 1986).

de Vos, G., 'Ethnic pluralism: Conflict and accommodation', in G. de Vos and K. Romanucci-Ross (eds), *Ethnic Identity: Cultural Continuity and Change* (Palo Alto, CA: Mayfield, 1975).

Vrasidas, C., 'Interpretivism and Symbolic Interactionism: "Making the Familiar Strange and Interesting Again" in Educational Technology Research', in W. Heinecke and J. Willis (eds), *Research Methods in Educational Technology* (Charlotte, NC: Information Age Publishing, 2001), pp. 81–99.

Welsh Assembly Government, *Iaith Pawb: A National Action Plan for a Bilingual Wales* (Cardiff: Welsh Assembly Government, 2003).

Welsh Language Board, *The Welsh Language Use Surveys of 2004–2006* (Cardiff: Welsh Language Board, 2008).

Who Does the Dishes? – by Ian Homer

4

Who Should Do the Dishes Now? Revisiting Gender and Housework in Contemporary Urban South Wales

DAWN MANNAY

Introduction

This chapter revisits Jane Pilcher's (1994) seminal work 'Who should do the dishes? Three generations of Welsh women talking about men and housework', which was originally published in *Our Sisters' Land: The Changing Identities of Women in Wales*. As discussed in the introductory chapter, I began revisiting classic Welsh studies as part of my doctoral study 'Mothers and daughters on the margins: gender, generation and education' (Mannay, 2012); this led to the later publication of a revisiting of Diana Leonard's (Barker, 1972) seminal paper 'Keeping Close and Spoiling in a South Wales Town' (Mannay, 2013a).

Later, I then wrote a paper for *Contemporary Wales* (Mannay, 2014), which returned to Pilcher's (1994) work, two decades on from the original study, and explored the question of the division of household labour in contemporary south Wales, drawing upon data generated in a study of mothers and daughters residing in a Welsh, marginalized, urban housing area. This chapter returns to that paper, revisiting and updating the key arguments and adding visual images, which were created by Welsh women in my study to communicate their experiences in the domestic sphere.

The chapter argues that in contemporary Wales, the domestic sphere remains a site of inequality, where women are negotiating the impossibility of being both in full-time employment and meeting the ideology of the 'Welsh Mam'. Furthermore, the work of women and the accompanying expectations have moved from being peripheral to becoming central; this places women in a psychological impasse where they identify themselves as 'lazy' when they cannot simultaneously fulfil these roles to the unreachable standards of the new respectable working-class femininity.

Background

According to the historian Beddoe (2000) the lives of Welsh women have been shaped by Nonconformity, religion, industrialization and a virulent strain of patriarchy, which have meant that in Wales, more than in other parts of Britain, women have been denied access to the public sphere. However, today women are far more visible in the labour market and have seen a brief period of gender parity in the National Assembly, which engendered a government responsive to the issues of women (Chaney et al., 2007). Such developments suggest that, perhaps, gender roles in Wales are being challenged. However, examining demographic evidence provides a more conventional picture.

Women's average hourly pay was 10.9 per cent lower than that of their male counterparts in 2006, reinforcing the concept of the gendered pay gap (WAG, 2008). In chapter eight of this collection, Caroline Lloyd discusses the contributory factor of widespread loss of female manufacturing jobs in Wales, and the expansion of low-wage jobs in the service sector for both men and women. In the following chapter, Alison Parken explores how low-waged work contributes to gendered inequalities in relation to the new 'Equal Pay Duty', and demonstrates the ways in which women in the most disadvantaged social groups in Wales fare significantly worse in employment and earnings than their male counterparts.

These gendered inequalities are also evident in Welsh public life. In 2003, the National Assembly had a world-first perfect gender balance of 50 per cent men and 50 per cent women; and 56 per cent of the Welsh Government cabinet seats were occupied by women. However, the ratio now stands at 58 per cent men to 42 per cent women, with only 27 per cent of cabinet seats being filled by women (EHRC, 2014). Paul Chaney, in chapter eleven of this book, critically reflects on the progress made following the espousal of gender mainstreaming during the early years of devolution and questions whether the implementation of devolution has served the pursuit of equality.

Furthermore, in other sectors of Welsh public life women only made up 9 per cent of Welsh council leaders, 16 per cent of secondary head teachers and none of the chief executives of Wales's top 100 private companies. These statistics suggested that 'progress towards getting more women into positions of power is far too slow' (EHRC, 2009, p. 3). In 2014, these figures were revisited and the percentage for Welsh council leaders remains unchanged, whilst a more recent survey of 100 companies operating in Wales found a diminutive rise in which 2 per cent record women chief executives (EHRC, 2014, pp. 9–10). Nevertheless, the report paints a stark picture of Wales, which illustrates that 'women are largely missing from the decision-making tables across most areas of our daily life' (EHRC, 2014, p. 3). If gender equality in public life is 'far too slow' and the gendered pay gap a persistent inequality, then perhaps we need to examine the situation of Welsh women in their private lives.

The ideology of the women enclosed inside the assumed safe space of the home is the traditional legacy that most girls inherit and there is a significant divide between boys' and girls' use of space (Dodman, 2003; Furlong and Cartmel, 1997; Griffin, 1985; Skelton, 2000; Tucker and Matthews, 2001). Accordingly, this chapter examines the positioning of mothers and daughters within the confines of the home and the moral boundaries that lay out respectable and acceptable benchmarks. Of course women are not cultural dopes without individual agency; however, as Butler (2004, p. 3) suggests, agency always exists within a paradox for it is opened by the fact that people are 'constituted by a social world' they never choose which can act to police women and trap them in patriarchal relationships.

As Page and Jha (2009) maintain, gendered labour divisions within the home are a cross-cultural phenomenon and in each of the seven countries that they researched, girls were given a larger proportion of family responsibilities and household chores than their male siblings. Wales is no exception. In her earlier study, Jane Pilcher (1994) explored housework across three generations of Welsh women and found that despite their greater rhetoric of egalitarianism women continued to have the main responsibility for housework, even when involved in paid employment.

Pilcher (1994) conducted interviews with families of Welsh women, mothers, daughters and adult-granddaughters between 1989 and 1990. She argued that the oldest generation of women – mothers – born around 1915, had been 'socialized to invest their female identities within the domestic sphere, as dictated by the cultural expectations of the time' (1994, p. 44), and that they claimed the responsibility of domestic work and resisted the idea of male participation despite the fact that their husbands had retired. The second generation – the daughters – had grown up in a different socio-economic climate and many had entered the workplace. For these women, Pilcher describes a pattern of continuity in that responsibility for the domestic sphere still fell to women and significant participation in the domestic sphere by men was resisted; however, there was a realization that their situation was inequitable and the domestic arrangement could be a 'bone of contention' (1994, p. 45).

The third generation – the granddaughters – born in 1967 had grown up in a society influenced by feminist ideologies and in their interviews the participants took up an egalitarian vocabulary, based on fairness and sharing. However, at the point of interview most of this group were still living at home and had not experienced living independently with a male partner: in this way their discussions were anticipatory and philosophical. Those young women who had married and left home maintained an egalitarian discourse; however, despite this rhetoric, their reported domestic routines suggested that they were in fact, largely responsible for housework, despite having outside employment. This led Pilcher to conclude that although 'younger generations of Welsh women may no longer be investing their identities in the domestic sphere ... they continue to invest their time and effort alongside paid employment' (1994, p. 45).

More recently, Warren (2003) argues that alongside a gender-based approach to the study of the domestic division of labour it is important to acknowledge the role of class. Analysing data from the British Household Panel Survey, Warren employs the categories of time-wealth and time-poverty to examine gendered and classed differentiations. Time wealth/poverty debates have largely been restricted to professional/managerial couples with little attention given to the experience of working-class families. Redressing this balance, Warren (2003) finds that working-class dual-waged couples were more likely to fall into the time-poverty category than their middle-class counterparts. Furthermore, women in these couples contributed a proportionally higher share of caring and domestic work than both their partners and women in professional roles, who can often afford to contract out domestic tasks.

Alongside the disparity in the actual physical engagement with domestic labour, contemporary research also documents the pervasive rhetoric of a false equity highlighted by Pilcher (1994). For example, Miller (2011) studied parenthood and in her interviews with both mothers and fathers she found that despite the presentation of egalitarian gender relations and social arrangements in their talk, the actuality was that everyday practices were inflected by traditional gendered expectations in which the woman was centralized as primary care giver. Similarly, Pahl (2005) conducted focus groups about patterns of money management within the household and found that participants' discourses offered a gloss of gender equality, but that beneath this rhetoric gender differences in spending responsibilities that discriminated against women were evident, particularly in relation to paying for children and childcare.

Again, exploring money management, Burgoyne et al. (2008) argue that while analyses of married couples have revealed gender-associated asymmetries in access to household resources, cohabitants are more likely to 'write their own scripts' according to their relational practices, with less emphasis on the traditional roles associated with marriage. Drawing on data from the International Social Survey Programme modules on Family and Changing Gender Roles, Vogler et al. (2008) also argue that cohabiting couples, particularly young childless and older post-marital partnerships, unlike married couples, keep money partly or completely separate. However, cohabiting parents tend to see their relationships as similar or equivalent to marriage and organize money in very similar ways to married parents.

This research, then, could suggest that gender issues are easily conflated with the ideological meanings of the institute of marriage, so that being a wife or a husband produces asymmetries, rather than simply gender. However, splitting of finances can in itself reinforce gender inequalities where one partner earns significantly more than the other, and the data discussed earlier in relation to gendered pay gaps would suggest the higher earner is generally the man. Furthermore, Vogler et al. (2008) recognize the ways in which parenthood presents itself as a catalyst for returning to more traditional gendered role taking and, returning to Miller (2011), the taking-up of the role of mother retains a duty of active care that is not as explicit in commonplace understandings of the role of fatherhood.

Polarities have been institutionally rooted in the marriage contract and the labour market, and today, household organization remains a crucially important dimension of intimate relationships, where everyday practices sit at the interface between the couple and the wider society. In this way, relationships mediate the extent to which gender inequalities in the labour market are transposed into inequalities within the home, and in both spaces it is women who are disadvantaged, despite post-feminist discourses of 'girl power' (May, 2008; McRobbie, 2008; Walby, 2011). These findings are reflected in the qualitative accounts of the mothers in the following discussion. The research setting often informs the interview questions that the researcher would ask, and in this study the images of places that were produced visually by the participants kindled my interest in their domestic spaces.

Research context

Mackay (2010) argues that the distinctiveness of Wales, in terms of its political life and culture, has grown considerably over the last decade: nevertheless, beneath the imagery of the definitive nation, Wales remains a complex and divided land. Wales is often presented as a country where locality, community and belonging are of particular importance but the nation can also be viewed as 'existing in relations of a paradox or antagonism' (Massey, 1994, p. 3). Such variation is captured in Balsom's three Wales model that distinguishes between Welsh Wales, British Wales and *Y Fro Gymraeg* (Balsom, 1985).

It is arguable whether or not Balsom's neat three-way geographical split is workable but there are distinctions drawn between urban and rural, Welsh-speaking and English-speaking, south and north and even the neighbouring town. As Day comments, 'It is striking how important geographical differences of place seem to be organising these perceptions of social difference. They imply that the individuals concerned possess a map of social variations, arranged according to the compass' (2010, p. 33). Place then, even within one nation, can be divided linguistically, culturally and economically.

Divisions of class are both powerful and pervasive, and one way of examining this class divide is through geographical distribution. Morrison and Wilkinson (1995) argue that polarization has a spatial dimension that is illustrated in the creation of new ghettos of prosperity and poverty that now dominate the Welsh socio-economic terrain; they term these divisions within Wales's towns and cities the 'Los Angelization' of socio-economic terrain to draw parallels with the inequalities found in American cities, epitomized by the growth of gated communities, which insulate the wealthy from the poor (Low,

2003). Morrison's and Wilkinson's (1995) ghettos are evident across Wales and, as Evans (2010) comments, this separation means that poverty can easily be overlooked by those with more resources who will rarely encounter those on low incomes.

In contemporary Wales, areas of deprivation become stigmatized and those of low socio-economic status become coded by their residence in the 'next-door yet foreign place where the other neighbours live' (Toynbee, 2003, p. 19). The research site Hystryd[1] forms what Day (2010, p. 37) would refer to as a 'distinct urban village', in some ways mirroring the key features of place and belonging associated with the rural village, illustrating a detailed familiarity, with sets of relatives living nearby.

However, Hystryd is not imagined as a rural idyll: it is an area of deprivation (Welsh Assembly Government, 2008), especially in terms of employment, and here the loss of localized heavy industry has meant that, borrowing from Trezise (2005, p. 17), the area could be remembered as a place 'where poverty surrounded you like a neck brace'. It is an area, then, that resonates with Michael Ward's and Dave Adamson's discussions, in chapters five and ten of this collection, where communities have become locked into a pattern of rising poverty and social exclusion: home to the girls and 'boys from nowhere'.

Place is both an heuristic mechanism, a quick fix, for placing ourselves and others and a 'social construct arising out of our interactions with others around us' (Scourfield et al., 2006, p. 15), but examining the co-ordinates of mothers' and daughters' social worlds in this study complicates the idea of a single Hystryd. For within Hystryd there are further complexities and a relational reconceptualization of identity. It is this multiplicity of place within a stigmatized ideal of singularity that I will explore in the chapter, examining the gendered distinctions that continue to define a woman's place. Focusing on the private space of the home, the chapter draws on discourses of acceptable working-class femininity (Davidoff, 1976; Mannay and Morgan, 2015; Skeggs, 2004), neoliberal notions of 'new motherhood' (May, 2008) and the pervasive disparity between the ideology of gender equality and the everyday engagement with domestic labour.

Methodology

The participants in this study were nine mothers and their nine daughters. Daughters were in one of three groups, the last year of primary school, the last year of compulsory education and post-compulsory education. Mothers of daughters in the two eldest groups tended to be born in the late 1960s, in line with Pilcher's (1994) youngest generation of interviewees, adult-granddaughters, born in 1967. The mothers of daughters in primary school were born in the late 1970s and are part of a younger generation than the participants in Pilcher's study.

The relationship between researcher and researched is key to the collection of reliable data (Pole, 2007): I previously lived in Hystryd, engendering a shared sense of geography, which positioned me as 'researcher near' and influenced the design of the study. Consequently, it was important to address my position as an indigenous researcher and make a deliberate cognitive effort to question my taken-for-granted assumptions of that which I had thought familiar (Mannay, 2010). In combination with earlier strategies (Delamont and Atkinson, 1995), I was influenced by research that employed participants' visual data to render the familiar setting more perceptible (Kaomea, 2003). Participants in this study used the data production technique of photo-elicitation, collage, mapping and narratives to express their perceptions of their social and physical environments, their everyday lives, reflections of their pasts, and aspirations and fears for the future.[2]

The practice of asking participants to explain the visual images that they create has become a common feature of social science research and the visual and narrative data produced were discussed in elicitation interviews, privileging the interpretative model of auteur theory (Rose, 2001). The notion that the most salient aspect in understanding a visual image is what the maker intended to show is often referred to as auteur theory (Rose, 2001), and in this study auteur theory was required on a practical level because the interpretation of the audience is not necessarily the same as the narrative the image-maker wanted to communicate: indeed it can often be markedly different (see Mannay, 2010).

These techniques proved useful within a participatory methodology and illustrated a potential for making the familiar strange (Mannay, 2010, 2013b); they also engendered in-depth qualitative accounts (Mannay, 2011; Mannay and Morgan 2013, 2015). Data presented were drawn from the wider research project that explored the everyday experiences of mothers and their daughters residing in Hystryd, and the analysis of visual, narrative and interview data drew from a psychoanalytically informed psychosocial approach.[3] In this chapter the analysis specifically applies the lens of gender to examine and foreground the 'place' of mothers and daughters in Hystryd, and explores the tension between the post-feminist discourses of equality (McRobbie, 2008; Walby, 2011) and the everyday negotiation of feminized identities in private space.

A woman's place ...

When I asked participants to create maps, collages and photographs for the 'place and space' data production many images focused on the domestic sphere and featured paraphernalia of the domestic. Images included irons, vacuum cleaners and cleaning products and such material culture was central to many of the mothers' interviews. Focusing on 'inside' and 'outside' of the home allowed an insight to the gendered space of everyday life within the home, and provided an opportunity to explore identity within domestic spaces.

It was apparent from the data produced that I could not consider place without thinking about gender divisions. In this chapter, I am not arguing that gender is important particularly in Hystryd, or that such gender divisions are necessarily place specific. Rather, I argue that gender divisions are particularly important in the everyday lives of the participants. The chapter demonstrates how individual experiences are intimately related to dominant and systemic features of social life within and outside Hystryd, and that despite the rhetoric of egalitarianism expressed by younger generations (Pilcher, 1994); as Melanie Morgan argues in chapter six of this book, women continue to operate within gendered spaces inside the confines of respectable femininity.

Housework – the busy mam

Many of the mothers constructed their ideas of 'place and space' with images of housework. Seven of the nine mothers interviewed created visual images for their 'place and space' data production and five of these mothers included images of household cleaning products or appliances with a total of thirteen such images across their collective visual data. Ironing seemed to hold a special position within the realm of housework and three mothers created images of irons for the visual data production, as illustrated in figure 4.1, and described working their way

Figure 4.1: 'It's not too bad with these irons they got now'

through great piles of clothes. Caroline[4] described ironing as her 'pet hate' but explained that she does not cut any corners, ironing sheets, pillows and quilt covers as well as clothes for five people. Caroline told me 'it's not too bad with these irons they got now' and joked 'I'm not there all day like I used to be, just half a day'.

All of the mothers in the study, apart from one, Nina, took complete responsibility for ironing. Where husbands, partners and children took part in housework activities ironing was not part of their remit. Only Nina breaks ranks by only ironing her own clothes and nothing else, and explained 'I've got *too much* to do'. Nina's 19-year-old daughter, Roxanne, is the only daughter in the sample to feature images of housework in her visual data and this reflects the delegation by Nina, meaning that she is responsible for cleaning her own bedroom and doing her own laundry. However, overall there seemed to be only minimal engagement with housework by the daughters in the study. Where mothers reported this assistance from their daughters or husbands it was often coached in terms of 'helping' and being 'as good as gold'. This help then was appreciated but not expected, unlike their work, and contrasted with the complete absence of support from their sons, a point discussed in the following section.

Legitimate 'wifework'

Social and moral identities are intricately bound up with parenting, and keeping the home clean is still considered essential, even in the prescribed ideal notion of 'new motherhood', depicting a woman who also holds down a full-time job (May, 2008). Pilcher (1994), exploring housework across three generations of Welsh women, found that the youngest women interviewed, who like Patricia were born in 1967, had been influenced by a society characterized by egalitarian and feminist ideologies. Despite their greater rhetoric of egalitarianism these women continued to have the main responsibility for housework, even when involved in paid employment, and this was seen as a source of tension within intimate relationships. However, despite having a part-time job and caring for her grandchildren, Patricia did not exhibit any overt tension in her talk around housework:

Patricia: I don't mind housework Dawn.

Interviewer: You don't mind it?

Patricia: No I don't, no I don't mind housework, like what stops me mostly is like time and things, you know?

Interviewer: Yeah.

Patricia: No I don't mind housework; I like a nice clean house.

Patricia invests her identity in the domestic sphere and the idea of cleanliness. The concept of cleanliness is intrinsically linked to the notion of maintaining a respectable working-class femininity (Davidoff, 1976; Skeggs, 2004). As Evans (2007) contends, dirt assumes a heightened importance when the metaphorical stereotypes of your class are muck, filth, dirt and waste products. In Wales, a country that many see as a colonized nation, such analogies can have a fervent and more sustained influence over the lives of women (see Aaron, 1994 for a full discussion of the moral imperative to adopt an English middle-class model of femininity put forward in the 1847 Report of the Commissions of Inquiry, which she argues had a pervasive influence over the identities of generations of Welsh women; also chapter two of the current collection where Jane Aaron revisits this earlier work). When I asked about who is seen as responsible for cleaning Patricia also described the designation of housework as if it had no gender distinctions:

Patricia: I don't think he thinks it's like women's work as such but [pause] the fact that I've always been home, I've always done it Dawn.

Interestingly, Patricia talked about what she thinks her husband 'thinks' and the point that she has always been home and her husband has always worked is a situation presented as an equitable split between working inside and outside the home. In the last few years Patricia has worked part time and acted as a childminder for her grandchildren, while her husband has remained in full-time employment and this change has been met with some support from her husband and daughter.

The adjective 'good' is used in Patricia's accounts to describe her husband's and daughter's housework.

> Patricia: No he's pretty good, I got to be fair he's pretty good, like if I've got to work, if I'm go to work in the morning and [my husband's] at home, it's clean when I come home ... You know like [my husband], wouldn't put the washing machine on and he wouldn't iron ... He's good like that and you know he wouldn't expect me to clean the bath out after him.

The housework of Patricia's husband is selective and seen as 'helping' Patricia, rather than as him having a direct responsibility for household chores, which is in keeping with previous research, where women were more likely to gain help with tasks, rather than for husbands to agree to accept ongoing accountability (Dempsey, 2000). Importantly, the peripheral activity of helping places the overall responsibility of domestic labour with the woman, and represents a condescending arrangement, whereby ownership of housework is ideologically and practically naturalized as a feminized activity.

In the same way, Patricia's 20-year-old daughter, Carla, helps. For Patricia, Carla is 'good as gold' and she will wash dishes and vacuum – a contrast to her younger brother who Patricia laughingly describes as a 'dirty Bertie'. The use of 'good' is interesting as it suggests that Carla and her father's engagement is both voluntary and appreciated: Patricia does not describe her own cleaning activities as 'good' and Carla does not attend to the subject of housework in her narrative data production or interview. Additionally, unlike the images of place produced by some of the mothers in the study, there are no images of cleaning utensils in Carla's photographs. For Carla, housework is not something that she feels she needs to represent in either photographic, narrative or oral data. On the contrary, for Patricia, housework is a cyclic inevitability that threads through the account of her everyday life.

> Patricia: 'Cause *whatever* you do *today*, tomorrow you got to do it again.

Although Patricia acknowledged the repetitive nature of housework, she maintained that this is part of the life she envisaged: an expected role of wifehood, motherhood and respectable working-class femininity, and a visible demonstration of her culturally presumed, innate capacity to care (Hollway, 2006).

Housework – the 'lazy' mam

As Warren (2003) maintains, even though women are contributing to the household income, the expectations within the household have not changed accordingly. When Juliet, also born in 1967, reflected back on her life she described it in terms of 'constant constant constant same old, all the time', referring to completing housework and looking after her partner and children. Although she has become the sole, full-time worker, working long hours, nothing has changed both in terms of the expectations of the rest of the family and her expectations of herself as illustrated in the following extract.

> Juliet: Yeah but you know my ideal would be to have a spotless house, you know, have it clean, have things put in its place, that is my ideal way of life [pause] and for some reason, I just can't seem to accomplish it.

Juliet takes responsibility for what she sees as domestic failure, it is only 'I' who 'can't seem to accomplish it', not the three children, all over sixteen years of age, or her partner, who although being too ill to carry on working in the building trade could complete light domestic work in the home. This theme of domestic responsibility is extended in the next quote.

> Juliet: I come home from work, do everything and then I'm sat on the settee for two, three hours [pause] in the evening being lazy.

When Juliet comes home from work she does 'everything', which here refers to the immediate everyday needs of preparing a meal, doing dishes and sorting out laundry, before she sits down for the evening. In this statement we are offered a reason for the failure to achieve 'a spotless house': Juliet's personal failure of 'laziness'. This disavowal of the importance and time-restraints of becoming the financial provider and Juliet's continued subservience to the ideology that cleanliness is her sole responsibility led me to challenge the fraught position that Juliet endeavours to negotiate. I asked about the responsibility of the rest of the family:

> Juliet: I suppose it's my own fault for doing it and not making them do it because yeah I think they don't think, that it is their job so, so yeah.

Again, self-blame was employed as a form of explanation and Juliet presented her family's lack of activity in the domestic sphere as a personal failing. Juliet was clearly not happy with the situation, her sadness and frustration was palpable and her collage was dominated by the paraphernalia of domestic bliss. In a central position in her collage is a timer or hourglass, illustrated in figure 4.2. It represents not only the daily struggle of trying to achieve an impossible ideal but also, as discussed earlier in the section, the reflection that her life has been and continues to be 'constant constant constant same old, all the time'.

Turgo (2010) conducted research in a fishing community in the Philippines where many women have taken on the role of breadwinner in response to changes in the wider economy. Turgo argues that while these women are extracting feminine dividends from the ongoing economic restructuring in the community, they are also complicit with their own subordination within the home. Like Juliet, these women have become the provider but continued to take ownership of the domestic sphere. According to Turgo this is necessary for them to be 'active players in maintaining the façade of "normalcy", the preservation of the structure of hegemonic masculinity, in their everyday lives' (2010, p. 165).

For Turgo, this act of subordination is a conscious one, a role they have to play given the societal structures that construct and constrain their lives, and he suggests that in this way it is a feigned subordination. The Philippines may seem a geographical leap, but in Wales, research has also been interested in the ways in which women endeavour to keep forms of lost masculinity alive. Walkerdine and Jimenez (2012) suggest that in the south Wales valleys the community reaction to loss of

Figure 4.2: Time

industry has often been one that demonstrates a commitment to keep everything going 'no matter what'.

Walkerdine and Jimenez (2012) describe interviews with women, in these marginalized communities, who talk about 'soldiering on' and describe how they will take any type of work, whilst their partners refuse employment that they categorize as feminine. Walkerdine and Jimenez (2012) note that women continue to employ the term 'breadwinner' for men who no longer win bread. For Walkerdine and Jimenez, these practices of femininity keep a sense of masculinity intact, at great cost to the women involved. However, the alternative, beyond the safety of these traditional, highly gendered roles, would be something new and, therefore, even more frightening.

Housework – the 'selfish' mam

This idea of subordination to wider, traditional and perhaps outdated structures that determine the requirements of acceptable femininity and motherhood is demonstrated in the account of one of the other mothers. Bethan, again, works full time and, like Juliet, she is frustrated by the hours she needs to spend undertaking housework. This is illustrated in the following extract:

> Bethan: You feel like you're throwing your life away just to make it look clean.

However, Bethan, a mother of a younger generation born in 1976, then went on to tell me how important it is to perform domestic work. This defence of domesticity is not a rationale cognitive model based on the avoidance of bacteria or a strategy to improve day-to-day organization, but rather a psychological defence against the stigma of being an inadequate partner and mother, as shown in the next conversation where I asked Bethan if she finds her share of responsibilities problematic:

> Interviewer: Yeah, mm, and you don't *mind* with the *hoovering* and *washing*, you, or is it like a bone of contention?

> Bethan: *No* it's not a bone of contention, because I'm working full time that little bit that I'm doing [pause] makes me feel like I'm still a Mum.

> Interviewer: The cooking?

> Bethan: Yeah . . . And the *washing up* and the *hoovering*, I like to do it sometimes [pause] because I still feel like I'm *doing something* for my *children*, I'm . . . For where *they live* [pause] does that *make sense*?

79

Interviewer: Yeah.

Bethan: I'm not just going out to work and being a *selfish* Mum, and earning the money and sitting on my arse and doing *nothing*.

Interviewer: Yeah.

Bethan: I suppose it's *pride* for myself really, just to be able to say, look I can work full time and look after *my kids*, and sort of maintain a *home*.

As Menjivar observes, while 'women may experience the empowerment of earning a wage and deciding how to spend it … they also face the disempowerment of recreating conditions of gender inequality in the home so as to maintain an idealised (class-specific) union' (2006, p. 93). For Bethan, who was living as a single mother before meeting her current partner, there is a need to manage a moral presentation of the self (May, 2008). The ideology of the 'good wife' can replace the stigma of the 'single mum' and, more importantly, taking on domestic tasks offers an opportunity to display a normative femininity characterized by her 'capacity to care' for her children (Hollway, 2006).

As Bethan told me, she wants to 'still feel like I'm *doing something* for my *children*'. The role of financial provider is not enough, as illustrated by Bethan's portrayal of 'being a *selfish* Mum, and earning the money and sitting on my arse and doing *nothing*', a point that is not made as a contradiction in terms. This mirrors Juliet's account where resting after work is seen as lazy and again not being able to perform the ideology of the mythical and untenable goal of single-handedly combining full-time work and being a domestic goddess.

In order to attain this form of idealized femininity, there may then be a need to guard against the involvement of partners in the domestic sphere, acting as a 'gate keeper' (Maushart, 2001) to maintain the adage that 'a woman's place is in the home'. In a post-feminist society that offers the illusion of choice, women can supposedly 'have it all' (McRobbie, 2008; Walby, 2011); however, the discourses that promote employability and equality have not erased the physical and psychological work of more traditional positioning so that women feel they are obliged to 'do it all'.

Even where husbands and partners took on a domestic role that was well received by mothers in the study, their cleaning was still seen to impinge on their own role and the way their standard of cleaning was perceived by others.

Tina: Yeah he does help, I'll probably come across as a *lazy bitch* now.
[laughs]

Tina, born in 1977, is happy that her partner will share the domestic responsibilities but the idea that such equitable arrangements position her as a 'lazy bitch' has to be defended against and explained. Therefore, even if an even-handed engagement with housework can be sustained in the home it can still have social and psychological consequences for those involved. In this way, in Hystryd, the accounts of these mothers indicate that although women may have 'time off' to be 'a selfish Mum' in the labour market, their 'place', where they belong, concretely and ideologically, is firmly at the kitchen sink.

Conclusion

Writing in the 1980s, Morris (1987, p. 64) argued that Welsh women's role in the domestic sphere was their traditional one, and that the domestic role has proved enduring despite their entry into employment. For Morris (1987), the very nature of part-time work meant that women's role in the domestic division remained undisturbed. In contemporary Wales, for women working full time, these inequalities often remain undisturbed and crystallized as the pathway to legitimate wifehood and motherhood.

The traditional roles of domestic division of labour is not challenged by women's employment and the reality is the double-shift, where the myth of the 'Welsh Mam' (Rees, 1988), alongside the bread-winning Mam, have become the dual expectations of acceptable working-class femininity. In the late 1980s there was an argument that women's traditional role in Wales would appear to be little different to twenty years ago, 'in so far as it has been changed it has been added to' (Winckler, 1987 p. 66). Data presented here suggests that contemporary Wales is resonant of both continuity and addition.

In Pilcher's (1994) study, women born in 1967 demonstrated the rhetoric of egalitarianism but in everyday life these women continued to have the main responsibility for housework. Data in this study have illustrated the ways in which women born in the 1960s and later in the 1970s retain this responsibility for the domestic sphere. However, while Pilcher (1994) reported that younger generations of women were, at least ideologically, less likely than their mothers and grandmothers to invest their identities in the domestic sphere, in the present study we see women re-investing their identities in the domestic sphere.

Different identities and roles are assumed according to their time and place, and in a local and global climate where working-class male employment has become destabilized then perhaps this has engendered a return to traditions as a way of stabilizing the home within wider destabilization: the sacrifice of new femininities to protect traditional masculinities (Turgo, 2010; Walkerdine and Jimenez, 2012). In the accounts in this chapter, the rhetoric of egalitarianism and equality has been silenced and replaced with a discourse of inadequacy: where when the impossibilities of new femininity – full-time job, perfect mother, domestic goddess (May, 2008) – are not achieved, women are blaming themselves and identifying themselves incongruously as the lazy but bread-winning Welsh Mam.

If we ask 'who should do the dishes now?' the answer from many women may be 'we should', an answer with a conviction that was absent in earlier times. In Pilcher's study the hope for equality was visible, if not in the physical tasks of domestic work, in the possibilities of the adult-granddaughters' talk. This discourse was influenced by feminist and egalitarian ideologies; however, the power of this message seems to have weakened, perhaps because the ideology was not met with the participation, time and effort of the elusive sharer. In public life there has been a shift in the visibility of women in Wales, but behind closed doors many women remain physically, psychologically and symbolically embedded in a never-ending stack of dirty dishes.

Acknowledgements

I would like to acknowledge the participants who made this chapter possible, and also Professor John Fitz, Professor Emma Renold and Dr Bella Dicks for supervising the related research project. I am grateful to Dr Elin Royles and Dr Paul Chaney and the reviewers for their encouragement and invaluable comments on earlier versions of this chapter. The doctoral research project from which this paper is drawn was titled 'Mothers and daughters on the margins: gender, generation and education' and was funded by the Economic and Social Research Council, Award No. PTA031200600088.

Notes

[1] The name Hystryd is fictitious and it was chosen to maintain the anonymity of the area.

[2] The technique of mapping is an activity where participants are asked to draw a representation of a specific geographical space of journey; collage offers participants to make a visual representation of their lives from a collection of images; photo-elicitation techniques allow participants to take a series of photographs that form the basis of an interview discussion. In this study participants were each provided with art materials and/or cameras and asked to make a series of visual productions depicting meaningful places, spaces and activities. Data produced then formed the basis of an interview where I engaged in a tape-recorded discussion with each participant. Further discussion of the technique can be found in Mannay (2010). In narrative approaches, stories provide an analytical frame for the study of mental life as well as the study of social conditions. In this study participants were asked to write narratives from the retrospective perspective of their childhood self describing who they wanted to become, their positive possible self, and who they feared becoming, their negative possible self. This activity was repeated from the perspective of the present and participants again wrote a narrative of possible positive and negative selves.

[3] Psychosocial approaches are concerned with psychological development in, and in interaction with, a social environment. A seminal text for exploring psychosocial inquiry is J. Henriques et al. (1998), and its application in my own writing can be seen in Mannay (2013a).

[4] Women's names employed in the paper are pseudonyms chosen to maintain participants' anonymity.

References

Aaron, J., 'Finding a voice in two tongues: gender and colonization', in J. Aaron, T. Rees, S. Betts and M. Vincentelli (eds), *Our Sisters' Land: The Changing Identities of Women in Wales* (Cardiff: University of Wales Press, 1994), pp. 183–98.

Balsom, D., 'The three-Wales model', in J. Osmond (ed.), *The National Question Again* (Llandysul: Gomer, 1985).

Barker, D., 'Keeping Close and Spoiling in a South Wales Town', *Sociological Review*, 20/4 (1972), 569–90.

Beddoe, D., *Out of the Shadows: A History of Women in Twentieth-century Wales* (Cardiff: University of Wales Press, 2000).

Burgoyne, C., Barlow, A. and Sonnenberg, S. J., *Financial management practices in non-traditional heterosexual couples: Full Research Report ESRC End of Award Report, RES-000-22-1471* (Swindon: ESRC, 2008).

Butler, J., *Undoing Gender* (Abington: Routledge, 2004).

Chaney, P., Mackay, F. and McAllister, L., *Women, Politics and Constitutional Change* (Cardiff: University of Wales Press, 2007).

Davidoff, L., 'The rationalization of housework', in D. Barker and S. Allen (eds), *Dependence and Exploitation in Work and Marriage* (London: Longman, 1976), pp. 121–51.

Day, G., 'Place and belonging', in H. Mackay (ed.), *Understanding Contemporary Wales* (Cardiff: University of Wales Press and The Open University, 2010), pp. 25–58.

Delamont, S. and Atkinson, P., *Fighting Familiarity: Essays on Education and Ethnography* (Cresskill, NJ: Hampton Press, 1995).

Dempsey, K. C., 'Men and Women's Power Relationships and the Persisting Inequitable Division of Housework', *Journal of Family Studies*, 6/1 (2000), 7–24.

Dodman, D. R., 'Shooting in the City: An Autobiographical Exploration of the Urban Environment in Kingston, Jamaica', *Area*, 35/3 (2003), 293–304.

Equality and Human Rights Commission (EHRC), *Who Runs Wales 2009?* (Cardiff: EHRC, 2009).

——, *Who Runs Wales 2009? A Lost Decade – No Change* (Cardiff: EHRC, 2014).

Evans, G., *Educational Failure and Working Class White Children in Britain* (London: Palgrave Macmillan, 2007).

Evans, N., 'Class', in H. Mackay (ed.), *Understanding Contemporary Wales* (Cardiff: University of Wales Press and The Open University, 2010), pp. 125–58.

Furlong, A. and Cartmel, F., *Young People and Social Change* (Buckingham: Open University Press, 1997).

Griffin, C., *Typical Girls? Young Women from School to the Job Market* (London: Routledge Kegan & Paul, 1985).

Henriques, J., Hollway, W., Urwin, C., Venn, C. and Walkerdine, V., *Changing the Subject: Psychology, Social Regulation and Subjectivity* (London: Routledge, 1998).

Hollway, W., *The Capacity to Care: Gender and Ethical Subjectivity* (London: Routledge, 2006).

Kaomea, J., 'Reading Erasures and Making the Familiar Strange: Defamiliarising Methods for Research in Formerly Colonized and Historically Oppressed Communities', *Educational Researcher*, 32/2 (2003) 14–25.

Low, S., *Behind the Gates: Life, Security and the Pursuit of Happiness in Fortress America* (New York: Routledge, 2003).

Mackay, H., 'Rugby – an introduction to contemporary Wales', in H. Mackay (ed.), *Understanding Contemporary Wales* (Cardiff: University of Wales Press and The Open University, 2010), pp. 1–24.

McRobbie, A., *The Aftermath of Feminism: Gender, Culture and Social Change* (London: Sage, 2008).

Mannay, D., 'Mothers and Daughters on the Margins: Gender, Generation and Education' (unpublished PhD thesis, Cardiff University, 1998).

——, 'Making the Familiar Strange: Can Visual Research Methods Render the Familiar Setting more Perceptible?', *Qualitative Research*, 10/1 (2010), 91–111.

——, 'Taking Refuge in the Branches of a Guava Tree: The Difficulty of Retaining Consenting and Non-consenting Participants' Confidentiality as an Indigenous Researcher', *Qualitative Inquiry*, 17/10 (2011), 962–4.

——, 'Keeping Close and Spoiling: Exploring the Significance of "Home" for Family Relationships and Educational Trajectories in a Marginalised Estate in Urban South Wales', *Gender and Education*, 25/1 (2013a), 91–107.

——, '"Who Put That on There ... Why Why Why?" Power Games and Participatory Techniques of Visual Data Production', *Visual Studies*, 28/2 (2013b), 136–46.

——, 'Who Should do the Dishes Now? Exploring Gender and Housework in Contemporary Urban South Wales', *Contemporary Wales*, 27/1 (2014), 21–39.

——, 'Doing Ethnography or Applying a Qualitative Technique? Reflections from the "Waiting Field"', *Qualitative Research*, 15/2 (2015), 166–82.

—— and Morgan, M., 'Anatomies of Inequality: Considering the Emotional Cost of Aiming Higher for Marginalised, Mature Mothers Re-entering Education', *Journal of Adult and Continuing Education*, 19/1 (2013), 57–75.

—— and ——, 'Doing Ethnography or Applying a Qualitative Technique? Reflections from the "Waiting Field"', *Qualitative Research*, 15/2 (2015), 166–82.

Massey, D., *Class, Place and Gender* (Cambridge: Polity Press, 1994).

Maushart, S., *Wifework: What Marriage Really Means for Women* (London: Bloomsbury, 2001).

May, V., 'On Being a "Good" Mother: The Moral Presentation of Self in Written Life Stories', *Sociology*, 42/3 (2008), 470–86.

Menjivar, C., 'Global Processes and Local Lives: Guatemalan Women's Work and Gender Relations at Home and Abroad', *International Labour and Working-Class History*, 70 (2006), 85–105.

Miller, T., *Making Sense of Fatherhood: Gender, Caring and Work* (New York: Cambridge University Press, 2011).

Morris, L., 'The household in the labour market', in C. C. Harris (ed.), *Redundancy and Recession in South Wales* (Oxford: Blackwell, 1987).

Morrison, J. and Wilkinson, B., 'Poverty and Prosperity in Wales: Polarization and Los Angelization', *Contemporary Wales*, 8 (1995), 29–45.

Page, E. and Jha, J. (eds), *Exploring the Bias: Gender and Stereotyping in Secondary Schools* (London: Commonwealth Secretariat, 2009).

Pahl, J., 'Individualisation in Couple Finances: Who Pays for the Children?', *Social Policy and Society*, 4/4 (2005), 381–91.

Pilcher, J., 'Who should do the dishes? Three generations of Welsh women talking about men and housework', in J. Aaron, T. Rees, S. Betts and M.

Vincentelli (eds), *Our Sisters' Land: The Changing Identities of Women in Wales* (Cardiff: University of Wales Press, 1994), pp. 31–47.

Pole, C., 'Researching Children and Fashion: An Embodied Ethnography', *Childhood*, 14/1 (2007), 67–84.

Rees, T., 'Changing Patterns of Women's Work in Wales: Some Myths Explored', *Contemporary Wales*, 2 (1988) 119–30.

Rose, G., *Visual Methodologies* (London: Sage, 2001).

Scourfield, J., Dicks, B., Drakeford, M. and Davies, A., *Children, Place and Identity* (London: Routledge, 2006).

Skeggs, B., *Class, Self and Culture* (London: Routledge, 2004).

Skelton, T., 'Nothing to do, nowhere to go? Teenage girls and "public" space in the Rhondda valleys, south Wales', in S. Holloway and G. Valentine (eds), *Children's Geographies: Playing, Living, Learning* (London: Routledge, 2000).

Toynbee, P., *Hard Work: Life in Low Pay Britain* (London: Bloomsbury, 2003).

Trezise, R., *Fresh Apples* (Cardigan: Parthian, 2005).

Tucker, F. and Matthews, H., 'They Don't Like Girls Hanging Around There': Conflicts Over Recreational Space in Rural Northamptonshire', *Area*, 33/2 (2001), 161–8.

Turgo, N., '"*Bugabug ang dagat*": local life in a fishing community in the Philippines' (PhD thesis, Cardiff University, 2010).

Vogler, C., Brockmann, M. and Wiggins, R. D., 'Managing Money in New Heterosexual Forms of Intimate Relationships', *Journal of Socio-Economics*, *Special Edition on the Household*, 37/2 (2008), 552–76.

Walby, S., *The Future of Feminism* (Cambridge: Polity Press, 2011).

Walkerdine, V. and Jimenez, L., *Gender, Work and Community after De-industrialisation: A Psychosocial Approach to Affect* (Basingstoke: Palgrave Macmillan, 2012).

Warren, T., 'Class and Gender-based Working Time? Time Poverty and the Division of Domestic Labour', *Sociology*, 37/4 (2003), 733–52.

Welsh Assembly Government (WAG), *Welsh Index of Multiple Deprivation 2008: Summary Report* (Cardiff: Welsh Assembly Government, 2008).

Winckler, V., 'Women and Work in Contemporary Wales', *Contemporary Wales*, 1 (1987), 53–71.

A Post-industrial Welsh Landscape – by Ian Homer

5

'Placing young men': The Performance of Young Working-class Masculinities in the South Wales Valleys

MICHAEL R. M. WARD

Introduction

At the end of the millennium, Scourfield and Drakeford (1999) published an article exploring the concept of masculinity in relation to Wales and what it meant to be a 'Welshman'. Over a decade later, their article, 'Boys from Nowhere: Finding Welshmen and Putting Them in their Place', remains a rare contribution because of its focus on masculinities in the nation, a topic that has received scant interest within the social sciences. Scourfield and Drakeford (1999) asked key questions about the way social and local factors may combine alongside language, culture, history and politics to shape the formation of masculinity in Wales. The authors argued that the changing nature of masculinity should be a part of 'any rounded scrutiny of the new Wales itself' (Scourfield and Drakeford, 1999, p. 15).

This chapter revisits Scourfield and Drakeford's 'call to arms' for empirical research into men's lives in contemporary Wales. Drawing on a longitudinal ethnographic study with young men, aged 16–18, in a de-industrialized community in the south Wales valleys, I present the results of an 'active investigation of the way in which men are constructed' in the nation (Scourfield and Drakeford, 1999, p. 15). Given the diversity of the country, in terms of those who speak the Welsh language, social-class dynamics and the north/south/urban/rural divide, I suggest that young men in Wales can only be analysed within separate historical and geographical contexts, and through the social construction of gender within specific places in the nation. This focus on the local enables 'the messiness of layered subjectivities and multi-dimensional relations in particular localities' (Hopkins and Noble, 2009, p. 815) to be explored, highlighting how the histories of place, class and gender impact on young lives in one marginalized Welsh locale.

Context and methods

My two-and-a-half-year ethnographic study examined how social, economic and political changes have impacted on young working-class men's lives in the south Wales valleys (Ward, 2015). In particular, I was interested in how these processes have altered transitions to adulthood and the relationships that exist between education, work and future aspirations in a de-industrialized community. This chapter draws on the time I spent in the town of Cwm Dyffryn[1] observing and interacting with young men, aged 16–18, within and beyond educational settings, and as the research progressed, beyond the town itself. The research involved participant observation supported by extensive fieldnotes, focus group interviews, ethnographic conversations and more formally recorded one-on-one interviews.

The ethnography draws and builds on UK ethnographies conducted with young men over the past half century (Lacey, 1970; Willis, 1977; Brown, 1987; Mac an Ghaill, 1994; Parker, 1996; Nayak, 2003) and other research in the UK and beyond that has studied masculinities within and beyond the school setting (Martino, 1999; Frosh, Phoenix and Pattman, 2002; McDowell, 2003; Kenway, Kraack and Hickey-Moody, 2006; Pascoe, 2007; Roberts, 2013). It should be noted here that these UK-based studies are, in fact, English-based studies, something this research sought to address by providing a Welsh perceptive on the issue. It also draws on the symbolic interactionist tradition of understanding gender as a performance, which takes place through everyday interaction in multiple settings (Goffman, 1959, 1976, 1977; West and Zimmerman, 1987; Schrock and Schwalbe, 2009).

During the fieldwork, I found that masculine identities were performed in various ways within and outside the school that seemed to continue the industrial and cultural legacy of the region, but to also contradict it. I identified that there were three distinct friendship groups who I termed The Valley Boiz, The Geeks and The Emos (see Ward, 2014a, b, 2015), who seemed to represent these continuities and changes particularly clearly. A common strategy for presenting young men's subject positions within ethnographic and masculinities research has been through the use of friendship groups. However, Francis (2000) and Swain (2006) have suggested that whilst friendship groups demonstrate that multiple versions of masculinity may exist in a singular setting, they often appear too static and simplistic, and limit the portrayal of the multifaceted nature of 'real life'. Consequently, friendship groups have a tendency to produce typologies and they often fail to show the ways in which young men move between groups.

Whilst I recognize these difficulties, I employed friendship groups as a starting point for a number of reasons.[2] First, while young men employ multiple performances of self, and can move in and out of friendship groups, many of these performances still occur within 'teams' of individuals (Goffman, 1959). Consequently, it is important to recognize the power of friendship groups. Secondly, the friendship group enables overt performances of masculinity within these 'teams' to be examined. Thirdly, this framework also allows comparisons from this south Wales-based study to other geographical locations, acting as a point of cross-reference throughout the field of masculinities research.

The research site, Cwm Dyffryn, was in an area of Wales that was once a major contributor to the British coal industry (Williams, 1985) and one of the largest industrial centres in the country, employing up to a quarter of a million men, one-third of the Welsh labour force (Smith, 1984; Egan, 1987; Francis and Smith, 1998). A strong division of labour characterized these communities, where distance from anything seen as 'feminine' was essential for a strong masculine identity and which would enable the communities to survive (Walkerdine, 2010). Men earned respect for working arduously and 'doing a hard job well and being known for it' (Willis, 1977, p. 52). These roles were often seen as heroic with punishing physical labour that involved different degrees of manual skill and bodily toughness, creating a tough, stoic masculinity (Kenway and Kraack, 2004). Male camaraderie was established through physicality and close working conditions underground, and maintained through jokes, story-telling, sexist language and banter. Camaraderie was further supported through social institutions such as miners' institutes, chapels, pubs, working men's clubs and sports. Rugby union and, to a lesser extent, boxing and football still hold powerful positions in the culture of the locale influencing those who play it, those who watch it, those who reject it and those who are deemed unfit for it (Holland and Scourfield, 1998; Howe, 2001; Harris, 2007).

After the Second World War, despite the nationalization of the industry in 1947, coal mining in the region continued to weaken and large numbers of collieries were closed. During the 1980s and 1990s, the region underwent rapid de-industrialization due to the economic restructuring policies of the Conservative government led by Margaret Thatcher (Williams, 1985; Smith, 1999; Day, 2002). This acute collapse, coupled with the decline of the manufacturing industry, led to a drastic increase in economic inactivity (see Fevre, 1999). These industrial losses were accompanied by the erosion of traditional apprenticeships and youth training schemes, which would have supported these industries and provided a platform into adulthood and other forms of manual employment.

The area is now characterized by a 'triangle of poverty' (Adamson, 2008, p. 21), with low levels of educational attainment and high levels of unemployment, health inequalities and poor housing across the region. Young people from the area have also become subject to social stigmatization (Ward, 2014c), with 6.7 per cent of those aged between 16 and 24 recorded as claiming Job Seekers Allowance (ONS, 2014). It is often the case that young people must move out of the area not only to find employment, but also to use the educational skills they have gained. For young people who remain within the locale, the prospects of getting jobs are extremely low and highly competitive.

Cwm Dyffryn, and the south Wales valleys more broadly, are examples of localities strongly rooted in the modern industrial era, which are experiencing difficulties in transforming economically, socially and culturally to cope with a post-industrial society. The conditions described above have had a significant impact on how masculinity has been shaped and re-shaped within this environment. The following sections outline the differential ways in which young Welsh men are negotiating acceptable masculinities with these changing conditions.

The Valley Boiz: the re-traditionalization of white working-class masculinities

The Valley Boiz were a large group of white, working-class young men who were all born and brought up in Cwm Dyffryn, and their friendship developed as they progressed through secondary (high) school. The Valley Boiz' anti-school behaviours and negative attitudes to education were similar to those documented in other ethnographic studies of working-class young men of a similar age (Willis, 1977; Mac an Ghaill, 1994; Nayak, 2003). However, there were a number of differences between The Valley Boiz and these other studies of young men.

The Valley Boiz persevered with the profoundly contradictory process of continuing in post-16 education after their General Certificate of Secondary Education (GCSE) exams. This decision clashed with the traditions of the local community and their general anti-school behaviour; however, returning to school enabled the group to delay uncertain employment futures for a further year or two. The school was also a safe and familiar space for the young men, which provided access to a small amount of money in the form of the Educational Maintenance Allowance (EMA).[3]

The Valley Boiz were a large friendship group; however, there were other young men who were loosely affiliated with them and joined them for nights out in the town, drinking or driving around in their cars as they grew older. The core members of the group comprised of Dai, Birdy, Jonesy, Shaggy, Clive, Hughesy, Davies, Brad, Cresco, Tomo and Bunk.[4] The group dynamics were fluid and others such as Jimmy, Frankie, Bakers and Ian (see Ward, 2015) also joined the group on occasions. As the young men progressed into and through the school's sixth form (year 12 and 13), their friendships changed and some ended due to arguments, fights, the development of deeper relationships with girlfriends or moving out of Cwm Dyffryn to different educational institutions.

The legacy of the region's industrial past was evident in their family backgrounds with the young men speaking of relatives who had worked in the coal industry or related occupations, such as working in coal cleaning plants or driving lorries delivering coal. Their fathers, who had grown up in the industry's decline, had continued the tradition of working-class occupations by entering other male-dominated jobs in the building trade or haulage. A small portion of the group had families who owned their own businesses such as Birdy's family who ran a local post office and Tomo's father who co-owned an electrical factory employing twenty-three people. Others like Dai and Jonesy were a bit unsure as to what their parents did or were reluctant to admit to it. For example, all Jonesy could tell me was that his father 'worked in a big office somewhere in Cardiff', which as far as he was concerned was enough and not terribly important in defining his father to him.

The situation of the young men's female family members was more varied, with mothers being described as 'housewives', cleaners, clerical workers and retail assistants. Some, like Dai, had older sisters in higher education. Brad was a little unsure of his mother's exact job title, but he said she worked as an 'assessor' in the local college. Brad was perhaps indicating here that she was involved in some form of teaching or training role. However, none of their parents had any experience of higher education (apart from Brad's father who had attended university briefly in his late twenties before dropping out) and the majority of the young men were in receipt of the EMA. While a contradictory class position was evident for a few of the young men due to their parents' slight upward mobility, as a group these boys come from traditional, white, working-class families. However, their relatively stable family backgrounds (only Jonesy had parents who had divorced) and employment histories indicate that these boys were quite distinctive from those of their counterparts who had totally disengaged from schooling at the age of sixteen and who were not involved in education, employment or training (NEETs).

I first encountered the young men in the spring of 2008, when they were in the final weeks of compulsory schooling and contemplating their impending futures. When asked during a group interview what they planned on doing after their GCSEs, some of these aspirations became clear whilst others less so.

Bunk:	Apprenticeship.
MW:	Ok you want to tell me a bit about that?
Bunk:	I've applied for one with Ford and Quick Fit …
MW:	So that's work as well as college or …
Bunk:	Yeah …
Tomo:	That be good that is, be paid to do an apprenticeship!
Bunk:	I think Quick Fit was like £280 a week …
MW:	Ok sounds good …
Hughesy:	… stay on and see about something.
Brad:	I'm going to go to the sixth form till Christmas so I can go skiing again and err then I'll go and work with my old man then …
MW:	Shaggy what about you then …
Shaggy:	Whatever happens …
MW:	OK whatever happens …
Birdy:	I want to go to uni cos of the girls …

Bunk had already looked into a modern apprenticeship and reported that he had applied for two different schemes with national motor vehicle companies. Tomo seemed impressed with this and illustrated that he had some background knowledge about the modern apprenticeship because he realized that it is accompanied by a paid wage. The validation for Bunk's choice comes through the ability to earn whilst studying in an acceptable (male-dominated) industry, reproducing an idealized form of masculinity, which for the others in the group is the performance to be maintained. Those who are not sure what they want to do but have decided to stay on in education, like Hughesy, Brad and Birdy, validate their choices in different ways, reconfiguring their macho-front performance. Hughesy expresses nonchalance without committing to anything, whilst Brad justifies his decision to return to the sixth form purely because he can go skiing again[5] and will then go to work with his father in an acceptable manual occupation as a floor tiler. Birdy was the only one of the group to look beyond the immediate future by suggesting he wanted to go to university. However, he justifies this quickly by saying 'because of the girls'. His aspirations are validated by emphasizing (hetero) sexual motives, rather than academic ones.

With a heritage of working-class family backgrounds and recognizable manual skills, educational qualification leading to occupations, which could be gained through apprenticeships or training schemes, were deemed most desirable. However, it was not just their family backgrounds and the industrial heritage of place that had an impact on their views of education and what constituted acceptable performances of self: interactions of the friendship group within these spaces also contributed to the construction of acceptable masculinity.

Whilst The Valley Boiz attended sixth form regularly (as their attendance had to be proven to receive their EMA), they did not always attend every lesson, as they should have, and often opted to sit around the common room chatting about girls and plans for the weekend or making use of computers in the library to surf the internet. During lessons their interactions with their teachers were very casual and banter was often exchanged about football or rugby results. Even in the almost empty classrooms (there were only around half a dozen students on their courses) The Valley Boiz sat at the back of the room as far away from the teacher as they could. Resonant of their compulsory school days, they still exhibited an indifference to being close to the front of the classroom, which might have meant being seen by the others as over-investing in the lesson and therefore gaining a derogatory label as a swot or a geek. Sitting at the back of the class also meant that chatter could occur whilst out of earshot of the teacher where a certain amount of 'piss taking' and sexual storytelling occurred during the lessons (Parker, 2006). A clear example of this can be seen when Hughesy recounts a tale from the weekend's activities during a group experiment in an applied science lesson.

The boys began taking 'the piss' out of Hughesy about an incident with a caravan. I asked to hear more about this and Hughesy told me eagerly. He'd been out on a Saturday night in the town and 'pulled' an older woman in a nightclub. After getting a kebab (which he'd dropped all over his black shirt) he'd gone home with her. But instead of being invited into her house, she took him into a touring caravan that was parked outside it. When he awoke in the morning (with scratches all over his back he was happy to tell us) he had no idea where he was. Alongside the 'rough bird' he had 'pulled' there were a few Doberman dogs in the caravan which he said looked 'fucking scary!' He called everyone on his phone to try and get a lift home, but only Clive had answered and gone to collect him in his car, at 8:30am on the Sunday morning. Clive had commented that Hughesy had sounded 'well quiet' and shy on the phone and as Hughesy wasn't sure exactly where he was, it took him a while to find him. Hughesy admitted not calling her again and lying to her about his age. He told her he was in university so that she would think he was older and would sleep with him. [Field notes]

Three things seem to be occurring here in the telling of this tale, which continues the macho-front performance. First, The Valley Boiz are engaging with a practical task and whilst carrying it out are reproducing normative expectations of heterosexual prowess. By interacting around a practical task, a sanitized older world of industrial work is being re-traditionalized in the classroom space. Secondly, through storytelling Hughesy occupies an honoured position and reaffirms dominant myths about what constitutes a 'real man'. As Goffman (1959, p. 44) contends, the impression of a particular character is 'idealized in several different ways'. Hughesy is enjoying being the centre of attention and his desires are shared by the others. Hughesy portrays himself as a hero: he went through dangers (the Dobermans), incurred injuries (the scratches on his back) and needed to be rescued from the ordeal by his friend (who drives to find him) after the event. His story is also validated by this rescue, as some of the tale is authenticated by Clive. Finally, the sexual objectification of the girl in the story is complete when Hughesy states that he did not call her again and admits to lying to her, in order to sleep with her. This incident strengthens the group identity and acts as a collective normalizing practice, by reinforcing myths about the roles of traditional masculinities in the locality and through emphasizing a heterosexual prowess.

This transformation of the industrial base of the region has led to changes in the relationship between work and masculinity. Yet the attitudes to work and identity are still intrinsically connected to their community and their family biographies. To be a 'proper' boy or man from the valleys, an archetype of masculinity associated with an older world of industrial work, must be outwardly performed through 'masculine' affirming practices associated with certain educational subjects, engaging in physical and aggressive behaviours and certain ideas of male embodiment. The expulsion of the feminine or homosexuality is an essential aspect in this performance and enables The Valley Boiz to perform their masculinities through re-traditionalizing practices, which re-transmit the traditional values of the locale through pain, heroism and physicality. These practices, which Scourfield and Drakeford (1999) also highlighted, are often seen as key to a Welsh man's identity and to diverge from them can be problematic. I now turn to two groups of young men who did diverge from these normal scripts and highlight some of the issues that they faced.

The Geeks – the performance of studious working-class masculinities

The Geeks friendship group consisted primarily of Leon, Gavin, Ruben, Scott, Nibbles, Alan, Sean, Ieuan, Sam, Sin and Nixon. Apart from Sin, who was of Chinese heritage, all were white and had been born in the town, and when I met them, in year 11, they had the highest grades in their year group. In the extracts below, a 'geek' is described by the young men themselves as someone who does not participate in sports and is more interested in video games, films and comics:

Sam: Get a sporting accolade and you're already like the greatest person ever.

Alan: If you don't do sport in school you're like …

Sam: … a geek …

Sean: … yeah a geek basically. [Group interview]

MW: So do you play a lot of video games then?

Sean: Yeah, I'm a geek I am, I love games!

MW: So are you really a geek like when you say you are?

Sean: Yeah I love all the geeky things, like um games, films um …

MW: … you're well into your films are you?

Sean: Ah yeah! Graphic novels, comics, things like that. [Individual interview]

As Sean indicates here, being defined as a geek was evident in more subtle ways than just being positioned as academically successful. In year 11 some of The Geeks were smaller in stature and less physically developed than many others in their year group, making them easy targets for bullying. They arrived at lessons on time with their own pens and pencil cases, did their homework and carried their books and other equipment in bags, which others in their year group did not always use. Along with this compliance to the rules, they correctly adhered to the school dress code of white shirts, with red ties, black V-neck jumpers, black trousers and black shoes. This uniform was accompanied by neat haircuts and, for some, horned-rimmed glasses or braces on their teeth, which completed the stereotypical geek persona. These artefacts then operate as forms of 'expressive equipment' (Goffman, 1959, p. 32) and marked The Geeks with their own recognizable identity.

Whilst The Geeks adhered to school rules, others in their year group sought to disrupt uniform policy and replace compulsory items with one's own. It was common practice to replace the standard black V-neck jumper with a round neck one, because this then meant that the school tie could be removed and it would go unseen by teachers. Other attempts by The Geeks' peers to disrupt school rules included replacing shoes with trainers, wearing hooded jackets and baseball caps, and adorning their bodies with flashy rings, chains and single earrings or studs. A large group of pupils who were registered on sports subjects were also allowed to wear a tracksuit instead of the regular uniform. This process not only validated a specific form of masculinity based on sporting prowess by the educational institution itself (Mac an Ghaill, 1994), but also acted as a symbolic marker of status, which The Geeks did not have access to and were therefore 'othered' as a group for not belonging to the sporting elite.

After achieving good GCSE grades, all The Geeks returned to the school's sixth form. The subjects chosen by The Geeks to study were predominantly in the arts, natural sciences, maths and IT. The Geeks had been in the top sets for all their core subjects at GCSE level and even though they were a close group of friends, they were fiercely competitive over their grades. They also all harboured aspirations to go to university. This is not to say that others in their year group did not aspire to go to university or gain well-paid and meaningful employment, but for The Geeks this seemed to be of paramount importance to their projected futures. For example, Sam planned on spending a year in America studying:

Sam: Journalism is what I'd like to get into at the moment.

MW: Alright.

Sam: And I'd like to go to America as well for my university course.

MW: So you've thought a little bit down the line where you want to go?

Sam: Yeah I have done a bit of research into it and they do offer it in some of the English universities and the exchanges into American universities, so I'll aim for that first … if I get rejected I'll just go lower down the ladder.

MW: So you've thought about going to uni then?

Sam: Yeah [shouts] I am going to uni! [Individual interview]

Sam's final statement demonstrates a powerful sense of agency: he is not constrained by place and his ambitions illustrate a willingness to move on. His determination to find a way to his goals by attending different universities if his first choice is unavailable is also clear. Arguably, for Sam, attending university is a way to gain a hegemonic form of masculinity (Connell 1995) so often denied him and other boys like him who have invested in academic capital in this community.

The Geeks' family biographies often contributed to their positive outlook on academic qualifications. Ruben, Nixon, Ieuan and Leon had fathers and mothers who had some experience of higher education and were employed in professional occupations. Other parents owned their own businesses in the form of garages (Sean) and takeaway food shops (Sin). However, there were also some parents who worked in more traditional working-class occupations such as lorry drivers (Scott) and caretakers (Sam); or were unemployed (Gavin, Alan). Three of the boys (Scott, Ieuan and Gavin) said that their mothers stayed at home and described them as housewives. Sadly Nibbles's mother had died when he was fourteen and his step-dad (his biological father had left the family years before) was on long-term incapacity benefit after being injured in an accident whilst driving a lorry.

Although some of these young men's parents could be seen as employed in middle-class occupations, my justification for using the term 'working class' to refer to these young men as a group is that I feel it is important to recognize the inequalities that they experienced by coming from a deprived locale. Having a parent who is a teacher in a de-industrialized, marginalized area is very different to having a parent who is a teacher in a more affluent area (see Weis, 1990). Consequently, it is important that the geo-demographics of place are considered when defining class and how successful boys from poorer communities experience education (Burrows and Gane, 2006). I now want to turn to a final group of young men who further illustrate the diverse performances of masculinity in south Wales.

The Emos – the performance of 'alternative'
working-class masculinities

The key members of The Emos friendship group were Bruce, Clump, Jelly Belly, Jack and Tommy.[6] Over the time I was acquainted with them, and as their educational pathways changed, other young men and women were introduced to the group. Jenkins, Dai and Billy-Joe became friends with Clump and Jelly Belly at a local further education (FE) college and Brittany and Rosie also became part of the wider group when they became romantically involved with Clump and Bruce. The young men performed together in different bands playing music in pubs and clubs across the region and were part of a global youth culture often referred to as the 'alternative' scene.

The 'alternative' scene revolves around a combination of guitar-based bands stemming out of broad genres of non-mainstream music that transcends the globe (Moore, 2005). 'Alternative' can be used as an umbrella term for a music scene with fluid, flexible boundaries, which can incorporate many sub-divisions of punk, different forms of heavy and extreme metal (Harris, 2000), hard-core, glam, thrash, grunge, riot grrrl (Moore, 2010), emo (Peters, 2010) and the Goth scene (Hodkinson, 2002). Multiple forms of dance and violent body movements, such as moshing, slam dancing and crowd surfing, accompany the live arena with many of these activities being carried out in spaces known as 'pits' (Tsitsos, 1999; Riches, 2014).

The broad scene is also marked with different clothing fashions, but these are frequently combined together to make a complex appearance. These incorporate tight or over-sized jeans, T-shirts with slogans or band logos on them, canvas or chunky trainers, heavy boots, dark or colourful belts with big buckles, hooded jumpers and jackets. Hair is often straight and long (sometimes pulled down over one eye) and dyed in various shades, but usually black. Tattoos, facial and other body piercings are also popular. Leisure pursuits or 'extreme' sports that are loosely associated with the music, such as skateboarding, BMX riding, surfing and snowboarding, also accompany the scene. Holly Kruse argues that the loose term of 'alternative' music also means that 'local identities and traditions interact with relatively coherent trans local frames of reference' (Kruse, 1993, cited in Hodkinson, 2002, p. 27). The shared task of networks, communications and commerce can connect people with each other.

In keeping with this scene and using Goffman's (1959) dramaturgical framework to understand this interaction order, one of the ways these young men's personal front performance of masculinity was displayed was through their distinctive style of clothing. When not in school uniform, they tended to dress in baggy trousers or very tight skinny jeans, with dark T-shirts that had their favourite band logos on them and big baggy hooded jumpers. The Emos tended to have long hair which was dyed a variety of bright colours and sometimes, but not always, pulled down over their eyes. Their bodies were also adorned with piercings in their eyebrows, ears, tongues, noses and even though the base of the neck. Even in their school uniform, they stood out with these symbolic representations of the 'alternative' scene, and the young men were constantly reprimanded by teachers for breaking uniform policy.

As they grew older, ever more elaborate tattoos were added on their arms, legs and bodies, further enabling them to showcase their allegiance to the 'alternative' scene. However, embracing this scene caused alienation within their schools and colleges from both teachers and their peers. They were often bullied in the wider community because of the way they dressed, their hair styles and the variety of body piercings and colourful tattoos that made them stand out as they transgressed accepted patterns of behaviour and masculinity. While this bricolage of styles acted as an unofficial group 'uniform', its contradictions to a more traditional working-class culture highlights the plural nature of young working-class masculinities in Wales and how gender is produced and performed within this space.

At school, teachers and their peers referred to the group as 'emos', something the popular press and other forms of media have sought to mock (*Guardian*, 2006) and vilify (*Daily Mail*, 2012) when writing about the 'dangers' of non-mainstream youth (Peters, 2010). The Emos did enough to 'get on' in school and achieved a mid-range of GCSE grades (see Brown, 1987; Roberts, 2013). However, they all said that they hated the way they were treated in school and the majority of the group left after their GCSEs to undertake a variety of music- and arts-based courses at an FE college. Bruce and Tommy did opt to return to school to undertake A levels, but they continued to feel out of place. This feeling of alienation resulted in Tommy leaving before he had completed his course, so only Bruce remained to complete his final year. Between lessons Bruce used to distance himself from the rest of his year group and escape to the art department to work on his art project or play his guitar, preferring being on his own to mixing with his peers.

Alongside the alienation experienced within the school, The Emos felt that they did not fit in with the town of Cwm Dyffryn. Their involvement with the different aspects of the 'alternative' scene attracted unwanted attention within the locality.

Jack: Yeah, it used to be bad, and used to be annoying, because everyone hated each other but it's a bit better now cos everyone's grown up a little bit now.

Clump: Yeah used to get heaps of shit everyday in like Year 7 ...

MW: Who did?

Bruce: Us, cos we're different to everyone else so we just got shouted at ... called names but now in Year 11 we get hardly any of it. [Group interview]

Jack, Clump and Bruce frame the bullying as occurring in the past and therefore make it safe by indicating that it 'used to be bad' and that now, as they are all older, they 'get hardly any of it'. In this way, The Emos are able to distance themselves from any negative feelings associated with this bullying or how it may have affected their self-esteem and attitudes to school in general. Outside school the bullying took a more violent turn. They explained that on certain occasions when they were out at night, they felt threatened and intimidated when they came across other young men drinking alcohol in parks or in the street.

Jack: Like, yeah, wherever we go out, cos we don't wanna go out drinking round the street, say we wanna go up the country park sitting on the swings like that and a load of piss heads (drunks) will walk up like.

Bruce: Yeah I can guarantee that you'll go out on a Friday night and you're guaranteed to see loads of um.

Jelly Belly:	It's like they can't enjoy themselves.
Clump:	Like drink after drink just to get smashed and …
Bruce:	[cuts in] … the bad thing then is that you're walking through them you're a bit weary of things.
Tommy:	You walk past some of um and they'll go [aggressive tone] 'can I have a fag en butt' [can I have a cigarette then] and if you don't have a fag you're fucked!
Bruce:	Yeah that's it like, no fag or lighter they start on you!
Jelly Belly:	Me, him [points at Clump] and Jenkins [not present] right got jumped on down the skate park because we didn't have a fag or nothing, they kept shouting at us, about 15 of um coming on to us.
MW:	Did you manage to get away?
Jelly Belly:	Well all them lot, Jenkins and Clump run off!
Clump:	Yeah I had to! I got head butted!
MW:	Really? Hang on, start again!
Jelly Belly:	Well as Jenkins and Clump run off they all chased um, I stayed there for a little bit and they all went, then when I jumped down [off the skate ramp] they were all round the corner, about 14 of them and then I got jumped again! [Group interview]

In keeping with other studies of marginalized masculinities (Connell, 1995), The Emos were subordinated by others for not adhering to the normative masculine practices of Cwm Dyffryn. Over the course of the study The Emos voiced their concerns about the bullying and harassment; however, instead of seeing themselves as victims, The Emos attempted to frame their experiences as heroic narratives. As Jelly Belly states '15 of um coming on to us' – it is clear that he sets himself up as trying to battle back against the odds in the face of intimidation and to hold onto his pride. He does not talk about the pain that these beatings may have caused him, physically or emotionally, again adding to his heroic narrative and proving that he has the ability to suffer and take a beating. This is potentially also about the reinforcement of a minority marginalized status through the numerical terms of the bigger group of 'them' versus the smaller outside group of 'us'.

Conclusion

The chapter has shown that young men perform their working-class masculinities in different ways before various audiences and spaces, illustrating the multifaceted nature of one community at one particular level of Welsh society. This was something Scourfield and Drakeford (1999) argued was needed in order to understand not just the inhabitants of Wales, but also the lives of those with and without power. This would, they suggested, enable us, as a nation, to critically explore the social processes surrounding the construction, production and reproduction of masculinities. In this chapter, these processes have been exemplified through separate but interlinked friendship groups. Re-traditionalizing older masculine practices through selecting specific 'masculine' educational subjects and engaging in risky leisure activities is, for The Valley Boiz, a way to hold onto a legacy of the industrial past and to maintain a connection to their community. The more studious performances of masculinity through academic achievement is a way for The Geeks to find solace from a community that they do not feel they belong to, and an escape route to a more successful future. And, the more 'alternative' non-normative performances of manhood, played out through the musical interests and leisure pleasures of The Emos, offers another route to escape from the de-industrial community, but also produces a troubled and risky subject position.

Despite industrial changes, a particularly 'hard' form of working-class masculinity in this de-industrial community is still the default reference point. This form of masculinity is interlinked with family histories, gender, class and place and has consequences for those who adopt or deviate from this script. However, this chapter demonstrates that for different young men it is also a divergent identity and one that can be enacted, banished or resisted in multiple ways. Importantly, place and local cultures within Wales continue to be of significance in a time of global uncertainty, but within the limits of place and during different social interactions, individual young men, despite structural inequalities, can be seen as active agents in their own construction of identity, as the boys from nowhere find and define themselves as contemporary Welshmen.

Notes

1   A pseudonym.
2   See Ward (2015) for the stories of other young men in this year group.
3   Although the coalition government announced the end to the EMA in 2010 with no new claims eligible after January 2011 in England, EMA continues in Wales, Scotland and Northern Ireland (see *www.studentfinancewales.co.uk* (accessed 18 March 2015)).
4   Nicknames or slightly modified surnames e.g. Hughes to Hughesy, or first names such as David to Dai were used to refer to each other. This practice of shortening names has a long tradition in south Wales and I suggest it was another link back to the male camaraderie that developed alongside the growth of heavy industry. Some names were also chosen by the respondents.
5   Despite being situated in a highly deprived community, Cwm Dyffryn High School ran an extensive programme of school trips with skiing and foreign-language trips to Europe every year.
6   Participants chose their own pseudonyms, many of which reflect their musical tastes. Bruce chose his because it was the name of the lead singer of one of his favourite bands, Iron Maiden, and Jack chose his after the musician Jack White.

References

Adamson, D., 'Still Living on the Edge?', *Contemporary Wales*, 21 (2008), 47–66.

Brown, P., *Schooling Ordinary Kids, Inequality, Unemployment and the New Vocationalism* (London: Tavistock, 1987).

Burrows, R. and Gane, N., 'Geodemographics, Software and Class', *Sociology*, 40/5 (2006), 793–812.

Connell, R. W., *Masculinities* (Cambridge: Polity, 1995).

Daily Mail, 'Stoned to death for being an emo: Ninety Iraqi students killed for having strange hair and tight clothes', *Daily Mail* (2012), *www.dailymail.co.uk/news/article-2112960/90-students-Iraq-stoned-death-having-Emo-hair-tight-clothes.html#ixzz2vf50y7a5* (accessed 11 March 2014).

Day, G., *Making Sense of Wales* (Cardiff: University of Wales Press, 2002).

Egan, D., *Coal Society: History of the South Wales Mining Valleys, 1840–1980* (Cardiff: Gomer Press, 1987).

Fevre, R., 'The Welsh Economy', in D. Dunkerley and A. Thompson (eds), *Wales Today* (Cardiff: University of Wales, 1999), pp. 61–74.

Francis, B., *Boys, Girls and Achievement: Addressing the Classroom Issues* (Oxford: Routledge Falmer, 2000).

Francis, H. and Smith, D., *The Fed: A History of the South Wales Miners in the Twentieth Century* (Cardiff: University of Wales Press, 1998).

Frosh, S., Phoenix, A. and Pattman, R., *Young Masculinities: Understanding Boys in Contemporary Society* (Basingstoke: Palgrave, 2002).

Goffman, E., *The Presentation of Self in Everyday Life* (New York: Doubleday, Anchor Books, 1959).

——, 'Gender Display', *Studies in the Anthropology of Visible Communication*, 3 (1976), 69–77.

——, 'The Arrangement between the Sexes', *Theory and Society*, 4 (1977), 301–31.

Guardian, 'The web's fourth most dangerous word? Emo', *Guardian* (2006), *www.guardian.co.uk/technology/blog/2008/aug/06/thewebsfourthmostdangerous* (accessed 25 February 2015).

Harris, J., 'Cool Cymru, Rugby Union and an Imagined Community', *International Journal of Sociology*, 27/3/4 (2007), 151–62.

Harris, K., 'Roots? The Relationship between the Global and the Local within the Extreme Metal Scene', *Popular Music*, 19/1 (2000), 3–30.

Hodkinson, P., *Goth: Identity, Style Subculture* (Oxford: Berg, 2002).

Holland, S. and Scourfield, J., 'Ei gwrol ryfelwyr. Reflections on body, gender, class and nation in Welsh rugby', in J. Richardson and A. Shaw (eds), *The Body and Qualitative Research* (Aldershot: Ashgate, 1998), pp. 56–71.

Hopkins, P. and Noble, G., 'Masculinities in Place: Situated Identities, Relations and Intersectionality', *Social and Cultural Geography*, 10/8 (2009), 811–19.

Howe, P. D., 'Women's Rugby and the Nexus Between Embodiment, Professionalism and Sexuality: An Ethnographic Account', *Football Studies*, 4/2 (2001), 77–91.

Kenway, J. and Kraack, A., 'Reordering work and destabilizing masculinity', in N. Dolby et al. (eds), *Learning to Labor in New Times* (New York: Routledge Falmer, 2004), pp. 95–109.

——, —— and Hickey-Moody, A., *Masculinity beyond the Metropolis* (Basingstoke: Palgrave, 2006).

Kruse, H., 'Subcultural Identity in Alternative Music Culture', *Popular Music*, 12/1 (1993), 31–43.

Lacey, C., *High Town Grammar, the School as a Social System* (Manchester: Manchester University Press, 1970).

Mac an Ghaill, M., *The Making of Men: Masculinities, Sexualities and Schooling* (Buckingham: Open University Press, 1994).

Martino, W., '"Cool boys", "Party Animals", "Squids" and "Poofters": Interrogating the Dynamics and Politics of Adolescent Masculinities in School', *British Journal of Sociology of Education*, 20/2 (1999), 239–63.

McDowell, L., *Redundant Masculinities* (Oxford: Blackwell, 2003).

Moore, R., 'Alternative to What? Subcultural Capital and the Commercialization of a Music Scene', *Deviant Behaviour*, 26 (2005), 229–52.

——, *Smells Like Teen Spirit, Music Youth Culture and Social Crisis* (New York: New York University Press, 2010).

Nayak, A., *Race, Place and Globalization, Youth Cultures in a Changing World* (Oxford: Berg, 2003).

Office for National Statistics (ONS), *Local Authority Profile, Rhondda, Cynon, Taff, Local Authority* (2014), *www.nomisweb.co.uk/reports/lmpla/194615 7398/report.aspx* (accessed 19 August 2014).

Parker, A., 'Sporting masculinities: gender relations and the body', in M. Mac an Ghaill (ed.), *Understanding Masculinities* (Buckingham: Open University Press, 1996), 126–38.

——, 'Lifelong Learning to Labour: Apprenticeship, Masculinity and Communities of Practice', *British Educational Research Journal*, 32/5 (2006), 687–701.

Pascoe, C. J., *Dude you're A Fag: Masculinity and Sexuality in High School* (Berkeley: University of California Press, 2007).

Peters, B. M., 'Emo Gay Boys and Subculture: Post Punk, Queer Youth and (Re) Thinking Images of Masculinity', *Journal of LGBT Youth*, 7/2 (2010), 129–46.

Riches, G., 'Brothers of Metal! Heavy Metal Masculinities, Moshpit Practices and Homosociality', in S. Roberts (ed.), *Debating Modern Masculinities, Change, Continuity, Crisis?* (Basingstoke: Palgrave Macmillan, 2014), pp. 88–105.

Roberts, S., 'Boys will be Boys … Won't They? Change and Continuities in Contemporary Young Working-class Masculinities', *Sociology*, 47/4 (2013), 671–86.

Schrock, D. and Schwalbe, M., 'Men, Masculinity and Manhood Acts', *Annual Review of Sociology*, 35 (2009), 377–95.

Scourfield, J. and Drakeford, M., 'Boys from Nowhere: Finding Welsh Men and Putting Them in their Place', *Contemporary Wales*, 12 (1999), 3–17.

Smith, D., *Wales! Wales?* (London: George Allen and Unwin, 1984).

——, *Wales, A Question for History* (Bridgend: Poetry Wales Press Ltd, 1999).

Swain, J., 'Reflections on Patterns of Masculinity in School Settings', *Men and Masculinities*, 8/3 (2006), 331–49.

Tsitsos, W., 'Rules of Rebellion: Slam Dancing, Moshing and the American Alternative Scene', *Popular Music*, 18/3 (1999), 397–414.

Ward, M. R. M., '"I'm a Geek I am": Academic Achievement and the Performance of a Studious Working-Class Masculinity', *Gender and Education* (2014a) 26/7, 709–25.

——, '"We're different to everyone else": Contradictory working-class masculinities in contemporary Britain', in S. Roberts (ed.), *Debating Modern Masculinities, Change, Continuity Crisis?* (Basingstoke: Palgrave MacMillan, 2014b), pp. 52–69.

——, '"You get a reputation if you're from the valleys": The stigmatization of place in young working-class men's lives', in T. Thurnell-Read and M. Casey (eds), *Men, Masculinities, Travel and Tourism* (Basingstoke: Palgrave MacMillan, 2014c), pp. 89–104.

——, *From Labouring to Learning, Working-Class Masculinities, Education and De-industrialization* (Basingstoke: Palgrave 2015).

Walkerdine, V., 'Communal Beingness and Affect: An Exploration of Trauma in an Ex-industrial Community', *Body & Society*, 16/1 (2010), 91–116.

Weis, L., *Working Class without Work: High School Students in a De-industrializing Economy* (New York: Routledge, 1990).

West, C. and Zimmerman, D., 'Doing Gender', *Gender and Society*, 1/2 (1987), 125–51.

Williams, G. A., *When Was Wales?* (Harmondsworth: Penguin, 1985).

Willis, P., *Learning to Labour, How Working Class Kids Get Working Class Jobs* (Farnborough: Saxon House, 1977).

II

Education, Labour Markets and Gender in Wales

Beautiful *by Tasha Harvey*

*This beautiful girl I knew just
started high school
Bullied just because she walked
into the classroom
Pushed on the floor and kicked in
the face
Trying to cut herself with a
shoelace
She's beautiful no matter what they
say
She's beautiful in every single way
She's beautiful, she's beautiful
All she wanted was to be accepted
Instead she was the only one
affected
Eleven years old and starving
herself
As the years went on it was about
her health
Being anorexic and skinny to the
bone
Still people picked on her because
she was alone
Day after day thinking that it would
end*

*And for them to stop and just be her
friend
She's beautiful no matter what they
say
She's beautiful in every single way
She's beautiful, she's beautiful
Sixteen years old and being in a
hospital bed
Just laying there while she's trying
to be fed
Nothing seemed to work because
her system started to shut down
A few days later she was buried in
the ground
She wrote a letter three weeks
before she left
To Mum and Dad and this is what it
said
Don't cry for me just stay strong
I'm in your hearts where I
belong
I couldn't put you through my pain
but I promise I will see you again
some day
She's beautiful no matter what they
say*

She's beautiful in every single way
She's beautiful, she's beautiful

She's beautiful no matter what they say
She's a beautiful angel in heaven

Music and media webcontent is hosted on the following websites:
www.molgroup.org.uk/ourchangingland and
https://www.youtube.com/watch?v=A93uWd6FAjc.

Balancing Academic Study and Motherhood – by Ian Homer

6

Re-educating Rhian: Experiences of Working-class Mature Student Mothers

MELANIE MORGAN

Introduction

In this chapter, I revisit Pam Garland's (1994) work, 'Educating Rhian: experiences of mature women students', which was originally published as chapter six in the edited collection *Our Sisters' Land: The Changing Identities of Women in Wales*. Garland's research looked at the changing identities of thirty mothers in north Wales during their time as students at the University College of North Wales (UCNW), Bangor (now Bangor University). Garland was interested in exploring the reasons why women chose to become mature students, and the importance and meaning that they attached to their multiple roles at that stage of their lives. The study was also interested in how this transition affected their personal relationships and self-image.

The participants in Garland's study offered a constellation of reasons for their participation, including a desire for self-fulfilment, confidence, intellectual development, a career or career change. For some, this was bound up in dissatisfaction with purely domestic roles or a desire to contribute economically to the family unit. Garland concluded that the timing of their decision to enter higher education was intrinsically linked to their current life situation, and particularly the perceived needs of the family: more than half the women surveyed cited 'the children becoming more independent' as the largest influence on their decision. Within the sample, there were variations in perceptions of when children became more independent, thus freeing mothers to pursue other interests. In particular, the younger mothers in the sample tended to see children as dependent for a much shorter period of time in relation to their older counterparts, some of which saw their children as dependent until their late teens or until they left home. Garland linked this phenomena to the increasing participation of mothers in the labour market and related change surrounding understandings of motherhood from generational perspectives. She concluded that 'family matters' and domestic issues were at the forefront of women's concerns throughout their educational transformation, the home front remaining a site of main responsibility with studentship being an additive role and identity. This chapter returns to Garland's study, revisiting and updating some of her key arguments and drawing on my Economic and Social Research Council-funded doctoral study, 'Class, Motherhood and Mature Studentship: a Psychosocial Exploration', to communicate the experiences of Welsh women mature students in higher education in contemporary Wales.

Background

The title of Garland's original chapter, 'Educating Rhian', is taken from the 1983 film 'Educating Rita', the story of a working-class mature student woman who embarks upon higher education to study literature in order to better herself. The substitution for the name 'Rhian' then evokes this famous film and its issues from a uniquely Welsh perspective. The focus of this chapter is a review of contemporary experience for other 'Rhians' in higher education in south Wales, considering what might have changed in the past twenty years, what might not have changed and the ways in which women experience and negotiate educational transitions.

Despite debates regarding process, transformation of identity is currently of significant interest within the social sciences (Brooks and Wee, 2008). Indeed, within modern Western society, understanding the life course as a linear trajectory of appropriate ages and stages of participation has become contested. As Giddens (1991) asserts, plurality of choice means that adult individuals are now invited and expected to be many things during their lifetime: 'we are not what we are, but what we make of ourselves' (Giddens, 1991, p. 75) and as Kennedy (2001, p. 6) asserts, 'individuals are compelled to take greater control over the kinds of social identities they wish to assume ... because once powerful solidarities such as class, occupation, church, gender, and family are slowly declining in their ability to define our life experiences'. Against the backdrop of contemporary neo-liberalism, sexual liberation, emancipation from patriarchal ideologies of oppression and new technologies have offered opportunities for women, which mean that they no longer have to confine themselves to a particular life course and given sets of identities at particular points in time. This shift has coincided with a change in the landscape of post-compulsory education in Britain, which has been transformed to a mass system of higher education and an overall increase in access to and participation in higher education. As a result of this expansion, higher education is no longer just the domain of middle-class school leavers, and the student population has become far more diverse in terms of age, class, gender, race, life experience, occupational profiles and caring responsibilities with numbers of mature students increasing steadily (Mercer, 2007; Marandet and Wainwright, 2006).

Labour government aims (DfEE, 1998) of fostering a civil society, promoting citizenship and bolstering both the family and community through higher education supported this expansion via education policy initiatives such as 'lifelong learning' and 'widening participation'. As a government initiative, Widening Participation was central to New Labour's higher education policy, the rationale for which has been framed around both economics and social justice. In terms of the former, recent shifts from industry and manufacturing towards a knowledge-based economy has acted as an incentive for many governments in the developed world to invest in their citizens and academic institutions in order to produce world-class research, compete in global markets, gain economic prosperity and individual wealth (DfES, 2003). In terms of the latter, the British government now also views universities and colleges as providing a more social role, the 2003 White Paper emphasized their 'vital role in expanding opportunity and promoting social justice' (DfES, 2003, p. 4) and providing more social equality through the inclusion of disadvantaged groups (DfES, 2003).

In Wales, twenty years on from 'Educating Rhian' much has changed. In terms of the economy, the shift from heavy industry and manufacturing to service industries and the knowledge economy, although reflecting national patterns, has had massive implications for both place and people (see Adamson and also Lloyd this volume). In their work in 'Steeltown', a post-industrial community, Walkerdine and Jimenez (2012) explored the consequences that this process had for the identity of the townspeople and the threat to their ontological security that this engendered. In terms of feminist and egalitarian discourses, the imagined place of women has altered and, ideologically at least (see Mannay this volume), women's roles and worlds go beyond the family and the domestic, shifting their visibility in other arenas such as work and higher education: it is important to consider what new opportunities are afforded in the landscape of Welsh higher education.

Higher education in Wales

In Wales, against the backdrop of neo-liberalism, there has been 'an ideological commitment to ensure access to higher education to a wide demographic of participants from a range of social backgrounds' (Mannay and Wilcock, 2015, p. 50). The review of higher education in Wales (Welsh Government, 2009) presented social justice and widening access as its core aims, and the Higher Education Funding Council for Wales (HEFCW) has invested considerable funding in projects of widening participation (Taylor et al., 2013). These policy initiatives have brought some gains for non-traditional students and accordingly they have been conceptualized as a vehicle 'to secure inclusion, progression and success in higher education to enable learners across all age ranges and backgrounds, who face the highest social and economic barriers, to fulfil their potential as students' (HEFCW, 2014, p. 4).

The HEFCW Reaching Wider regional partnerships model was an initiative set up in Wales to develop the educational progression and attainment of young people from disadvantaged backgrounds that focused on raising the aspirations of disadvantaged young people (Hill and Hatt, 2012). Similarly, the Universities Heads of the Valleys Institute (UHOVI) emerged as a programme to recruit students from areas of low economic productivity and educational exclusion. Specifically, the programme aimed to contribute to the regeneration of a former heavy industrial area in Wales known as 'the valleys', improving job prospects and the quality of life for those living and working in the region (Saunders et al., 2013).

However, despite these policy initiatives, it is important to consider that as non-traditional students, mature learners face complex psychological and structural barriers to accessing and completing higher education, which are well versed within the social sciences

(Lucey et al., 2003; Mannay and Morgan, 2013; Mannay and O'Connell, 2013; Reay, 2010; Rose-Adams, 2013; Thomas, 2002; Ward, 2014; Walkerdine, 2013). The difficulties experienced by marginalized higher education students have been mapped by academics and practitioners, employing diverse theoretical models and methodological approaches (Lucey et al., 2003; Skeggs, 2010; Reay, 2010; Mannay, 2013; Walkerdine, 2013). This corpus of work has illustrated the costs of divided learner identities along the lines of social class, and it is also important to explore issues of gender, which has also been a concern of my doctoral studies, as outlined in the following sections.

Class, motherhood and mature studentship

Concerned with identity, Garland's research illustrated the everyday experiences: 'the struggling and juggling' of life as a mature student and mother in north Wales in the early 1990s. My own research, within south Wales, was also concerned with issues of identity for mature student mothers in higher education; however my focus is class specific, concerned with working-class experiences only. The doctoral research on which I draw explored the psychosocial dimensions of aspiration, motivation and participation in higher education, acknowledging its relational and affective nature. The participants all resided in marginalized urban and rural locales and were recruited from three university sites in south Wales; however, the shared geographical location, class and gender did not make my participants a homogenous group. Although considered a distinct group, there is much heterogeneity in the category of mature students both in terms of intersectional identities and individual biographies. As Waller (2005, p.115) argues, 'Mature students are a diverse and heterogeneous group, with the "reality" of their experience(s) being too complex, too individually situated, for meaningful representation otherwise.' For Waller (2005), historically academic literature has made 'overly simple generalisations' about this group by focusing on social categories rather than subjective experience. The biographical turn in social research, however, has been able to start to address this and is evident in the work of Britton and Baxter (1999) and Wilson (1997). This subjective experience of mature students in higher education is vital both in academic theorization and in terms of policy, since whilst as a category the term 'mature student' is useful in relation to political arithmetic, it does nothing to address how to attract and maintain older students, and how aspiration and motivation is enabled or constrained by intersectional categories of class, gender, race and individual biographies, within cultural contexts at particular points in time.

In my study, the mothers' ages ranged from early twenties to late thirties. These differences in demographics are also reflected in biographies and identities. Although the women shared a self-identity as working-class, mature student mothers, there is much diversity within these intersectional categories, which is of significant importance in terms of identities and subjectivities. Nevertheless, categorized in terms of education and employment, the thirteen women who participated in my study fall into three broad groups: those studying at undergraduate level, those pursuing Masters or vocational level qualifications and those undertaking doctoral studies.

Whilst the women were all clearly 'clever' and most would acknowledge this in themselves since childhood, often this was not fully reflected in their educational attainment at the time of leaving school. Due to the relational context of their childhood, sometimes due to trauma or family dynamics and lack of parental expectation, to different extents aspects of support and care, which enable motivation, aspiration and success, were unavailable.

In the first group, women were undergraduates in higher education for the first time, undertaking degrees following an access course, their work history varying widely from none to having always previously worked in manufacturing/care/service industries, to one participant having owned her own successful optician business. About half the women in this group tended to almost drift into higher education following access courses, greatly supported and mentored by college tutors and careers advisors who often rallied 'getting them onto' courses at their local university. For the other half, their learning choices and aspirations were more specific and their applications more autonomous; however, they still centred on local universities.

Motherhood involves ties that bind in many ways, and the inability to travel great distances because of family responsibilities and lack of money has to be considered as a constraining factor. Additionally, reliance on informal childcare due to lack of financial resources also meant making choices based on convenience. For all except one, moving home to attend a university of choice was not even a consideration. The exception to this was Jennifer, whose transition to university was meticulously planned and inherently risky, involving a move for herself and her children from England to Wales, where she had no friends or family, in order to study a ceramics course. The university she attended was her second choice, after the university in London she considered the best, and planned to attend, withdrew their course.

In the second group, having already recently completed an undergraduate degree some women were undertaking further Masters or PGCE qualifications. Once again their work history varied widely from caring, through to a high-profile purchasing role in the diamond industry abroad. While for the women in this group moving was not considered, travelling further to attend university became both a consideration and a possibility, particularly to attend a Russell Group University. Although one woman did move closer to the university once her course had started, this was based on convenience and a desire to distance herself from past difficult relationships with her mother and ex-partner. She was also familiar with relocation, having emigrated alone from South Africa some years earlier.

In the third group, having attended university at a traditional age, other women were returning to university in their thirties to undertake PhDs or post-graduate qualifications in order to progress career or change career direction, having already experienced varied and rewarding (qualified) work. These women had very formulated plans in terms of their studies and future aspirations and had invested much time and effort in their applications for bursary funding. Having previously attended other universities around the country, they were well aware of the capital that attending a Russell Group University carried, and this guided their selection of institution.

There was a significant variation in the extent to which the women were 'marginalized' by their working-class status. This seemed to be influenced by their relationship status and biographical history, the number of children they had and their previous employment history. Some women considered they had adequate material resources and income, some managed on state benefits, whereas others struggled on benefits and low-paid work, their children existing in poverty like many other in Wales (see Adamson in this volume). What surprised me was that several mothers reported that their financial position had benefitted since they became students, they were better off than they had been and were adequately supported by the various bursaries, grants and loans available to them as learner mothers. In particular, the child tax credits available to mothers working sixteen hours apparently made a considerable difference to their financial circumstances. This of course is relative and perceptions of having adequate resources are inherently subjective.

In terms of their motherhood status, in general, the women took the main responsibility for the care of their children and the domestic sphere. Exceptions to this were Justine, who was divorced and shared care with her husband, with the children living between houses; Jayne, whose mother and husband took on the main responsibilities in this area; and Ruth and her husband who shared responsibility, her husband working part time. All had children of school age, their ages ranging from fifteen months to seventeen years of age. Five women had babies/ toddlers, most were under ten and the women had between one and five children. Out of the thirteen women, all except three – Ruth, Lynfa and Kim – had experienced single motherhood.

Then and now

Within the women's narratives, there were many resonances with Garland's findings in relation to personal change and self and identity; the highs and lows of participation in higher education; the importance of relationships with other mature students; and the ways in which the women managed the multiple roles centralized around the 'greedy' institutions of family and university (Edwards, 1993, p. 62; Currie et al., 2000). Whilst Garland's mothers were all at various stages of the family life cycle, with just over half having children of school age and just under a fifth having children under the age of five, the patterning of the family in my own study was rather different. Each of the thirteen participants had school-age children, nine had children under five, two having a child under one year. Of particular note and in contrast to the mothers in Garland's study then is the way in which the mothers, in my own study, were willing to embark upon higher education and take on the mantle of juggling motherhood and studentship simultaneously, whist their children were still dependent as babies, toddlers and nursery age.

In terms of Garland's question – 'Why am I putting myself through this? Why now?' – the participants in my study presented a diverse set of responses. However, to demonstrate some of the complexity of these answers, within the short space of this chapter, I shall focus on data with one participant, Tanya, who I have discussed in more detail along with other participants' accounts elsewhere (see Mannay and Morgan, 2013; Mannay and Morgan, 2015). Tanya was selected as, although this journey is unique to Tanya, her story broadly captures some important themes across the women's accounts of transition, which are particularly pertinent for this chapter, as they are able to demonstrate points of convergence and divergence with Garland's original study, providing an insight into aspiration, motivation and the everyday negotiations of identity though an affective lens, for one contemporary 'Rhian' in south Wales.

Introducing Tanya

Tanya is a 34-year-old single mother of two sons, aged fourteen years and fifteen months old, who was in the third year of a nursing degree at a local post-1992 university. Tanya resides in Milburn,[1] a council estate in the south Wales valleys, a community notorious for high levels of deprivation and pathologized both locally and in wider media. However, in recent years, much work and funding, from the Welsh Government and National Lottery, has gone into community regeneration of the area, particularly in terms of education. There have been initiatives to develop aspirations, led by local community role models, and Tanya could be understood as a success story, an exemplar as a member of the community in terms of educational and social mobility.

Life before education

Tanya left school with no educational qualifications and worked as a barmaid at a local club. At twenty years old, Tanya became pregnant but the pregnancy was unplanned and her boyfriend left her for another woman, whom he had also made pregnant. Tanya describes her life after her first son was born as centred on cleaning and caring for the needs of her baby and her family as illustrated in the following extract.

> I would go to my mother's ... I would clean my house in the morning and then go down there [Tanya's mother's house] and clean her house, then I would go to my Nan and see to my Nan, go back to my mother, make tea, come home put the baby to bed – do it ... sort everything out – do it all again the next day and that was it until [son] was about nine.

Tanya's account suggests an identity centred on motherhood, family and the domestic sphere. It is a form of idealized Welsh working-class femininity that is central and prolific in many post-industrial communities, echoing the legend of the 'Welsh Mam' (Rees, 1988). However, as Hollway (2006, p. 8) reminds us 'women who are mothers are not only mothers' and there came a point when Tanya wanted to move into a space outside the routines of the acceptable working-class femininity and the ideology that motherhood is a mutually exclusive enterprise.

Education, aspiration and affect

As Garland found in her study, women with dependent children often experience academic study as particularly challenging (Marandet and Wainwright, 2006), and gendered expectations around household chores and childcare mean that academic study is often viewed as an 'extracurricular' activity or hobby, to be fitted into but not disrupt an already busy schedule. Some of the partnered women in my research spoke of 'sharing' or partner's 'helping' with household chores; however more than half the women were either not in relationships or not residing with partners at the time of interview and thus 'sharing' was either not an option or came in the form of help from their own mothers. In order to manage conflicting demands, time needs to be strategically negotiated and planned, and this is particularly problematic for single parents (Osborne et al., 2004).

When available, support systems of wider family members and friends are often asked to help out with childcare, and thus academia is pursued depending upon the cooperation of others and under conditions of constraint. Mothers in education often discuss experiencing feelings of guilt, which are expressed in terms of neglecting or compromising their familial relationships and role as mother. In terms of both gender and class, then, there are some important implications for subjectivity, and although Tanya discusses the positive factors of entering education in the extracts below, this journey is not without cost:

> I'd get up in the morning – I'd still do my cleaning – put [son] to school and it was like switching off then ... you had a purpose to get up and do something ... New Year's Eve and I was thinking good God this time last year I would have been out, because I had been out every New Year's Eve and I was sitting there holding my head, I remember holding my head thinking I am stuck in here – but I thought no, I will do it, I will ... I'm pleased to tell you, you have been accepted. Well I just burst out crying ... I was hysterical ... and I was going oh thank you, you don't know how much all this means to me and all this – I feel emotional telling you.

Tanya could be understood as a poster girl for the regeneration project; however, as Walkerdine (2011) suggests, addressing issues of intergenerational poverty and social mobility via higher education is far more complicated than raising aspiration. For the working-class subject, the discovery of aspiration and desire to succeed can be felt as threatening to self and others creating tensions between autonomy and belonging, safety and risk, stasis and transition: a complicated cultural and psychosocial phenomenon (Walkerdine and Jimenez, 2012).

Tanya's transition is one laden with affect and her desire to be a nurse is not experienced in a straightforward way for she is deeply ambivalent, torn between expectations of her centred around her old life and identity – 'I would still do my cleaning' – and the possibility of new becomings, being someone else, somewhere else. Although thrilled at being accepted to university and managing to stay in education to pursue her nursing degree, Tanya has become a 'border crosser' (Lucey et al., 2003) and cultural and gendered expectations around motherhood are a constant threat to her studentship: both a source of anxiety and conflict. For Tanya, it is not a lack of aspiration that is problematic, but rather the complex relations and practices within which Tanya's aspiration is ensconced or anchored (Walkerdine, 2011).

In their study, Britton and Baxter (2001) found that managing conflict and changes to identity were more arduous to working-class mature students than their middle-class counterparts, and that negotiating alteration in family relationships was particularly difficult for female students in comparison to males. The following extract highlights the precarious nature of Tanya's position and illustrates the complex set of emotional and relational challenges inherent to working-class upward social mobility. Tanya describes a day when her son was ill, she was pregnant and just before going into her first year examinations she received an abusive telephone call from her sister.

> Some things she has said. It is awful. Dreadful what she has said – like phoning social services, you should be ashamed she said, you should be in the house with the baby ... you shouldn't be in uni and I said Scott [partner] what can I do, I can't win – whatever I do is wrong, it's not, it's not good enough ... I do feel guilty coz like I said to Scott, even a few weeks ago – I am finishing, I am quitting, I said I need to go back to what I used to be before – my mother, I need to be there all the time and doing. He said Tan you can't, you can't and then I convince myself I gotta, I gotta finish, I can't do this anymore – I should be there for my family. But I think well I can't be
> ...

Despite having the support of her boyfriend at the time, wider family expectations, envy and culturally gendered discourses around mother-hood collided with Tanya's own ambitions and desires with painful effect. Judgement and conflict from her sister and the threat of state intervention elicits guilt and a longing for her old life, which Tanya manages by trying 'not think about it … try to block it out and carry on'. Indeed this was manifest during our interview when Tanya managed her sister's constant phone calls, thirteen in one hour, by blocking them out and carrying on – she managed to ignore them far better than I. Since early on in her educational journey, Tanya experi-enced education as a 'place to switch off … before having to come back to reality'. Despite the tensions that her degree has created and exacer-bated, for Tanya education is simultaneously a place where she feels she can escape and in that respect, university has become a place of safety.

Strength and survival

Tanya sought support from another woman student on her course who was living locally to her and in similar circumstances. This advice and guidance developed into a reciprocal arrangement whereby the women studied together and 'bounced off each other'; learning became a shared endeavour and their relationship developed into a firm friendship, with-out which Tanya claims she could not have completed the first undergraduate year. Her position in higher education became more precarious when her maternity leave meant that she had to join the next year's cohort. However, this situation was eased via both women's stra-tegic planning and a social networking site engendered a virtual relationship that acted as a point of contact and meant that on her return from maternity leave Tanya once more had a woman, connected to her community, she could identify with and share her journey. When Garland's (1994) chapter was published online social networking was not commonplace; however, Tanya's account resonates with previous literature that has highlighted the value of online support systems for non-traditional students in Wales (Mannay and Wilcock, 2015).

When Tanya returned to her studies, coming from the previous year's cohort positioned her as 'the expert', and she gained much pleasure and satisfaction from providing advice and guidance to other students. These relationships also developed into friendships and having her support recognized and appreciated (unlike at home) was very much valued by Tanya. During my visits, Tanya showed me the cards and notes of encouragement, thanks and congratulations that the women had exchanged, which demonstrated the salience of their relationships in sustaining their academic journeys.

Understood within the context of the post-industrial communities, of which these women are a part, these connections are important as they gain strength and support through their sameness and they provide a sense of belonging, of keeping together, of continuity and safety. They are in fact drawing on the same resources that, historically in times of difficulties, held their communities together. The women have themselves established an informal system of 'paying it forward' or generalized reciprocity. It is this mutual and acknowledged support that is a key element to Tanya staying in higher education. In psychoanalytic terms the women may be understood as transitional objects, which allow Tanya to feel safe – contained or held (Bick, 1968; Walkerdine, 2010, 2011), giving her a continuity of being as she moves forward in her educational trajectory whilst simultaneously anchoring herself to her past and her culture. Sadly, these informal support networks are not always available or easily accessed. Their absence could be assumed to result in the affective pull of one's old life and identity to become stronger, preventing movement and change but providing continuity and security in the safety of familiar identities and ways of being.

Conclusion

In revisiting Garland's (1994) study in *Our Sisters' Land*, this chapter sought to provide a contemporary view of the lives of mature student mothers in Wales, through the story of Tanya, pointing to the structural and psychological barriers faced in their participation in higher education in contemporary Wales. Butler (2004, p. 3) has suggested that agency is paradoxical: 'If I have any agency, it is opened by the fact that I am constituted by a social world I never choose.' Thus, for Tanya, and the other women in my sample, being a mature student had to be accommodated within their wider lives, lives that are gendered, classed and often mismatched to the world of higher education. Their educational transitions involved surmounting significant barriers in engaging in formal learning; barriers that were frequently at the level of the psychosocial, rendering them invisible and beyond the categorization necessary for institutional support (Mannay and Morgan, 2013).

Tanya has successfully, but not painlessly, negotiated the journey into and through higher education and her account offers insight into the everyday negotiations and strength, which have achieved this position of success. For Tanya, it was the informal support network system that offered a point of contact with someone like herself that was central in providing the motivation to carry on in higher education. This anchoring to the past, by befriending peers with similar historical and cultural heritage, both face to face and through social networking sites, allowed Tanya to move forward in her educational journey. In terms of institutional policy, this would suggest that it could be useful to instigate informal networks and peer buddy systems within universities as a support system for mature learners entering higher education, and through personal experience of being involved in a mature student coffee club (see Mannay and Edwards, 2015), I am aware of the tacit and nuanced support this offers mature learners, both academically and pastorally.

The demographic data of my mother participants, in comparison to Garland's, suggests that women in contemporary south Wales are embarking upon higher education much sooner, whilst their families are still very young, dependent and in need of much 'mothering'. Whilst ideologically at least this reinforces feminist ideas around equality, since these mothers are marginalized and have no resources with which to purchase additional childcare, nor domestic help around the home, it may well be that caught within neo-liberal discourses of self betterment and of 1990s feminist 'girl power', women in Wales are set up to try to achieve impossible standards of selfhood and motherhood. Additionally, as Wilson and Huntington (2005) maintain, shifts in government policy away from redistributive models of welfare support and towards models focused on economic growth have meant that traditional ideas of motherhood and child rearing have been sidelined in favour of women's participation in the labour market and economic independence.

Resonating with the findings presented in chapter four in this volume, the themes and findings discussed here paint a problematic picture emerging within the rhetoric of egalitarianism and equality. Kennedy (2001, p. 6) asserts that 'individuals are compelled to take greater control over the kinds of social identities they wish to assume'; however, aspiring to juggle the demands of two greedy institutions – motherhood and studentship (Currie et al., 2000) – within such a demanding stage of the family life cycle, although achievable, is not without cost for marginalized mothers in Wales. As Mannay explained in chapter four, 'when the impossibilities of new femininity – full-time job, perfect mother, domestic goddess (May, 2008) – are not achieved', there is potential for perceived 'failure' and 'inadequacy' both being levelled at and internalized by individual women in south Wales. For Garland (1994), 'family matters' and domestic issues were at the forefront of women's concerns throughout their educational transformation and they remain sites of contention for new cohorts of Rhians who attempt to negotiate the higher education landscape in Wales.

Note

[1]   The name Milburn is fictitious and it was chosen to maintain the anonymity of the area.

References

Brooks, A. and Wee, L., 'Reflexivity and the Transformation of Gender Identity: Reviewing the Potential for Change in a Cosmopolitan City', *Sociology*, 42 (2008), 503–21.

Bick, E., 'The Experience of the Skin in Early Object Relations', *International Journal of Psychoanalysis*, 49 (1968), 558–66.

Britton, C. and Baxter, A., 'Becoming a Mature Student: Gendered Narratives of the Self', *Gender and Education*, 11/2 (1999), 179–93.

—— and ——, 'Risk, Identity and Change: Becoming a Mature Student', *International Studies in Sociology of Education*, 11/1 (2001), 87–102.

Butler, J., *Undoing Gender* (Abingdon: Routledge, 2004).

Currie, J., Harris, P. and Thiele, B., 'Sacrifices in Greedy Universities: Are They Gendered?', *Gender and Education*, 12/3 (2000), 269–91.

Department for Education and Employment (DfEE), *The Learning Age: A Renaissance for a New Britain* (Sheffield: DfEE, 1998).

Department for Education and Skills (DfES), Aimhigher website (2003), *www. dfes.gov.uk/aimhigherprogramme/index.cfm?i_pageId=1&s_pageType=l evel2* (accessed 17 January 2004).

Edwards, R., *Mature Women Students: Separating or Connecting Family and Education* (London: Taylor Francis, 1993).

Garland, P., 'Educating Rhian: experiences of mature women students', in J. Aaron, T. Rees, S. Betts and M. Vincentelli (eds), *Our Sisters' Land: The Changing Identities of Women in Wales* (Cardiff: University of Wales Press, 1994), pp. 107–21.

Giddens, A., *Modernity and Self-Identity: Self and Society in the Late Modern Age* (Cambridge: Polity, 1991).

Higher Education Funding Council for Wales (HEFCW), 'Strategic Approach to Widening Access of Higher Education 2013/2014 to 2015/2016, Circular W14/32HE' (Cardiff: HEFCW, 2014).

Hill, M. and Hatt, S., *Review of Widening Access and Reaching Wider Strategies in Wales* (York: Higher Education Academy, 2012).

Hollway, W., *The Capacity to Care: Gender and Ethical Subjectivity* (London: Routledge, 2006).

Kennedy, P., 'Introduction: globalization and the crisis of identities?', in P. Kennedy and C. Danks (eds), *Globalization and National Identities: Crisis or Opportunity?* (New York: Palgrave, 2001), pp. 1–28.

Lucey, H., Melody, J. and Walkerdine, V., 'Uneasy Hybrids: Psychosocial Aspects of Becoming Educationally Successful for Working-class Young Women', *Gender and Education*, 15/3 (2003), 285–99.

Mannay, D., 'Keeping Close and Spoiling: Exploring the Significance of "Home" for Family Relationships and Educational Trajectories in a Marginalised Estate in Urban South Wales', *Gender and Education*, 25/1 (2013), 91–107.

—— and Edwards, V., 'Coffee, Milk and a Sprinkling of Sand: an Initiative to Assist Non-traditional, Mature Students form Supportive Networks in Higher Education', *Proceedings of the Forum for Access and Continuing Education 2014 Annual Conference* (London: Forum for Access and Continuing Education, 2015).

—— and Morgan, M., 'Anatomies of Inequality: Considering the Emotional Cost of Aiming Higher for Marginalised, Mature, Mothers Re-entering Education', *Journal of Adult and Continuing Education*, 19/1 (2013), 57–75.

—— and ——, 'Doing Ethnography or Applying a Qualitative Technique? Reflections from the "Waiting Field"', *Qualitative Research*, 15/2 (2015), 166–82.

—— and O'Connell, C., 'Accessing the Academy: Developing Strategies to Engage and Retain Marginalised Young People on Successful Educational Pathways', *Socialine Teorija, Empirija, Politika ir Praktika – Social Theory, Empirics, Policy and Practice*, 7 (2013), 133–40.

—— and Wilcock, C., 'What Students Want? Exploring the Role of the Institution in Supporting Successful Learning Journeys in Online Distance Education', *Widening Participation and Lifelong Learning*, 17/1 (2015), 49–63.

Marandet, E. and Wainwright, E., *An Analysis of the Learning Needs and Experiences of Students with Dependent Children at Brunel University* (London: Brunel University, 2006).

May, V., 'On Being a "Good" Mother: The Moral Presentation of Self in Written Life Stories', *Sociology*, 42/3 (2008), 470–86.

Mercer, J., 'Re-negotiating the Self through Educational Development: Mature Students' Experiences', *Research in Post-Compulsory Education*, 12/1 (2007), 19–32.

Osborne, M., Marks, A. and Turner, E., 'Becoming a Mature Student: How Older Potential Applicants Weigh the Advantages and Disadvantages of Embarking on a University Course', *Higher Education*, 48 (2004), 291–315.

Reay, D., 'Identity making in schools and classrooms', in M. Wetherell and C. T. Mohanty (eds), *The Sage Handbook of Identities* (London: Sage, 2010), pp. 277–94.

Rees, T., 'Changing Patterns of Women's Work in Wales: Some Myths Explored', *Contemporary Wales*, 2 (1988), 119–30.

Rose-Adams, J., 'Leaving University Early: Exploring Relationships between Institution Type and Student Withdrawal and Implications for Social Mobility', *Widening Participation and Lifelong Learning*, 15/2 (2013), 96–112.

Saunders, D., Marshall, H., Cowe, F., Payne, R. and Rogers, A., 'Developing Higher Education in South Wales: The Emergence of the Universities Heads of the Valleys Institute', *Journal of Adult and Continuing Education*, 19/1 (2013), 76–100.

Skeggs, B., 'Class, culture and morality: legacies and logics in the space for identity', in M. Wetherell and C. T. Mohanty (eds), *The Sage Handbook of Identities* (London: Sage, 2010), pp. 339–60.

Taylor, C., Rees, G., Sloan, L. and Davies, R., 'Creating an Inclusive Higher Education System? Progression and Outcomes of Students from Low Participation Neighbourhoods at a Welsh University', *Contemporary Wales*, 26 (2013), 138–61.

Thomas, L., 'Student Retention in Higher Education: The Role of Institutional Habitus', *Australian Journal of Educational Policy*, 17/4 (2002), 423–32.

Walkerdine, V., 'Communal Beingness and Affect: An Exploration of Trauma in an Ex-industrial Community', *Body and Society*, 16 (2010), 91–116.

——, 'Neoliberalism, Working-class Subjects and Higher Education', *Contemporary Social Science*, 6/2 (2011), 255–71.

——, 'Using the Work of Felix Guattari to Understand Space, Place, Social Justice, and Education', *Qualitative Research*, 19/10 (2013), 756–64.

—— and Jimenez, L., *Gender, Work and Community after De-industrialisation: A Psychosocial Approach to Affect* (Basingstoke: Palgrave Macmillan, 2012).

Waller, R., '"I Call Myself a Mature Student. That One Word Makes All the Difference": Reflections on Adult Learners' Experiences', *Auto/Biography*, 13/ 1 (2005), 53–76.

Ward, M. R. M., 'I'm a Geek I am: Academic Achievement and the Performance of a Studious Working-class Masculinity', *Gender and Education*, 26/7 (2014), 709–25.

Welsh Government, *For Our Future – The 21st Century Higher Education Strategy Plan for Wales* (Cardiff: Welsh Government, 2009).

Wilson, F., 'The Construction of Paradox? One Case of Mature Students in Higher Education', *Higher Education Quarterly*, 51/4 (1997), 347–66.

Wilson, H. and Huntington, A., 'OHS in the Nursing Workplace: Accountability and the Management of Stress', *The Journal of Occupational Health and Safety: Australia and New Zealand*, 21/2 (2005), 113–20.

Credentials and the Chameleon – by Ian Homer

7

Private Lives Used for Public Work: Women Further Education Teachers in Wales

Introduction

Six women teachers employed in the contemporary Further Education (FE) sector in Wales are the focus of this chapter. The discussion draws on qualitative data from an Economic and Social Research Council (ESRC) funded project as part of the extension to Wales of the Teaching and Learning Research Programme (TLRP). The Learning and Working in Further Education Colleges (ESRC/TLRP, 2008) research involved an ethnography of seven different college campuses over a period of two years.[1] This fieldwork generated volumes of observational field notes, expanded accounts, journal entries and interview transcripts from students and teachers. To date, the study provides the only detailed ethnographic investigation of FE sites in Wales (Salisbury, 2012; Salisbury and Jephcote, 2009, 2010; Salisbury et al., 2009).

The chapter revisits some key themes from my earlier chapter 'Chasing credentials: women Further Education teachers and in-service training', from *Our Sisters' Land*, which considered six unqualified female FE teachers and their altruistic or instrumental motivations for undergoing formal in-service teacher training (Salisbury, 1994). The FE sector in Wales has undergone much change over the last two decades against a background of increased politicization of education in general. Politicians' claims that schools and colleges were failing to prepare young people adequately for the 'world of work' (Hodgson and Spours, 1999) led to numerous reforms: a remodelling of qualification structures, the 'incorporation' of colleges of FE in 1993 and new funding regimes, which inaugurated an era of external accountability, regulation and control (Hyland and Merrill, 2003; Gleeson et al., 2005). So the FE landscape in Wales, with its drive for efficiency, value for money and greater accountability, is a markedly different landscape to that experienced by the women in the early 1990s when the fieldwork for 'Chasing credentials' was undertaken.

The project investigated the experiences of learning and working in FE colleges in Wales and followed the learning journeys of twenty-seven teachers and forty-five students over two years. This chapter focuses on six women teachers who had been employed as FE teachers from between four and fifteen years, teaching a range of vocational courses and A-level subjects. Each of the women discussed here was passionate about supporting their students to secure qualifications. All of them were also striving for self-improvement and were engaged in various types of continuing professional development and acknowledged that they were 'chasing credentials'.

The following sections explore how the teachers negotiated managerial imperatives, institutional bureaucracies and engaged in principled infidelity to enable students to proceed and attain the qualifications for which they were enrolled. Teachers illustrated a particular ethic of care and the chapter presents the ways teachers' emotional labours are deployed across different situations in their day-to-day working lives as they strive to credentialize their students and themselves. In being authentic role models for their classes as lifelong learners themselves, and sharing their learner biographies with their student audiences, each of these women teachers is supplying a crucial but under-acknowledged part of the programmatic endeavour for FE learners. The chapter discusses contemporary experiences and perspectives of women teachers in the Welsh FE sector in Wales and makes comparisons with earlier research from the mid-1990s.

The teachers

The rationale behind the selection of these six individuals is quite simple: of the twenty-seven teachers recruited these six were enthusiastic lifelong learners all engaged in the pursuit of a qualification. During data analysis this fact, along with their agentic stances, set them apart. Furthermore, each of them participated fully in all aspects of the two-year project, wrote regular journal entries, offered me, as the

Table 7.1: Vignettes of the six women FE teachers and their 'credentials'

Name & age	Marital status: Married-M Single-S	Children's ages	No. of years teaching in FE part time	No. of years teaching in FE full time	Teaching subjects	Occupational history before teaching	Qualifications & credentials	Current studies and credential sought
Carys 43	M	28, 21	3	4	Business studies /IT	Clerk – secretary, mother, carer	HND/BA PGCE (FE)	GSCE Welsh adult evening class
Debra 39	S	-	-	15	Sociology & psychology	Tax office clerk/ temp	BA, PGCE (FE) OU Diploma	Completing dissertation for MA (Ed) (Open University)
Mary 45	M	21, 17	2	6	Animal care	Zoo & pet shop assistant, kennel owner, mother	HND, Cert. Ed. BEd	Enrolled for distance M.Ed
Charlotte 27	M	-	1	3	Numeracy, health & social care	Play scheme leader, youth club worker	BSc Psychology, PGCE (Primary)	OU module on autism spectrum D Ed Psych (applicant)
Helen 42	S	-	-	15	Health & social care, biology	Nurse	RGN B N (Nursing) BSc PGCE (FE)	Completing modules on Ed D.
Penny 45	M	25, 22	3	10	Computer studies, IT	Secretary	BSc Cert. Ed.	GCSE Italian adult evening class

ethnographer, complete access to their lessons and materials and participated in at least two audio-recorded semi-structured interviews.
Typically, like twenty-four of the twenty-seven teachers sampled, each
of the six women was a 'late entrant' to teaching (Sikes et al., 1985),
having joined the FE workforce following employment in other occupations. Marriage, fairly early motherhood and time spent raising a
family characterize the later learning trajectories of Carys (43), Mary
(45) and Penny (45), who each 'returned to learn' as their children
became less dependent.[2] Each of them studied initially part time for
BTEC and HND qualifications and with success moved on to part-time
degree programmes delivered by their local university.

In contrast, Debra (39) and Charlotte (27) moved from school sixth
forms with good A levels directly into university, both pursuing social
science degrees. Helen (42) entered nurse training and when nursing
became an all graduate profession she studied part time for a BSc in
nursing and again for a BSc in behavioural science, eventually deciding
to pursue a PGCE (FE) full time to enter the teaching profession. The
six women totalled between them nine years of part-time and fifty-three
years of full-time employment, teaching a range of academic and
vocational courses. Table 7.1 provides a biographical overview for each
participant.

Like Mannay's (2013) 'homebirds' both Carys and Mary had
remained in the localities of their birthplace and always lived near their
respective workplaces. They had not only attended the FE college
themselves as mature students, but had returned to teach in the
departments that they themselves had thrived in. As credible champions
of lifelong learning there was an acknowledgement that by moving 'to
the other side of the desk' both had become positive examples of
women who gained from returning to education.

> I know that I am a positive role model ... I tell them, 'just look at me. If I can
> do it so can you!' I don't mind telling them that I left school as soon as I
> could, that the school had written me off, that I had my son when I was
> rather young! I shared quite a lot with them really, and when they're flag-
> ging it's what they need to hear. [Carys]

The women recognized that FE offered a second chance for people to
pursue training, improve their basic skills and study for a qualification.
With its catchy internal rhyme the phrase 'return to learn' was a
commonly used term with special significance when discussing older
learners and those over nineteen who may have been caught up in the
'revolving door' (Roberts, 2005) of benefits-linked welfare-to-work

schemes and low-paid jobs. The women's abilities to empathize with mature students and understand their situations were frequently apparent in observational fieldwork. One 32-year-old male student of Mary's animal care course, Joe, described himself as 'severely dyslexic' at initial interview and in subsequent informal conversations.

> In the library I sit with the three Animal Care students who have set about their task to find some good diagrams of a dog's innards. They are well focussed, pouring over and flicking through six books ... Joe pipes up, 'Will you lot check my spellings again 'cos Mary [teacher] says it's a good idea? She knows that when you're copying down from books it can come out wrong because she's dyslexic too. She always gets someone to check her diagrams.' Amy teases Joe saying that she will, but only if he buys her a bar of chocolate! ... Joe explains to me later over coffee that 'Mary tells us all that she's dyslexic too! I don't feel so bad about the stuff I hand in then, she understands.' [Field note extract]

Teachers' biographical disclosure and willingness to share details of their private lives, their learning disabilities, their chequered school histories, the arrival of untimely babies and events from their wider lives were appreciated by their students who saw their teachers as role models who had also had their different struggles with life, relationships, employment and learning. Establishing sound relationships at the start of a course was seen as the main function of the induction period and from the outset these women were prepared to share their 'private lives for public good'. In so doing, each felt able to succeed in their teaching and nurturing roles precisely because they were capable of building relationships with their students.

Relationships and pastoral work

A predominant theme across the student interviews was the way in which teachers were perceived as having to be available and approachable. This was understood as a right of students who also had and expected individualized learning plans (ILPs), regular one-to-one tutorials and individualized teaching. Wales' Ten Student Entitlements (WAG, 2002) were published in student handbooks, on posters and explained during formal induction programmes, reinforcing the notion that students were clients to be provided for.

Teachers described how they worked at relationships and engaged in lengthy, difficult pastoral work outside contact hours, revealing a strong emotive concern for their students as individuals with lives outside college, as well as learner identities inside subject departments. A complete lunch break was a rare luxury, and the women shared the issues students bring into college for them to sort out. Charlotte, the youngest and least experienced teacher amongst the women, had been shocked by the 'horrendous personal situations' she was made aware of in what was only her fourth year of teaching.

This year, I guess a lot of my students have got some big problems – they've come from backgrounds, they've got alcoholic mothers … one of my students, her mother was murdered … a lot of them have had abuse, sexual abuse and whatever. It just goes on, you know, and I've got lots of asylum seekers.

Students share delicate and personal information with their teachers and although all six women knew on entering the profession that pastoral work would be part of their role, without exception, none of them had expected the volume of it and the extent that this would consume their time. Carys, whose open door policy and approachability kept her extremely busy, recounted a conversation with her male line manager who commended her: 'He made no bones about it! He said, "Well Carys, let's face it, you're so good at it [pastoral care] so the students choose you to share their problems with – you and the other women staff. The men get off lightly.' Carys was not alone in feeling ambivalent about others' expectations that she will nurture and care for students while her male colleagues appeared to be free from such responsibilities. Debra also resented the way male colleagues in her department quite readily 'passed over the complex student cases and problems', though as a teacher of sociology, she also recognized that having an open door and dedicated office hours was perhaps a visible demonstration of her culturally presumed, innate capacity to care (Hollway, 2006). Like the Canadian women academics studied by Acker and Webber (2014) and the HE personal tutors researched by Huyton (2014), these women FE teachers were aware that many of their pastoral efforts were invisible in the metric of workloads and contact hours, and yet each engaged willingly in a service that went well beyond just teaching and assessing their students. The diversity of tasks and encounters was made visible in their journals, those of their students as well as the ethnographic fieldwork. Escorting distressed students to the counselling service or arranging medical referrals were typical actions of these caring women who also loaned (gave) money for bus fares, a hot lunch and generally responded to many human needs and upsets. The complexity of younger and older students' lives and the ways these impacted upon these teachers' work and roles was striking.

Mary explained why she always gets into college 'early at 8.00am or even before that to be *there* for students' and describes how her week begins and some of the help that is required before she can begin the business of teaching:

> Monday mornings are hell because you come in Monday mornings and there's ... 'so and so's been in a fight' or 'so and so's mother's thrown them out'. Or 'so and so thinks she's pregnant' ... 'so and so's fallen out with their boyfriend'... it's all Monday mornings. *Guaranteed*! Before half past nine, right ... something catastrophic's happened right or somebody's got sacked, or somebody can't get any grant money [...] So that's the start of the week. [Interview, Mary]

The weekly group tutorials were deemed inadequate to support the diverse range of problems that students presented and the women increasingly gave individual one-to-ones in their non-contact time and lunch breaks to address students' needs. Students across the age range appreciated their teachers' efforts and often drew sharp contrasts with their experiences at school.

> [In college] they care about us. In school you were just part of a class. They really want us to do well here. This year, it didn't matter if staff were busy, they would always make time for me or tell me. [Student focus group, A-level art]

> I like the more personal relationships in college we call teachers by their first names and this seems to make it easier to ask for help. Everything seems more open and less reserved. I think you can speak to teachers in college in private, on your own more easily; they are a more available to you than teachers in school. [Student journal 1, Melissa, Health Studies]

Reflecting their concerns with the 'whole' person, some women teachers defended students against demanding parents and employers whose intrusive phone calls in lessons disrupted learning and important formal assessments.

> Students ... can be pulled out of class because ... they've got to go home to look after a two year old. And I'm thinking, don't they [parents] realize they're taking [their] education and chance away ...? [Interview, Carys]

> I grabbed her mobile and rang the Burger Bar back immediately. I said 'Hello, I am Kylie's teacher at college [name]. I am afraid she has an assessment which is being filmed this morning and she has to present. She'll be

able to come to work today but not until this afternoon.' The student was in tears, worried that the manager didn't believe her. Anxious that she'd lose the job. It was an assessed presentation and it could not be missed. She was so grateful that I stood up for her. That sort of thing happens a lot. [Interview, Helen]

In the fieldwork, I came across numerous incidents that directly impacted on college life and on a more routine basis there were many interruptions in class from mobile phones and texts relaying, for example, the heart attack of a student's mother, the news of an absent classmate's positive pregnancy test. The complexity of students' wider lives and details came into the classroom with them. The teachers showed a particular empathy for mature students, many of whom were women involved in the 'double shift' (Davidoff, 1976, and see Mannay and Morgan this volume).

Emotional resilience and an ethic of care

The pressures that teachers were operating under were exemplified in their responses to a structured journal entry narrating 'A day in life of a FE teacher'. Some teachers provided a detailed hour-by-hour, sometimes minute-by-minute, record of a given day. An extract from Helen's journal captures vividly an emotional encounter:

10.50 am. Arrive back in my office to find one of second years in tears, a young gentleman. Very complicated issue concerning a mental health-related problem. Student is 18 – cannot inform parents – no counsellor is available. Child protection issue could be involved here as well with a sibling. All middle management are unavailable as is the head of student services. 2.5 hours later and still with the student, feeling emotionally drained after listening to all concerns from the student and supporting him as much as I could. Made him coffee in office, talked, chocolates given to him to munch with coffee. I am concerned student may harm himself – and yet there is no one to support me in this other than 1 meeting with one middle manager I located. It seems I've done everything I could here – a relief but I still feel it could have been dealt with better. No marking done in my duty time [11.00 a.m. to 2 p.m.] as planned today. [Journal, Helen]

Teachers described the emotional struggles they experience. These emotions provide evidence of the complex relationship of teaching and caring: irritation and frustration with students who arrived late, who are ill equipped or who have not brought in their coursework and who have missed submission dates; disappointment about those who drop out or sadness for those who experience tragedy, an unwanted pregnancy, health scares or personal, domestic difficulties. And joy and pleasure at how individuals respond to encouragement and demonstrate achievement or progress. Having to mask and disguise negative emotions, that is, conduct 'emotional labour' (Hochschild 1983; Hargreaves, 1998; Isenbarger and Zembylas, 2006) was a skill that all of the women had developed so as to negotiate and enable productive interactions in their learning spaces (see also Salisbury, 2014).

Many classroom practices are the result of FE teachers anticipating how they think their students will respond to different teaching and learning strategies, or the way they set up or organize the learning setting. Charlotte, for example, is acutely mindful not to expose the vulnerability of the students with poor numeracy:

> I have students who don't know their three times table and can't tell the time and things like that. And, to enable a student to be able to tell the time because they're 16 and they should know that is good it makes me feel like I'm putting something right ... There is this kind of, they never wanted to admit they couldn't do it in the first place and they don't make a big deal of it and I don't make a – try not to make a big deal of it. Because there is definitely that feeling of 'I'm embarrassed that I can't do this' ... I mean that's the thing that's uppermost in my mind usually with maths with foundation classes – is how do I say to the student now, 'okay this is wrong, you need to do this' but without making them look stupid or feel stupid. And they're so defensive anyway and so I suppose all of my psychology comes in big time, in terms of building up a relationship with them. My style is to build the relationship up and their trust. And that pays off and it definitely pays off in terms of them being *safe* in maths. [Interview, Charlotte]

Whilst Charlotte had been shocked and privately upset and angry that students had left compulsory schooling with such limited skills, she managed her emotions, fronted up a confident 'we can do this attitude'. Her ethic of care and grasp of her students' vulnerabilities underpinned her enthusiastic teaching to these social care girls in their compulsory numeracy lessons.

The women were emotionally resilient teachers and they tended to have a firm sense of moral purpose about their work, speaking often of their own deep sense of reward from 'turning someone round – getting them to believe in themselves' (Debra) and 'putting something back into the sector which benefited me and seeing my efforts help someone else make it' (Mary). Such remarks appeared to support the widening access, inclusion and participation agenda of UK and Welsh

Government (SEU, 1999; WAG, 2001). These women formed 'solidary relationships' (Lynch, 1989), engaged in emotional labour and believed in looking after 'the whole student', solving personal difficulties and nurturing and protecting their students in order to liberate them for the tasks of learning. The teachers manage both their own hearts (their feelings and emotions) and the hearts of their students (their emotional well-being, self-esteem and anxieties) in order to manage their students' motivations and engagement in learning. With an 'holistic focus' they embrace the view of FE as a client-centred service.

Overworked and under scrutiny

Four of the six women revealed that their work/non-work boundaries were blurred, and they admitted that achieving a better balance would help them gain an improved sense of professional autonomy in their teaching roles. Mary and Penny explained that they checked e-mails late into the night: 'I don't do college work all evening but before bed I often find myself opening my inbox and responding to emails and before I know it, it's well past midnight!' (Mary). Penny described how she responded covertly to e-mails at weekends because her husband 'hates the fact that I put in masses of unpaid and unrecognized over-time'. This backstage, off-site working was a norm and supports Gornall et al.'s (2014) point that much important work in education is conducted in temporal margins and hidden spaces. These teachers accepted long working hours, tackled blizzards of e-mails after normal hours and lived with the expectation of colleagues and students that they would be accessible over an extended week. Charlotte and Debra saw themselves as good collegial citizens 'servicing' needy students willingly but doing their best, with frequent failure, to construct an on campus working day of 8.30 a.m. to 5.30 p.m.

The women discussed a growing sense of being over managed and under surveillance, which resulted in stress (see also Dixcy and Harbottle, 2014; Jephcote and Salisbury, 2008; Salisbury, 2014). Alongside many other FE colleagues they felt pressured by the requirements to produce more visible and impressive course material and learning outcome documentation. The ever-present pressure to recruit and retain students, sometimes regardless of their ability or performance, was also felt keenly. At the micro level of the college the teachers were critical of the fact that much work was 'driven by numerical data' with middle managers having to regularly undertake 'curriculum area audits by subject'.

A college's 'target fetishism' was said to have 'distortive effects' (Gray, 1994; Coffield, 2008) on teachers' activities. The privileging of particular indicators was seen as an outcome of punitive funding regimes and most perceived the impacts of national macro policy in the form of outside inspection and data gathering for audit, to detract from what they saw as their core roles in teaching and supporting students. The women lamented that 'grappling with the data prevents you from preparing for teaching' (Debra). Carys was particularly frustrated with excessive time spent 'breaking down the raw figures to show the truth' and technological acceleration had impacted significantly on administrative and core teaching work for these teachers, altering the tempo and rhythm of their work.

The women gave accounts of having their lessons 'observed and scored' by their peers and being 'performance reviewed' by their line managers; without exception, all six women felt under close scrutiny. In fact, a clear sense of their busyness and often 'over work' came through in the observational, interview and journal data. Penny thought that she and her departmental colleagues had 'bust a gut' to achieve their grade one Estyn report but were still left feeling undervalued. Pressure to take on administrative work left her no alternative but to:

> fob off the students by giving them research work to do ... Time constraints mean that I am cutting corners and I know full well that I can teach in a much more absorbing way than I am forced to do by circumstances.

This dedicated teacher was unhappy when she knew she could do better for her IT students and admitted her discomfort: 'I find myself having an identity crisis – am I a lecturer, here to educate my students or simply someone for whom educating students is a by-product of learning how to cook the books to improve students statistics?' Penny's strong sense of professional identity was challenged by managerial imperatives and, in a similar way, Debra's was also. The heavy-handed way her senior managers were 'throwing their weight around' she thought was 'un-collegial, unprofessional and totally ignored the dignity at work policy'. A field note extract depicts the tension she experienced.

> Debra has had her annual review meeting and today she has been given a hard copy of the college's analysis of her teaching quality and her students' evaluations. She waves a printout and shows me how student evaluation data have been presented to all staff. Her students have not *all* been positive. There are other data sheets too on student retention, attainment,

performance and she is clearly upset by the footnotes to some tables which specify her targets for 2007 … She is most cross at having been interrupted while teaching an A-level revision class and taken outside her room for a 'corridor conversation' in which the manager gave her this paperwork, 'so that I could read it in my break at 11 and be ready for the diaried formal meeting at 11.15!' [Field note extract]

The women responded imaginatively to try to reconcile conflicts between the performative demands of monitoring systems and what they felt to be in the best interests of their students. Debra compensated for the disrupted revision lesson by giving – on the same day – a lunch-time catch-up session in which she distributed two model answers (essays she had written and typed herself) and a packet of digestive biscuits 'to keep the students sustained'. It has been argued that the dilemmas professionals face are chronic and serious because there is no simple translation between institutional obligations and ethical obliga-tions, between 'doing my job' and 'doing the right thing' (Cribb, 2005, p. 8). Some aspects of the teaching job involved the women doing things demanded by managers that they found ethically distasteful, examples being,

* *Directed* to mark only two drafts of student course work [Penny]

* *Instructed* to withhold [competitor sensitive] course availability informa-tion from part-time mature students thereby limiting vital course continuity information and career information [Debra]

* *Reprimanded* for texting absent students even when the intention is to ensure they receive their EMA [Education Maintenance Allowance] and improve likelihood of retention and completion [Mary, Carys, Charlotte]

* *Directed* to offer and provide individual tutorials of only 15 minutes dura-tion [Helen]

These teachers understood the concept 'assessment for learning' (Black and Wiliam, 2004) and continued to annotate several drafts of course-work with formative feedback to optimize their learners' attainments. They were also mindful that an individual's attendance data on class registers was compiled centrally and on a daily basis, as evidence for their EMA, and they did their best to generate data which would ensure that a 'needy' student got their £30 per week. The six women, along with many other teachers in the study, continually made decisions about compliance and when to subvert institutional rules or adopt a stance of 'principled infidelity' (Wallace, 2005).

Why pursue qualifications?

Many teachers complain of innovation fatigue, emphasizing that the FE sector is beleaguered by audits and targets (Clow, 2005; Coffield, 2008; Dixey and Harbottle, 2014; James and Biesta, 2007; Jephcote, 2014). Yet despite experiencing the effects of work intensification the six women appear to remain engaged in wider learning, though many occupational challenges contributed to their feelings of being 'time poor'. Hoyle's (1974) complimentary descriptive term 'extended professionality' applies to each one of them. There are no requirements in Wales as there are in England for FE teachers to undergo continuous professional development (CPD) and though colleges organize whole day events these are often generic and on topics like learning styles, e-learning or the Equality Duty, which reflect management priorities (Lloyd and Payne, 2012). The women participated in these and were well disposed to keeping up to date but they also sought out other courses, which better matched their needs and interests. Helen's altruism, sense of responsibility and avowed motive for pursuing her professional doctorate (Ed. D) studies is stated eloquently:

> I realize the effectiveness or ineffectiveness of my practical efforts as a teacher can have very significant effects on the life chances of the students whose needs I serve so I must always strive to improve my knowledge and skills … It's part of being a professional isn't it? There is such a thing as knowledge obsolescence!

Chasing credentials and undertaking CPD is perhaps a vehicle for achieving mid-life generativity and avoiding stagnation as Penny indicated enthusiastically: 'I thrive on doing courses and learning something new. I never want to stagnate!' For Penny, a GCSE Italian evening class would, she felt 'be good fun but also better equip me for the Welsh Bac. and it's Wales, Europe and the wider world elements which I have to teach'. Similar reasons were given by Carys for her pursuit of a GCSE qualification in Welsh; however, having been partly raised by a Welsh-speaking Nanna she admitted that she was 'actually reactivating and re-learning very rusty vocabulary … and it's much harder than I had expected especially the written exercises so I get my students to test me and they love it!' Pursuing a formal qualification is also a strategy for avoiding the erosion of a sense of professional autonomy – at least the sense of this – and to help build up a more professional identity:

> I am funding this Masters degree with the OU [Open University] myself for my own pleasure and of course at the same time self-improvement and it'll

also enhance my professional identity and strengthen my CV ... Of course, the college will reap the benefits of my new-found expertise in supporting SEN learners. [Debra]

Charlotte at twenty-seven anticipated a future helping young people not as a teacher, but as a professional psychologist and knew that this would mean upward social mobility. She intended to part-fund her three-year full-time educational psychology doctorate by continuing to teach evenings at college and, if necessary, do some private GCSE and A-level mathematics tuition. She had already applied once and was, as the study concluded, re-applying.

I've improved my chances of a successful application this year by completing an OU module on Understanding the Autism Spectrum. I've also done some volunteering at a youth centre with SEN teenagers on a deprived estate and obviously, I've now got an extra year's teaching experience under my belt. So fingers crossed that I'll be fit for purpose this time!

Their accounts left little doubt that these women perceived qualifications as cultural capital passports into employment or possibly higher education. There was a belief that qualifications would elevate their students beyond undesirable forms of dependency. A faith in the correlative relationship between the education system and the labour market prevailed not least because each of these women felt their particular credentials had currency for them. Disclosing biographical information came easily to Mary who took pains to stress this point:

I have shown all my students my own CV. They saw the big time gaps. I projected it [CV] onto the white board – you know my whole life was up there for them to see how I returned to learn initially part time then full time. They do have to see *real* examples of how learning pays off – particularly the girls and women.

These women orientated towards the post-feminist promise that young women can 'have it all' (Harris, 2004). Ideologies of upward social mobility prevailed and the transformative capacity of FE to help students on the ladder was a common belief. Four of these women saw themselves as direct proof and evidence that qualifications had labour market currency; two of them believed that to work effectively in the teaching profession required a disposition to learn and all six of them recognized the affordances of demonstrating their own status as learners to their students.

In the early 1990s, those women whose teacher training experiences I wrote about spoke candidly about motivations to qualify, their need to gain respect and acquire a 'more professional identity as a teacher' (Salisbury, 1994, p. 158). Some twenty years on, the present study identifies these same orientations. The women's various declared motivations for upskilling and their pursuit of new credentials were, in part, responses to concerns about having a more professional identity, being evaluated positively, seen to be performing effectively, as well as maintaining their employability and potential mobility in the always changing FE context. Employability, loosely defined as the ability to keep the job one has or get the job one wants (Rothwell and Arnold, 2007, p. 247), is a recent preoccupation of FE teachers with respect to their students. The women here all demonstrated an awareness of local labour markets for their students but were also mindful of their own careers. Attention to the internal labour market of their own colleges contributed to Mary's, Debra's and Helen's decision to pursue a higher degree, which would enhance their professional identity and set them apart. Helen recognized the buoyant demand for health and social care teachers UK-wide but accepted the impact of her domestic circumstances.

> Caring for older family members in a house that has been adapted makes me reluctant – no – unable – to move house or out of the area to a different job. I'll be here for some time so my plan is to build up my CV. [Helen, journal extract]

Debra, also single like Helen, found herself in an identical situation: an only daughter, now residing in the parental home to support them.

> I know that *sociologically*, I am seen as an 'ideal worker' in that until I have kids I am unconstrained by calls on my time outside of my workplace. I am a very private person about my living arrangements and prefer that the managers don't know my domestic details and that I return home to do the 'double shift'. [Debra, journal extract]

Future promotion and/or geographical mobility was clearly a contributing factor underpinning these two women's pursuit of higher qualifications.

In 'Chasing credentials' the six *un*qualified FE teachers were undertaking a university-based in-service teacher education course, thus they were thrust together in an enforced intimacy in their small cohort and came to share congruent vocabularies and perspectives readily. In contrast, the women in the present chapter were unknown to each other, came from five different college campuses and six distributed departments across south Wales and were already qualified

FE teachers. Perhaps not surprisingly, a key concern of both sets of women was to be an effective teacher. However, the latter contemporary group also set great store on caring and scaffolding their students to attain successful learning outcomes. This stance was influenced in part by the 'three Rs' (recruitment, retention, results) measures that each one of them was appraised against annually and which determined future course and college funding (Jisc, 2011b). Indeed, the latter group were employed in a radically different FE world than that which had existed in the early 1990s when Wales had twenty-six colleges of FE. In 2008 this had reduced to twenty-two and in 2015 mergers and reconfiguration has left Wales with just fifteen FE institutions.

Conclusion

It is not difficult to find commentaries that show that women teachers have improved their positions in schools, colleges and higher education considerably compared to the past. However, we should query this picture because women are still under-represented in the higher ranks in all sectors. A recent report revealed that whilst 58 per cent of women in professional occupations work in education, only 3 per cent of them are employed as senior managers (Parken et al., 2014, p. 29). More widely there is a paucity of women in public life in Wales as 'women are largely missing from the decision making tables across most areas of our daily life' (EHRC, 2014, p. 3; also see Chaney this volume). Chwarae Teg's (2014) report, *A Woman's Place in Academia*, throws a glimmer of positive light – albeit a tiny chink – on the FE sector in Wales. This survey of the fifteen colleges of FE and the eight universities in Wales revealed that top executive roles are dominated by men though four of the fifteen FE institutions have female principals. Of the 251 governors, eighty-one were women; and four women occupied the chair of governor's position (27 per cent). While some colleges had achieved or were approaching gender-balanced boards and leadership teams other colleges still had 'much work to do' (Chwarae Teg, 2014, pp. 3–15).

Considering the gender distribution of the ordinary FE classroom teachers in Wales is problematic. The numbers of men and women working at the chalk face as teachers in Welsh FE colleges is difficult to discern because since 2009/10 the data formerly collected by Staff Individualised Record (SIR) is now derived from the Financial Record.

Official data published annually as *Staff at FE institutions in Wales* is collected by the Department for Families, Education and Schools (DFES) and presents an interesting digest of statistical facts. During the year 2013/14, some 9,130 full-time equivalent staff were employed by FE institutions in Wales yet there is no disaggregation of the teacher numbers from tables which combine *all* staffing-support, general administration, technicians, premises and estates (Welsh Government, 2015). Of the teaching staff contracts, almost 70 per cent were part time and just under half were permanent, reflecting the pattern of courses that changes annually in response to local demand. Interestingly this proportion mirrors the type of enrolment in FE where around 70 per cent of learners attend part time (Colegau Cymru, 2014, p. 25). The Welsh Government has suspended the collection of data on FE college staff making it impossible to differentiate the trends or identify any patterns by gender for teachers. There is an urgent need for more nuanced data on male and female FE teachers, by contract type, age, qualification level and pay grade. England has more transparent data with the LSIS (2012) presenting a detailed analysis of the diversity profile of the FE workforce.

This chapter has drawn upon the journals, interviews and ethnographic field notes to convey an authentic picture of the work of women teachers in contemporary Welsh FE. The teachers' accounts of occupational challenges, of coping with the heterogeneous mix of students, their often demanding parents and employers as well as colleagues renders visible some of their typical, everyday realities. The discussion of their avowed motives for upskilling and credentializing combines together to provide a small 'window on the culture' (Cortazzi, 1993) of women teachers in the FE sector. In 2015, these women, like those I wrote about in the early 1990s, still remain a neglected and under-researched segment of the Welsh education workforce. Their invisibility in the currently available official statistics is a cause for concern. The Education Wales Act of 2014 established on 1 April 2015 the new Education Workforce Council (EWC) and the implementation of a single Education Workforce Register for Wales should improve this situation and the visibility of important teacher characteristics – not least that of gender.

Notes

[1] I am grateful to the women teachers who shared their biographies, journals and classroom experiences with me and to the ESRC/TLRP programme for funding the research project. Thanks to Sylvia Davies of Colegau Cymru for helpful discussions on women in the post-compulsory sector. Martin Jephcote and Gareth Rees of Cardiff University and John Roberts, University of Wales, Newport were members of the original project team.

[2] Pseudonyms are used throughout the article.

References

Acker, S. and Webber, M., 'Academia as the (Com)promised land for women?', in L. Gornall, C. Cook, L. Daunton, J. Salisbury and B. Thomas (eds), *Academic Working Lives: Experience Practice and Change* (London: Bloomsbury, 2014), pp. 199–206.

Black, P. and Wiliam, D., *Working Inside the Black Box: Assessment for Learning in the Classroom* (Bloomington, US: Phi Delta Kappan, 2004).

Chwarae Teg, *A Woman's Place in Academia* (Cardiff: Chwarae Teg, 2014).

Clow, R., 'Just Teachers: The Work Carried Out by Full-time Further Education Teachers', *Research in Post-Compulsory Education*, 10/1 (2005), 63–81.

Coffield, F., *Just Suppose Teaching and Learning Became the First Priority...* (London: Learning and Skills Network, 2008).

Colegau Cymru, *Response to the Consultation on the Single Education Work Force Register* (Cardiff: Welsh Government, 2014).

Cortazzi, M., *Narrative Analysis* (London: Falmer, 1993).

Cribb, A., 'Education and health: professional roles and the division of ethical labour', Paper presented at *C-TRIP Seminar 2: Professional Identities and Teacher Careers*, King's College London, 15 March 2005.

Davidoff, L., 'The rationalization of housework', in D. Barker and S. Allen (eds), *Dependence and Exploitation in Marriage* (London: Longman, 1976), pp. 121–51.

Department for Education and Skills (DfES), *Staff at Further Education Institutions in Wales: Statistical First Release* (Cardiff: DfES, 2015).

Dixey, P. and Harbottle, L., 'Teacher narratives of performativity and change', in L. Gornall, C. Cook, L., Daunton, J., Salisbury and B. Thomas (eds), *Academic Working Lives: Experience Practice and Change* (London: Bloomsbury, 2014), pp. 33–8.

Economic and Social Research Council (ESRC)/Teaching and Learning Research Programme (TLRP), *Inside Further Education: The Social Context of Learning: TLRP Research Briefing no. 52* (Swindon: ESRC, 2008).

Equality and Human Rights Commission (EHRC), *Who Runs Wales 2009? A Lost Decade* (Cardiff: EHRC, 2014).

Gleeson, D. and Shain, F., 'Managing Ambiguity: Between Markets and Managerialism', *Sociological Review*, 57/3 (1999), 461–90.

——, Davies, J. and Wheeler, E., 'On the Making and Taking of Professionalism in the Further Education Workplace', *British Journal of Sociology of Education*, 26/4 (2005), 445–60.

Gornall, L., Cook, C., Daunton, L., Salisbury, J. and Thomas, B. (eds), *Academic Working Lives: Experience Practice and Change* (London: Bloomsbury, 2014)

Gray, A., 'Contract Culture and Target Fetishism: The Distortive Effects of Output Measures on Local Regeneration Programmes', *Local Economy*, 11 (1994), 243–57.

Hargreaves, A., 'The Emotional Practice of Teaching', *Teaching and Teacher Education*, 14/8 (1998), 835–54.

Harris, A., *Future Girl: Young Women in the 21st Century* (London: Routledge, 2004).

Hochschild, A., *The Managed Heart: Commercialisation of Human Feeling* (Berkley: University of California Press, 1983).

Hodgson, A. and Spours, K., *New Labour's Educational Agenda* (London: Kogan Page, 1999).

Hollway, W., *The Capacity to Care: Gender and Ethical Subjectivity* (London: Routledge, 2006).

Hoyle, E., 'Professionality, Professionalism and Control in Teaching', *London Educational Review*, 3/2 (1974), 13–19.

Huyton, J., 'Personal tutoring in academic work', in L. Gornall, C. Cook, L. Daunton, J. Salisbury and B. Thomas (eds), *Academic Working Lives: Experience Practice and Change* (London: Bloomsbury, 2014), pp. 153–61.

Hyland, T. and Merrill, B., *The Changing Face of Further Education* (Falmer: Routledge, 2003).

Isenbarger, L. and Zembylas, M., 'The Emotional Labour of Caring in Teaching', *Teacher and Teacher Education*, 22 (2006), 120–34.

James, D. and Biesta, G., *Improving Learning Cultures in Further Education* (London: Routledge Falmer, 2007).

Jephcote, M., 'Further Education Teachers' Accounts of their Professional Identities', *Teaching and Teacher Education*, 25/7 (2009), 966–72.

——, 'Getting on with the job and occupational socialisation in Further Education', in L. Gornall, C. Cook, L. Daunton, J. Salisbury and B. Thomas (eds), *Academic Working Lives: Experience Practice and Change* (London: Bloomsbury, 2014), pp. 26–32.

—— and Salisbury, J., 'Being a Teacher in Further Education in Changing Times', *Research in Post-compulsory Education*, 13/2 (2008), 163–72.

Jisc, *How Can We Improve the Way Students are Assessed?* (2011a), *www.jisc. ac.uk/supportingyourinstitution/studentjourney/studentassessment.aspx* (accessed 17 April 2015).

——, *Retaining Students* (2011b), *www.jisc.ac.uk/supportingyourinstitution/ studentjourney/retainingstudents.aspx* (accessed 17 April 2015).

Learning and Skills Improvement Service (LSIS), *Further Education and Skills Sector: Summary Workforce Diversity Report* (Coventry: LSIS, 2012).

Lloyd, C. and Payne, J., 'Raising the Quality of Vocational Teachers: Continuing Professional Development in England, Wales and Norway', *Research Papers in Education*, 27/1 (2012).

Lynch, K., 'Solidary Labour: Its Nature and Marginalisation', *The Sociological Review*, 37/1 (1989), 1–14.

Mannay, D., 'Keeping Close and Spoiling: Exploring the Significance of "Home" for Family Relationships and Educational Trajectories in a Marginalised Estate in Urban South Wales', *Gender and Education*, 25/1 (2013), 91–107.

Parken, A., Pocher, E. and Davies, R., *Working Patterns in Wales: Gender Occupations and Pay* (Cardiff: Women Adding Value to the Economy (WAVE), 2014).

Roberts, K., 'Youth unemployment and social exclusion', in C. Pole, J. Pilcher and J. Williams (eds), *Young People in Transition: Becoming Citizens?* (Basingstoke: Palgrave Macmillan, 2005), pp. 116–35.

Rothwell, A. and Arnold, J., 'Self Perceived Employability, Development and Validation of a Scale', *Personnel Review*, 36/1 (2007), 23–31.

Salisbury, J., 'Chasing credentials: women Further Education teachers and in-service training', in J. Aaron, T. Rees, S. Betts and M. Vincentelli (eds), *Our Sisters' Land: The Changing Identities of Women in Wales* (Cardiff: University of Wales Press, 1994), pp. 141–60.

——, 'Vocational education and training: sites for qualitative study', in S. Delamont (ed.), *Handbook of Qualitative Research in Education* (Cheltenham: Edward Elgar Publications, 2012), pp. 143–57.

——, 'Emotional labour and ethics of care in Further Education teaching", in L. Gornall, C. Cook, L. Daunton, J. Salisbury and B. Thomas (eds), *Academic Working Lives: Experience Practice and Change* (London: Bloomsbury, 2014), pp. 47–56.

—— and Jephcote, M., 'Mucking In and Mucking Out: Vocational Learning in Animal Care', *Teaching and Teacher Education*, 26/1 (2010), 71–81.

——, Jephcote, M. and Roberts, J., 'FE Teachers Talking about Learning: Outcomes, Contexts and Methodologies', *Research Papers in Education*, 24/4 (2009), 421–38.

Sikes, P. J., Measor, L. and Woods, P., *Teacher Careers, Crises and Continuities* (Lewes: Falmer Press, 1985).

Social Exclusion Unit (SEU), *Bridging the Gap: New Opportunities for 16–18 Year Olds Not In Education, Employment or Training* (London: Stationery Office, 1999).

Wallace, M., 'Towards effective management of a reformed teaching profession', Paper presented at *C-TRIP Seminar 4; Enactments of Professionalism: Classrooms and Pedagogies*, King's College London, 5 July 2005.

Welsh Assembly Government (WAG), *The Learning Country: Vision Into Action* (Cardiff: Department of Education, Lifelong Learning and Skills, 2001).

——, *Extending Entitlement. The Ten Student Entitlements* (Cardiff: Welsh Assembly Government, 2002).

Welsh Government, *Further Education, Work Based Learning and Community Learning in Wales, 2013/14 (provisional figures)* (Cardiff: WG Knowledge and Analytical Services, 2014).

——, *Staff at Further Education Institutions in Wales, Statistical First Release* (Cardiff: DFES, 2015).

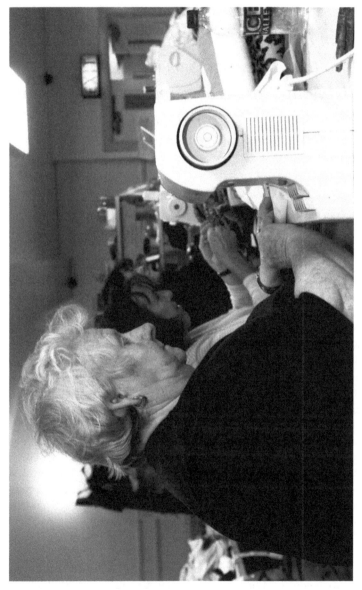

The Clothing Industry – by Ian Homer

8

From Low-wage Manufacturing Industries to the Low-wage Service Sector: The Changing Nature of Women's Employment in Wales

CAROLINE LLOYD

Introduction

In 1992, I published an article in *Contemporary Wales* that explored the issue of gender and skill in the Welsh clothing industry (Lloyd, 1992). This paper was drawn from my PhD research which focused on processes of restructuring and technical change in the sector (Lloyd, 1993). There was widespread concern at the time that the industry, then employing over 200,000 workers in the UK, could no longer compete with low-wage economies and was likely to fall into terminal decline. A counter-argument, however, was also being made that revival was possible if UK manufacturers were able to tap into retailers' growing interest in shorter runs of more quality, design-oriented fashions. The research sought to evaluate whether there was potential for the Welsh industry to restructure in a way that could lay the basis for renewal. A central part of the thesis involved an examination of the long-term effects on the industry of relying on low-paid female workers and the impact of computerization on occupational segregation.

In writing about the Welsh clothing industry, the typical response at the time was 'is there a clothing industry in Wales?' While Wales was not a traditional centre of the industry, as in the north-west, Leeds, the East Midlands and London, in 1901, there were over 43,000 jobs in clothing and the industry accounted for 18 per cent of all female employment (Lee, 1979). By 1990, there were still 11,300 workers, typically employed in larger factories, accounting for 2.4 per cent of female employment and 15 per cent of female manufacturing jobs. Although in the late 1980s many employers were fairly optimistic about the future, the outcome for the clothing industry and the women who worked in it has not been a happy story. In Wales, little remains of the industry, while across the UK it accounts for just 26,000 workers.

The chapter begins by revisiting some of the central findings presented in the original *Contemporary Wales* article. The next section charts what has happened to the Welsh clothing industry over the past twenty-five years, placing it in the context of the decline of manufacturing jobs across Wales, particularly for women. There then follows an examination of the failure of industrial and economic policy in Wales, and more broadly in the UK, to support the renewal of manufacturing. The clothing industry was typified by a high level of occupational segregation and endemic levels of low pay. It was hoped that these poor-quality jobs would be replaced by better-paid employment in new high-tech industries or in the service sector, with gender 'typing' of jobs gradually being broken down. The chapter compares the quality of work in the clothing industry with a number of service-sector jobs that are also situated towards the lower end of the occupational ladder. The evidence suggests that, on some measures, job quality has actually deteriorated. The final part of the chapter examines the prospects for improving the quality of work for women employed in these types of jobs in Wales.

The clothing industry in Wales

Although it was never regarded as an important centre, the clothing industry has a long history in Wales. Much of the industry was small scale until post Second World War, when companies responded to labour and accommodation shortages in traditional inner-city areas by establishing new factories in development areas, such as Wales (Hague and Newman, 1952). Regional aid was important in attracting large branch plants, which tended to concentrate on the simpler parts of assembly and production of long runs. One of the advantages of this change in location was that it allowed companies to transform their production processes. The use of highly sectional methods, where each garment was broken down into a series of small tasks, could increase productivity and substantially reduce the length and costs of training in an industry notorious for high-labour turnover (Wray, 1957).

By the late 1980s, the industry in Wales included over 100 companies employing at least 10,000 workers (ONS, 1990), 86 per cent of whom were women. Over three-quarters of the workforce were employed in factories with over 100 workers, and included branch plants of large multinationals, such as Courtaulds and Tootal (subsequently acquired by Coats Viyella), along with Welsh-based companies Morris Cohen (taken over by William Baird) supplying mainly to Marks and Spencer, and the headquarters and main factories of integrated manufacturer-retailer Laura Ashley. With the exception of Laura Ashley, these larger companies were typically covered by collective bargaining, with estimates of around 50 per cent of the Welsh clothing workforce being unionized (Short, 1987).

At the time, a number of large UK retailers were seeking to shift their business approach away from the intense price competition that had dominated the sector in the previous years to focus more on design, quality and variety. With the assistance of new computerized technologies, it was argued that quality and closeness to market would favour British manufacturers and provide the basis for a transformed sector (Zeitlin, 1988). The evidence presented (Lloyd, 1992) indicated that computerization had already started to break up areas of male dominance in pre-assembly (grading, marking and cutting) where jobs were traditionally occupied by 'skilled' men (see also Cockburn, 1985). A process of feminization was taking place as craft skills were being replaced by computer-aided manufacturing technologies, operated by lower-status and lower-paid computer operators or machine minders. Part of the attraction of computerization was not only the ability to reduce training times and wage costs but also to remove a powerful group of male craft workers who could seriously disrupt production. At the time of the research, 44 per cent of cutters were women. This process of feminization supported Coyle's view that the introduction of new technology is primarily the route through which women replace men.

> as the labour process is restructured and transformed, there is little compara-
> bility between old and new methods, between skilled and unskilled work,
> and between jobs which have been traditionally designated as men's and
> women's work. As this transformation is brought about in part by the intro-
> duction of new machinery, which changes the technical basis of the labour
> process, it appears to be the machine that eases women into men's jobs
> (1982, p. 23).

For other areas of production there was little change, particularly in machining where over 99 per cent of workers were women. Machining was a routine and low-paid job, described at the time as either 'semi-skilled' or unskilled. However, the job was certainly not without technical skill, as it normally took a year to learn to sew accurately and at a rapid pace. A few factories continued with the traditional 'make through' processes, whereby each machinist completed the whole of a garment. For the rest, tasks were broken down into cycles of one or two minutes which had to be repeated, in some cases, for weeks at a time. Speed and accuracy were crucial, as pay was based on piece rates, and any errors were identifiable and could be returned to the machinist responsible.

Machining was considered to be 'women's work', with a number of comments by clothing factory managers about the requirement for 'nimble fingers' or that their previous efforts at recruiting men had not been successful or that men would feel uncomfortable in an all-female environment. The few young men who were employed in one factory as machinists were using it as a basis for training to be a mechanic. There were no examples of female machinists being encouraged to follow a similar type of career pathway. While the traditional 'sex typing' of work was felt to be an important factor in continued occupational segregation, the issue of pay was also regularly raised. It was stressed that men would not work at the pay rates being offered for machinists in the clothing industry. As the regional union official argued:

> One of the biggest problems we have got to get men to even think about it is because of the low-wage because men have automatically got this idea in their head that's not a good wage and there's no way I'm going to work in a factory for 39 hours for that. (Official NUTGW, Lloyd, 1993, p. 214)

These assembly workers had neither the status, the training periods nor the pay that was associated with craft jobs in pre-assembly. Machinists in the UK were also quite distinctive from their counterparts in Germany, where the clothing industry was far more successful, focusing on quality and the export market. Steedman and Wagner (1989) found that workers in Germany were apprenticed for two or three years, working on a separate training sector. In the UK, trainees were typically put onto the production line after only six weeks and often left to find a 'trained' position in another company well before their training period was completed. Machinists in Germany took only two days to reach 100 per cent speeds after changing styles, they generally worked directly from technical sketches and made the whole garment. In the UK, it could take more than a week to reach normal productivity levels, despite the use of highly sectional methods of production.

Many employers in Wales complained about skill shortages among clothing workers, but it was broadly accepted that this was due to the low pay and the associated high levels of labour turnover. Workers were able to move to other clothing factories and, particularly in south Wales, to a range of foreign-owned light engineering plants. One of the discussion points was how to make the industry more attractive to workers, through, for example, working four days a week or introducing twilight shifts or improving pay rates. Tight labour markets, rather than union organization, was the crucial factor in pushing employers to reconsider their employment practices. However, the continued pressure emanating from powerful retailers to minimize costs meant that there was unlikely 'in the foreseeable future' to be change in either the sex typing of machinist jobs or their pay (Lloyd, 1992, p. 127).

The end of the clothing industry

Employers had been relatively optimistic about the future of the clothing industry in Wales; however, from the early 1990s, there were widespread factory closures as both retailers and manufacturers shifted production off-shore to cheaper labour countries. In 1990, forty-eight clothing factories each employed over 100 workers, by 2003 there were just ten. Between 1990 and 1995, Laura Ashley closed six factories, located in predominantly rural parts of Wales, as production was moved overseas to reduce costs. In the early 2000s, over a two-year period, William Baird and Dewhirst closed fifteen factories across Wales employing 3,000 workers. A number of companies, including William Baird, operated factories that were almost entirely dependent on contracts with Marks and Spencer. As this major buyer of UK clothing products dropped its preference for 'Made in Britain' and shifted to overseas suppliers, job losses in Wales were extensive (GMB, 2004). The ending in 2005 of the Multifibre Arrangement, which had set tariffs on clothing imports, accelerated this shift overseas. One of the last major closures was the Burberry factory in Treorchy in 2007. Today there are fewer than 500 workers in the clothing industry in Wales, and there are no manufacturing plants with more than twenty workers.

These changes were not unique to Wales and reflected wider developments taking place in the industry across the UK. In 1992 the industry employed 210,000 workers, and was one of the main manufacturing employers of women, accounting for 184,000 jobs. The shift to imports was a major factor in decline as the proportion of clothing sales sourced from overseas increased from 57 per cent in 1993 to 92 per cent in 2001 (Jones and Hayes, 2002). By 2014, there were just 26,000 clothing workers left in the UK. The decline in the clothing industry was much quicker and more extensive than in other comparable countries, such as Italy and Germany. Although employment continues to fall, there has been some gradual return of production to the UK. This revival has been linked to three main areas: technical textiles, such as protective clothing, workwear and sports clothing; fast fashion, which involves responding extremely rapidly to the latest demands and current seasons; and up-market 'British style' clothing (Skillset, 2011; Alliance Project Team, 2015).

Wales has been unsuccessful at capturing any of these markets, with the exception of some very small firms producing high-quality artesian-type clothing. Technical textiles, which requires substantial investment in research and development, is predominantly associated with north-west England, and employs far fewer people than traditional clothing factories. In contrast, fast fashion has been linked to those areas of manufacturing that have historically relied upon low-cost labour, predominantly ethnic minorities, and the substantial use of subcontracting and homeworking. A recent report by Hammer et al. (2015) found that fast fashion has revived the Leicester clothing industry but that this sector is highly price sensitive, offers small margins and requires extremely fast turnaround times. Online retailers are the major source of demand for fast fashion, consisting of 'large volumes of basic garments at fairly low margins in relatively small enterprises' (2015, p. 23). While technical textiles is aimed at the higher end of the market with limited requirements for machinists, Hammer et al. argue that fast fashion manufacturers appear only able to compete on the basis of illegal working, underpayment of the national minimum wage, lack of employment contracts, poor working conditions and the use of undocumented workers.

The role of industrial policy in Wales: the clothing industry and beyond

Historically state intervention to support the clothing industry across the UK has been rather limited and ineffective. The exception was during the Second World War when strict controls were introduced which fixed the price of clothing and rationed the quantity and type of clothes that could be manufactured. Restrictions on entry into clothing production and the protection of workers under the Essential Work Orders, which meant that they could not be sacked or leave their job and were ensured union wage rates and conditions, had a profound effect on an industry that had been highly fragmented and volatile (Board of Trade, 1947). The result was relative stability and prosperity, as companies placed greater emphasis on branding and increased their bargaining power in relation to retailers. The end of rationing saw the entry of new firms into the industry in the 1950s, a re-emphasis on fashion and a decline in the price of clothing. Retailers regained and enhanced their power in relation to manufacturers, reinforced by their increasing ability to source products from overseas.

The government's main role in the sector was the use of grants to encourage manufacturing plants to move to areas of industrial decline and in restricting imports from low-wage countries. Regional assistance was particularly important in attracting many clothing firms in the post-war period to set up branch plants in Wales. There was also some assistance over the 1960s and 1970s in relation to start-ups and investment in new technology and in subsidising vocational training. The main issue confronting many clothing manufacturers, however, continued to be their weak bargaining power in relation to a highly concentrated retail sector, and this issue was never seriously addressed. During the 1980s and 1990s, successive Conservative governments were ideologically opposed to industrial policy, arguing that deregulation, privatization, liberalization of markets, alongside some limited assistance to high technology industries, were the way to ensure economic success (Thompson, 2015). For the clothing industry, freeing up markets meant more international competition from low-wage countries, the removal of wage councils and weakening of trade unions, which further squeezed working conditions in the UK.

Wales suffered disproportionately during the recession in the early 1980s, reinforced by long-term decline in the coal and steel industries. As a 'special area for regional assistance' it was successful in the subsequent period at using regional aid to attract new foreign-owned manufacturing sites. While the UK lost around 30 per cent of manufacturing jobs during the 1980s, the decline in employment was much slower in Wales. Most of the incoming plants were in areas of light engineering, such as automotive components, office equipment and consumer electronics and many were Japanese-owned (Danford, 1999). These predominantly footloose branch plants were established in Wales for very similar reasons to the clothing factories many decades before: large grants, the availability of cheap land and low-cost labour. The jobs provided by these manufacturers were typically low-skilled, assembly-line work and were undertaken primarily by women.

As New Labour entered office in 1997, it was not only clothing that was relocating oversees but plants producing in other areas of light manufacturing were also shifting, first to Eastern Europe and then to Asia, in the search for cheaper labour. This transfer of employment was considered by the Blair government to be the inevitable outcome of globalization. The loss of these old traditional manufacturing jobs would, in the right conditions, be replaced by employment opportunities in high-tech industries and services within the UK's growing knowledge economy (see Lloyd and Payne, 2002). Interventionist forms of industrial policy were again rejected. It was not 'the Government's role to try to resist the profound structural changes affecting businesses', rather it was to focus on providing the skills, infrastructure and tax incentives to promote manufacturers that were at the leading edge offering innovative products at high quality (DTI, DfEE, 2002).

This approach to industrial policy remained similar to the Conservatives before them, that 'picking winners' was ineffective and rather than intervene strategically in particular sectors or firms, the aim was to make the UK a more attractive place to do business. Low levels of regulation in product markets, an attractive tax regime and 'the most flexible labour market in Europe' were believed to be central to improving productivity, encouraging innovation and start-ups and attracting inward investment. Skills were identified as the central lever to improve economic growth and address social exclusion (see Lloyd and Payne, 2002). This 'ideological' and interventionist-free approach to economic development (Cutler, 1992) enabled governments to avoid intervening directly in the market or adopting more directive roles in relation to specific industries.

Despite the predominant emphasis on investing resources in skills, there remained some support for the UK clothing industry, although it was estimated to be only about a quarter of that provided by other European governments (LATCF, 2003). Investment in research and development was targeted at technical textile organizations and universities in the north of England and had little impact in Wales. More

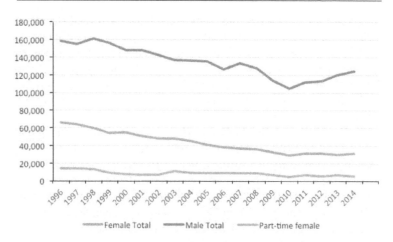

Figure 8.1: Manufacturing workforce jobs in Wales
Source: NOMIS, Labour Force Survey, ONS.

broadly, manufacturing employment continued to decline, particularly affecting women's jobs, as the clothing industry virtually disappeared followed by many of the foreign-owned branch plants. Between 1996 and 2014, women's employment in manufacturing in Wales more than halved from 66,000 to 31,000 (see figure 8.1). Wales had moved from a position of being one of the 'top performing' areas in attracting inward investment to one of the worst (WAC, 2012, p. 10).

Attempts were made to attract new investments into Wales but the quality of some of these new jobs was even more questionable than the 'low-skilled, assembly line jobs' that they replaced. Amazon, the online retail company, received Regional Selective Assistance Grants of £8.8 million to set up a giant distribution centre in Swansea. First Minister Rhodri Morgan stated that he was 'proud of the role that the Assembly Government had played in attracting Amazon to Wales' and that it was an 'iconic global company ... creating thousands of new jobs' (WAG, 2008). Subsequent investigations into the quality of work within the giant warehouse has revealed a range of low-wage jobs, harsh discipline, zero-hours contracts and the use of agency work and other forms of temporary employment. As Cadwalladr (2013) found, Amazon was considered locally to be 'the employer of last resort', however, the jobs were filled by builders, managers, IT technicians, electricians and marketing graduates: 'They are people who had skilled jobs or professional jobs, or just better-paying jobs. And now they work for

Amazon, earning the minimum wage, and most of them are grateful to have that.' These poor quality jobs were no longer just the preserve of women, as men dominate the increasingly low-paid areas of distribution and warehousing.

Similarly, working on the production line in food factories had been considered mainly 'women's work', but these jobs were also opening up to men (James and Lloyd, 2008). A meat processing plant was incentivized with £15 million of government grants to move to Merthyr Tydfil, with the promise of 'quality employment'. Tannock (2013) reports how the Secretary of State for Wales, William Hague, proudly spoke of 'seven hundred well paid jobs, here in Merthyr, exactly the right sort of jobs, in exactly the right sort of place' (BBC Wales, 1997, in Tannock, 2013). However, the factory quickly gained the reputation of a 'bad' place to work and by 2008 over 60 per cent of the workforce were estimated to be migrant workers despite high local unemployment (Tannock, 2013). Low pay, long and irregular shifts and lack of guaranteed hours linked to the use of agency work on zero-hours contracts were cited as the main causes.

More recently, there has been a growing recognition that Wales can no longer compete successfully for lower skilled assembly line work and that the policy focus should shift to supporting indigenous organizations. In 2009, the economic development minister, Ieuan Wyn Jones, stressed that, 'Wales is not going to compete in the future with large companies looking for a low cost, low wage economy' (BBC, 2009). The promise was that there would be a fundamental shift away from offering large grants to multinational companies towards a strategy based on building up research and design and the country's skills. However, policy initiatives designed to address the productivity gap with the UK and high levels of poverty have been dominated by the issue of improving low levels of employment participation and poor educational achievement in relation to the rest of the UK (see table 8.1 and table 8.2).

Despite evidence which suggested that skills accounted for only a small proportion of the productivity gap both between the UK and its major competitors, and between the UK and Wales (Pickernell, 2011), resources were poured into attempts to improve the education and training system. The results, in terms of qualification achievements, have been substantial. Over the last fifteen to twenty years, there has been a major transformation in the qualifications base of the Welsh population. In 2001 nearly 40 per cent of those of working age did not have a Level Two qualification (equivalent to five GCSEs A–C), compared to 24 per cent in 2013, with the difference to the UK dropping from four percentage points to 1.5 (see table 8.2). The proportion with some form of higher education has also expanded substantially from 22 per cent to 34 per cent. Greater participation of women in the labour market has seen overall employment levels increase, with mid-age women having higher rates than the same group in the UK (see table 8.1). Unfortunately, these improvements in qualifications and employment levels have not had the desired effect, neither stalling the growing levels of in-work poverty nor stimulating high-quality job

Table 8.1: Employment rate in the UK and Wales

Employment rate %	1996		2014	
	UK	Wales	UK	Wales
Total	70.0	66.5	72.3	69.5
Male	76.8	72.5	77.2	72.6
Female	63.4	60.5	67.4	66.4
Female aged 16–24	58.7	54.9	50.7	49.8
Female aged 25–49	70.9	69.2	75.4	76.3
Female aged 50–64	49.6	46.2	62.6	60.2

Source: StatsWales Labour Force Survey

Table 8.2: Highest level of qualification held
by working-age adults, UK and Wales

Qualifications*	2001		2013	
	UK	Wales	UK	Wales
None	16.4	21.5	8.7	9.7
Less than level 2	19.2	18.1	14.1	14.0
Level 2	20.3	21.8	19.3	20.3
Level 3	19.1	17.4	20.3	22.5
Level 4+	25.0	22.1	37.6	33.6

*Defined as 18–64 for males and 18–59 for females. Qualifications are allocated to NQF levels.
Source: StatsWales Labour Force Survey

growth. Instead, there has been a continued expansion of low-level service jobs, particularly in such areas as hospitality, retail and care.

Job quality: then and now

The clothing industry and many of the light engineering factories provided full-time employment for substantial numbers of women in south Wales and in some rural locations. Only 5 per cent of the women in the clothing industry worked part time, lower than any other region in the UK, and only 12.5 per cent of female manufacturing employment in Wales was part time (Census of Employment, 1987; figure 8.1). These manufacturing jobs were typically low paid and provided routine and repetitive forms of work. Low pay was a particular issue in the clothing industry, where minimum wages were set by the Clothing Manufacturing Wages Councils until their abolition in 1993. In 1992, the rate was just £102.86, at 34 per cent of average full-time weekly earnings. For those working in the unionized factories in south Wales, pay was somewhat higher, although average pay across the industry of £143 still represented less than 50 per cent of British average full-time earnings. Women's average earnings were just over 70 per cent of men's in the clothing industry, reflecting their segregation into the lower-skilled areas of machining.

The original study of the clothing industry (Lloyd, 1993) found that in south Wales, a large proportion of women were said to be the main earner in their family because of male unemployment in steel and coal. One clothing director explained: 'it's very, very repetitive. You must never lose sight of the fact that the only reason they are here is not because they like it but because just by accident or fate they live in this Valley' (Lloyd, 1993, p. 219). Turnover across the industry was high, particularly when there were alternative opportunities in the local labour market, with jobs in some areas available from better paying companies in light engineering, such as Orion, Sony and Revlon. The regional union official stressed that it was not the boredom that drove individuals from clothing companies but the lack of a decent basic wage.

> People don't mind being in a job where they have got to repeat things over and over and over, as long as they get the money at the end of the week. And women, in particular, are looking for something with a high basic rate of pay because of the situation with the men being unable to get the jobs in the area. (NUTGW official, Lloyd, 1993, p. 214)

Employers complained that workers would move from plant to plant in search of higher pay. One estimated that 40 per cent of machinists continually moved, while the other 60 per cent remained stable. In addition, there was an increasing number of lower-end service-sector jobs.

> When you get people like Tescos and whatever else offering the money they're offering these days for just filling shelves, coming into here in a piece work environment, it's not always the most attractive. (Production director, clothing manufacturer, Lloyd, 1993, p. 212)

High levels of absenteeism was also common in these factories as workers sought relief from intensive work regimes within an environment of weak collective organizations.

While these jobs were repetitive, highly intensive and poorly paid, the companies rarely used temporary workers, subcontractors or homeworkers. These larger factories in Wales were, therefore, somewhat different to some other areas of the clothing industry in the UK, particularly small firms employing minority ethnic workers, producing for the lower end of the market (Phizacklea, 1990). Part-time work was also rare and where it did take place was usually a reflection of a desire by employers to retain the skills of experienced machinists. Typically shifts were fixed and operated Monday to Friday, often with a half day on Friday. A typical work pattern was 7.50 a.m. to 4.40 p.m., Monday to Thursday and a 1.30 p.m. finish on a Friday. Blyton and Jenkins's (2012) study of the closure of the Burberry clothing factory fifteen years later than my own study showed similar work characteristics: pay just above the minimum wage and full-time, permanent contracts. Workers cited the benefits of the factory's proximity to their homes and the predictability of working hours, where over 95 per cent worked full time, Monday to Friday (2012, p. 32).

Since the early 1990s, there have been a number of positive developments for women in the labour market in Wales. Jobs in higher occupational categories have expanded, and women have benefited from the growth in health and education in providing professional and associate professional jobs (Owen, 2012). The higher share of public sector employment in Wales has been important in reducing regional disparities. Nevertheless, Wales, along with the north-east of England and Northern Ireland, has the smallest proportion of high-quality jobs in the UK (Jones and Green, 2009, p. 2481). One-quarter of workers in Wales are low paid, 27 per cent of women and 17 per cent of men, which is significantly higher than the UK average of 22 per cent. In

1975, the figure was less than 15 per cent and Wales was second only to London in having the lowest proportion of workers in low-paid jobs across the UK (Corlett and Whittaker, 2014). The main increase in low-wage work in Wales, as in other parts of the UK, occurred in the ten-year period from 1978 to 1988, primarily driven by an increase in male levels of low pay (Mason et al., 2008). The result, therefore, has been a narrowing of the gap between men and women, as higher-paid, unionized jobs in manufacturing, steel and coal have disappeared.

As the next chapter details, men and women are not necessarily undertaking the same type of jobs, despite the shift of men into low-paid work. Twenty-five per cent of women in Wales work in the typically low-paid jobs of care assistants, retail/cashier workers and in elementary service jobs, such as cleaning and catering. Low-paid men tend to have more varied jobs that also include working in retailing and hospitality, as well as more segregated areas such as warehousing and distribution, and in male-dominated positions of labourers and drivers (Parken et al., 2014). There is also considerable geographical diversity in low pay, with the south Wales valleys and more remote rural areas relying most on low-paid jobs. In Ogmore and Montgomeryshire, over one-third of men are in low-waged jobs, while less than 15 per cent are low paid in Cardiff and Flintshire. For women, Flintshire is one of the worst areas, with 42 per cent of jobs low paid, while 38 per cent are low paid in Blaenau Gwent. Only in Denbighshire is the rate of low pay less than 20 per cent for women (House of Commons Library, 2014).

While pay is only one aspect of job quality and replicates the experience of women in the clothing industry, there are other elements of many of today's low-paid jobs that offer some sharp contrasts. One of the main features is the shift to more insecure working time arrangements. Care work is an area that has seen substantial growth with the population ageing and the move towards more home care. There are 28,000 women working as care assistants and home carers in Wales, with estimates that 85 per cent of local authority domiciliary care workers are employed part time (Data Unit, 2014). Privatization of care work, and the more recent cuts to care budgets by local authorities, has seen widespread deterioration in pay and working conditions in this sector. Bessa et al. (2013) report that in domiciliary care in England, over half of care assistants are employed on zero-hours contracts. These contracts provide no guaranteed hours and leave the worker facing variations in working time and pay on a weekly basis, making it difficult to organize childcare and other non-work activities (TUC, 2014).

Rubery and Urwin (2011, p. 134) argue that behind these contracts is an assumption about care work: 'because it is primarily done by women who can still be treated as essentially casual or contingent workers, available for low-wage work without career prospects'. There is also evidence that a considerable proportion of domiciliary care workers are not even receiving the minimum wage.

It is estimated that at least 2.5 per cent of workers are on a zero-hours contract in Wales (ONS Labour Force Survey, 2014). While retail has long utilized part-time contracts, these types of zero-hours contracts appear to becoming more commonplace, alongside perhaps more frequently used 'short-hours contracts'. These latter contracts provide a 'core set' of hours to the worker, with the promise of additional hours when they are available. Wood and Burchell (2014) argue that these contracts generate uncertainty and worry about changes to hours and income: 'The insecurity often results in feelings of powerlessness and an inability to plan one's life.' A report from the TUC also raised the problem that if workers 'were assertive about what they wanted or complained about their treatment they would be offered fewer shifts and less work in the future or they would not get any work at all' (TUC, 2014, p. 22). Integral to these types of contracts has been variation in schedules and the longer opening hours of large retailers in the evening and at weekends. Associated with these changes has been a gradual elimination of pay enhancements for Sunday and bank holiday working in both retail and hospitality (IDS, 2014).

The stability in working time that was provided by clothing manufacturers is an important feature that has been missing from a range of jobs at the lower end of the service sector. Blyton and Jenkins (2012) found that the majority of female workers made redundant from the Burberry factory in 2007 moved into the care industry and retailing. These jobs were typically part time, with hours varying from week to week, and shifts being highly unpredictable in time and duration. They argued that Burberry had been 'regarded as a refuge from an increasingly casualised local labour market' (2012, p. 29).

Where now?

There is a growing recognition in Wales that there is a major problem with the quality of employment. Nevertheless, as in England, the policy narrative continues to focus on opportunities to access work and employment as the primary solution to poverty. A statement by the deputy minister for tackling poverty claimed that in-work poverty in Wales would be reduced by 'raising levels of attainment and increasing skills' which 'enable young people and adults to move into well-paid jobs' (Gething, 2013). Faced with nearly 500,000 Welsh jobs (close to 40 per cent of the total) that do not need a Level Two qualification, the issue is clearly one of lack of quality jobs rather than a poorly qualified workforce (Felstead et al., 2013).

While there are major issues of who has access to the better jobs in Wales, by geography, class, ethnicity and gender, there are simply not enough of them. The result is substantial levels of over-qualification in relation to the available jobs and an underutilization of the skills and qualifications that workers possess. These problems exist across the UK, but the situation in Wales is worse in terms of the extent of over-qualification, the proportion of low-wage jobs, the limited number of professional and managerial jobs and the preponderance of jobs at the lower end of the occupational hierarchy (Owen, 2012; Felstead et al., 2013). A change in public policy in Wales is beginning to emerge, with the living wage being adopted by Welsh Government, the health service and a number of local authorities. In addition, sustainable employment and training provision is being increasingly linked to public procurement, so that government contracts are not simply based on the lowest cost.

Nevertheless, there remain a number of features of the Welsh economy that encourage the creation and development of poor job quality, and which disproportionately affect women. In many cases, these reflect the broader UK regulatory and institutional environment. The unwillingness to establish the national minimum wage as a living wage, the undermining of trade unions and the lack of regulation of hours and employment contracts are all central (see also Williams and Jenkins, 2015). Some shift in political debate has taken place which recognizes the inadequacies of the minimum wage. However, the more difficult challenge is to deal with those employers who have been actively pursuing the use of more flexible contracts, such as zero-hours and variable-hours contracts. While the UK government has agreed to look at some of the conditions surrounding zero-hours contracts, a much more radical intervention has been implemented in France in response to growing concerns about the widespread abuse of part-time contracts. In 2014, legislation was introduced requiring all part-time jobs to be at least twenty-four hours per week, unless express written permission is given or the person is exempt such as a student. On a more fundamental level, in many other European countries, zero-hours contracts are only able to exist outside employment law in the informal economy. These types of policy responses to the growing insecurity at the lower end of the labour market are not even part of the debate in the UK.

The continued emphasis on flexible labour markets, which stems from the UK Government rather than from Wales, raises major issues in relation to tackling low pay and job insecurity. Lack of regulation allows employers the option of achieving competitive advantage by continuing to seek reductions in wage and conditions, as they push at the boundaries of what are considered to be acceptable forms of employment practices. Ongoing austerity measures and Welsh Government's limited willingness to shift away from traditional approaches to economic and industrial renewal add to these problems in the labour market.

Conclusion

Manufacturing in Wales offered women the opportunity to work full time, with stable hours, in a unionized environment. These were not particularly good jobs, with their repetitive and routine tasks and low pay, typified by conditions in the clothing industry. The loss of half of women's manufacturing jobs over twenty years to be replaced by work in the service sector, however, did not provide the promised improvement in the quality of work. The weakness of trade unions and lack of collective bargaining in many areas of private services have left workers reliant on their individual capacity to negotiate an increasingly flexible and insecure labour market. In the public sector, privatization and casualization has also contributed to deteriorating quality at the lower end of the labour market.

In the late 1980s, there was much discussion of skill shortages caused predominantly by workers moving in search of better paid employment. In these conditions, employers were forced to improve the quality of work in order to attract and retain employees. Ultimately these types of branch plants, with their focus on long runs of standardized products, were unable to compete with low-paid labour outside Europe. The indifference of successive UK governments to renew traditional manufacturing was apparent in the limited efforts made to encourage or develop the clothing industry in a new direction. Today, there has been a revival of interest in the industry but skill-development subsidies and small-scale research funding are too little and far too late. Women remain more likely to experience low-paid work than men. Nevertheless, the more profound change in the labour market has been the appearance of substantial numbers of low-paid men. Where once men in south Wales were claimed to have refused certain jobs that were not only considered 'women's work' but were too low paid for men, there is now far more 'equality' in who ends up in the worst jobs. Job segregation by sex, however, appears to remain strongly embedded at the lower end of the labour market, but with employers now also paying the minimum wage for classically 'male' jobs. It appears to be increasingly the case that employers have the upper hand when offering low-skilled jobs and there are few checks on how they manage their workforce.

There are some signs that issues of low pay and poor job quality are more prominent on the public policy agenda. Nevertheless, none of the main UK political parties have rejected the deregulatory approach in relation to the labour market, such that any intervention to strengthen the rights of both men and women is likely to be extremely limited. In some ways, employment conditions have deteriorated for those women who might have been working in a clothing factory twenty-five years ago but today are employed in a supermarket or a care home. This review, of the changing experience of women employed in lower-skilled jobs in Wales, suggests that the prospects for some sort of improvement in the quality of work remains bleak.

References

Alliance Project Team, *Repatriation of UK Textiles Manufacture* (Manchester: Report for the Greater Manchester Combined Authority, 2015).

BBC, '"Grants culture over" warns Jones', *BBC News Online*, 12 October (2009), *news.bbc.co.uk/1/hi/wales/8301385.stm* (accessed 17 November 2015).

Bessa, I., Forde, C., Moore, S. and Stuart, M., *The National Minimum Wage, Earnings and Hours in the Domiciliary Care Sector* (Leeds: University of Leeds, 2013).

Blyton, P. and Jenkins, J., 'Mobilizing Resistance: the Burberry Workers' Campaign against Factory Closure', *Sociological Review*, 60/1 (2012), 24–45.

Board of Trade, *Light Clothing*, Working Paper Reports (London: HMSO, 1947).

Cadwalladr, C., 'My week as an Amazon insider', *Observer*, 1 December (2013), *http://www.theguardian.com/technology/2013/dec/01/week-amazon-insider-feature-treatment-employees-work* (accessed 17 November 2015).

Census of Employment (Newport: ONS, 1987).

Cockburn, C., *Brothers: Machinery of Dominance and Technological Change* (London: Pluto Press, 1985).

Corlett, A. and Whittaker, M., *Low-pay Britain 2014* (London: Resolution Foundation, 2014).

Coyle, A., 'Sex and skill in the organisation of the clothing industry', in J. West (ed.) *Women, Work and the Labour Market* (London: Routledge and Kegan Paul, 1982).

Cutler, T., 'Vocational Training and British Economic Performance: A Further Instalment of the "British Labour Problem"?', *Work, Employment and Society*, 6/2 (1992), 161–83.

Danford, A., *Japanese Management Techniques and British Workers* (London: Mansell Publishing Ltd, 1999).

Data Unit, *Social Care Workforce Development Partnership (SCWDP) Workforce Data Collection 2013: The Findings* (Local Government Data Unit Wales, 2014).

Department for Trade and Industry, Department for Education and Employment (DTI, DfEE), *Opportunity for All in a World of Change: A White Paper on Enterprise, Skills and Innovation* (London: HMSO, 2002).

Felstead, A., Davies, R. and Jones, S., *Skills and the Quality of Work in Wales, 2006–2012* (Cardiff: WISERD, Cardiff University, 2013).

Gething, V., 'Written statement – Welsh Government's child poverty strategy progress report 2013', 29 November (2013), *http://gov.wales/about/cabinet/ cabinetstatements/2013/childpovertystrategyprogressreport13/?lang=en* (accessed 17 November 2015).

GMB, 'Written Evidence from the GMB: Manufacturing and Trade in Wales', *Select Committee on Welsh Affairs, Written Evidence* (London: Parliament, 2004), *www.publications.parliament.uk/pa/cm200405/cmselect/cmwelaf/329/ 329we02.htm* (accessed 17 November 2015).

Hague, D. and Newman, P., *Costs in Alternative Locations: The Clothing Industry*, National Institute of Economic and Social Research, Occasional Paper no XV (Cambridge: Cambridge University Press, 1952), pp. vii–73.

Hammer, N., Plugor, R., Nolan, P. and Clark, I., *New Industry on a Skewed Playing Field: Supply Chain Relations and Working Conditions in UK Garment Manufacturing* (Leicester: Centre for Sustainable Work and Employment Futures, University of Leicester, 2015).

House of Commons Library, 'Percentage of Employee Jobs with Hourly Pay Excluding Overtime below the Living Wage by Region and Parliamentary Constituency (place of work), UK, April 2013 and 2014' (London: ONS/ House of Commons, 2014).

Income Data Services (IDS), 'Pay, non-pay benefits, young people and the minimum wage', *A Research Report for the Low-pay Commission* (London: IDS, 2014).

James, S. and Lloyd, C., 'Supply chain pressures and migrant workers: deteriorating job quality in the UK food processing industry', in C. Lloyd, G. Mason and K. Mayhew (eds), *Low-wage Work in the United Kingdom* (New York: Russell Sage Foundation, 2008), pp. 211–46.

Jones, P. and Green, A., 'The Quantity and Quality of Jobs: Changes in UK Regions, 1997–2007', *Environment and Planning A*, 41 (2009), 2474–95.

Jones, R. and Hayes, S., 'The Economic Determinants of Clothing Consumption in the UK 1987–2000', *Journal of Fashion Marketing and Management: An International Journal*, 6/4 (2002), 326–39.

Leading Action for Textiles, Clothing and Footwear (LATCF), 'Attachment: 14, Item 20', Dumfries and Galloway Council (2003).

Lee, C., *British Regional Employment Statistics 1841–1971* (Cambridge: Cambridge University Press, 1979).

Lloyd, C., 'Tailor-made Occupations: A Study of Gender and Skill in the Welsh Clothing Industry', *Contemporary Wales: An Annual Review of Economic and Social Research*, 5 (1992), 115–29.

——, 'Restructuring and Technical Change: A Study of the Welsh Clothing Industry' (PhD thesis, University of Wales, College Cardiff, 1993).

—— and Payne, J., 'On the "Political Economy of Skill": Assessing the Possibilities for a Viable High Skills Project in the United Kingdom', *New Political Economy*, 7/3 (2002), 367–95.

Mason, G., Mayhew, K. and Osborne, M., 'Low-pay, labour market institutions and job quality in the UK', in C. Lloyd, G. Mason and K. Mayhew (eds), *Low-Wage Work in the United Kingdom* (New York: Russell Sage Foundation, 2008).

Office for National Statistics (ONS), *Size Analysis of UK Business*, Business Monitor PA1003 (London: HMSO, 1990).

—— *Labour Force Survey Employment status by Occupation, April–June 2014* (London, ONS, 2014).

Owen, D., *Working Futures 2010–2020: Summary Report for Wales* (London: UKCES, 2012).

Parken, A., Pocher, E. and Davies, R., *Working Patterns in Wales: Gender, Occupation and Pay* (Cardiff: WAVE Cardiff University, 2014).

Phizacklea, A., *Unpacking the Fashion Industry: Gender, Racism and Class in Production* (London: Routledge, 1990).

Pickernell, D., 'Economic development policy in Wales since devolution: from despair to where?', CEG Papers in Economic Geography (Cardiff: Cardiff University, 2011).

Rubery, J. and Urwin, P., 'Brining the Employer Back In: Why Social Care Needs a Standard Employment Relationship', *Human Resource Management Journal*, 21/2 (2011), 122–37.

Short, J., *The Garment Industry in Wales: A Report to the WDA*, Wales Cooperative (Cardiff: Development and Training Agency, 1987).

Skillset, *Sector Skills Assessment for the Fashion and Textiles Sector in Wales* (London: Skillset, 2011).

Steedman, H. and Wagner, K., 'Productivity, Machinery and Skills: Clothing Manufacture in Britain and Germany', *National Institute of Economic and Social Research*, 128, 1 (May 1989), 40–57.

Tannock, S., 'Bad Attitude? Migrant Workers, Meat Processing Work and the Local Unemployed in a Peripheral Region of the UK', *European Urban and Regional Studies*, 22/4 (2015), 416–30.

Thompson, G., 'Introduction', in G. Thompson (ed.), *Industrial Policy: USA and UK Debates* (Abingdon: Routledge, 2015).

TUC, *Women and Casualisation: Women's Experience of Job Insecurity* (London: TUC, 2014).

Welsh Affairs Committee (WAC), *Inward Investment in Wales, Eighth Report of Session 2010–12*, vol. 1 (London: House of Commons, 2012).

Welsh Assembly Government, 'First Minister praises Amazon for bringing jobs to Wales', press release, 17 April 2008.

Williams, K. and Jenkins, J., 'Challenging the concept that there can be fair employment with no guaranteed minimum hours', in TUC (ed.), *Debating Industrial Policy in Wales* (Cardiff: Wales TUC, 2015), pp. 19–22.

Wood, A. and Burchell, B., 'Beyond Zero-hours: Reducing the Misery of Insecure Hours', *Safety Management*, 1 September (2014), *https://sm.britsafe.org/ beyond-zero-hours-reducing-misery-insecure-hours* (accessed 17 November 2015).

Wray, M., *The Women's Outerwear Industry* (London: Duckworth, 1957).

Zeitlin, J., 'The Clothing Industry in Transition: International Trends and British Response', *Textile History*, 19/2 (1988), 211–38.

Paula at Eastmoors – by Ian Homer

9

Changes and Continuities: Women in Paid Work in Wales 1994–2014

ALISON PARKEN

Introduction

So much has changed for women in the Welsh labour market since Teresa Rees reviewed their position in *Our Sisters' Land* (1994). And yet, much remains the same. In 1994, Rees discussed how the decline of manufacturing and the growth of services (see also Lloyd this volume) had changed the gender composition of the workforce in Wales over the previous twenty years. From the vantage point of 2014, we now know that the period 1971 to 1991 was the most significant period of change for the decline of men's employment rates and the rise of women's (ONS, 2013b).

Rees reflected on how such changes might make significant in-roads into the breadwinner/homemaker 'ideal' for gender relations that had so shaped labour market participation in the twentieth century. Many more unmarried women were entering and staying in the labour market after marriage, and trying to re-enter the labour market after childcare. It appeared that labour-market structuring based upon men's pattern of full-time working over the lifetime, so that the employment contract was effectively underpinned by the marriage contract (Pateman, 1988; Gheradi, 1995), might be giving way to a dual-earner household model.

Today, this model is a necessity for households in Wales who are trying to avoid the in-work poverty trap (Kenway et al., 2013). However, the discussion here will demonstrate that despite significant changes in women's relationship to paid work, continuity with 1994 is evident as gender remains an organizing principle in the labour market and in welfare policy, affecting who does what and under what conditions in the workplace, and in the home (Osborn et al., 2000; Pfau-Effinger, 1998; Rees, 1994, 1999).

This chapter will reflect upon Teresa Rees's observations from twenty years ago, consider change since then and examine the present picture for women in paid work in Wales. Future change in industrial composition, education and the labour market will also shape women's future or, rather, futures, as the disparities between women who are doing well in the 'Top 3' occupational groups (senior managers, professionals and associate professionals) and those in semi-skilled or routine work at the bottom of the employment structure signify the need to consider differences between women as well as between women and men.

However, although it is as important to address socio-economic inequalities within disadvantaged groups as it is to close gaps between them (Hills et al., 2010), research in Wales found that, with the exception of higher-level educational outcomes for women, being a woman was still the most relevant marker of disadvantage across measures of employment, earnings, income and wealth. Being disabled, living in social rented housing or having Pakistani or Bangladeshi heritage brought additional disadvantage to women and men in employment (Joll et al., 2011, pp. 142–3).[1]

Rees (1994) observed highly qualified women entering the labour market in growing numbers; however, today, women, more often than men, work in jobs where the required skill level is below their qualification level (ONS, 2013b). Drawing on new Welsh data, and inequalities reviews such as the intersectional analysis of socio-economic inequalities (Davies et al., 2011) and secondary data analysis of gender segregation in occupations and working patterns in Wales (Parken et al., 2014), I will consider whether the hope, presaged in Rees's chapter, that the developing knowledge economy might address social inequalities through the greater provision of good quality work, has been realized (Walby, 2007; Parken and Rees, 2011; Brown, 2013; Felstead et al., 2013).

Teresa Rees called for a gender mainstreaming approach to equality that requires all policy actors and policy instruments to be employed in the *promotion* of equality (Rees, 1994, 1998; Verloo, 1999). This transversal policy approach to equality exceeds vertical legislative approaches to discrimination, and should be capable of addressing intersecting inequalities (Parken, 2010b). Equality mainstreaming was incorporated in the first Government of Wales Act 1998. Finally, then, this chapter will consider how, nearly twenty years on, the latest Welsh Specific Equality Regulations, introduced in 2012, might affect change for women in paid work in Wales.

Gender and participation in paid work

Gender, in the following analysis, does not refer to fixed or biological attributes but to one axis of social and economic stratification. Similarly, jobs are not assumed to be gender neutral but rather spaces where congruence with gender 'norms' are expected and unreflexively antici-pated by employers and employees (Acker, 1992; Adkins, 1995; McDowell, 1997; Parken, 2010a). We expect to align our subjective identities with already gendered jobs to be able to 'be ourselves' at work, performing forms of femininity or masculinity required by our jobs and mediated through class, region, age, sexual and ethno-religious identities (Leidner, 1991; Adkins, 1995; Parken, 2003).

Gender is a binary, informed by the oppositional positioning of masculinity and femininity within the institutions of heterosexuality (Parken, 2003). The male nurse and the female mechanic know that their job calls into question the social conventions associated with being a man or a woman and, consequently, their sexuality. In this chapter, gender is understood as an active process, one that we 'do' in everyday life in order to be intelligible, to ourselves and to others (West and Zimmerman, 1987; Butler, 1990). The picture under consideration here, then, is not based on personal or protected characteristics (Equality Act, 2010) but rather the outcome of institutional systems and practices producing advantage and disadvantage through social division.

Rees (1994) charted improved educational outcomes and increased participation in employment for women, the latter underpinned by the growth of the service economy in areas such as retail and business services, and an expanding public sector. She observed the rise of credentialism and the impact of this on the numbers of highly educated women entering the professions and deliberated on how women would negotiate workplaces where they would not be advantaged by the 'old boys' network, and where they might need to create new situational work identities to negotiate androcentric organizational work cultures (Cockburn, 1988; McDowell, 1997). She considered how women might manage the 'double-load', learning to balance responsibilities at work in combination with their traditional gender roles in the home.

These questions may appear outdated now, or even outdated then, but that is to forget that although working-class women have always worked (Crompton and Sanderson, 1990; Hakim, 1993, 1995), the breadwinner/homemaker ideal strongly underpinned the gendered division of labour between the public and private spheres, either side of the two world wars of the twentieth century. Its legacy in today's labour market is clear: a dual-earner model assumes full-time working patterns for men and a high proportion of part-time work for women.

In Wales, 43 per cent of women work on a part-time basis. Three-quarters of these part-time jobs are in low to low-middle skilled jobs such as sales, administration, personal services and elementary jobs (Parken et al., 2014). UK data shows that 46 per cent of women are employed in lower-middle skilled jobs (such as administration, caring and leisure and sales), compared to 24 per cent of men (ONS, 2013b, p. 10). Men are more likely to be employed in higher-skilled occupations, which are associated with higher pay (associate professional and technical and skilled trades) (ONS, 2013b, p. 10).

Women have therefore been considered to be a 'reserve army of labour', situated in jobs considered peripheral to a core of labour market jobs owned by men and more vulnerable to changes in the business cycle (Rubery and Rafferty, 2013). In this understanding, women's participation in work is dependent on employers' demand for flexibility in the lower-skilled sectors in which they are clustered, where poor job quality may lead to greater flexibility but also higher turnover (Felstead and Gallie, 2004, in Rubery and Rafferty, 2013, p. 416). Welfare policies to 'make work pay' can act as disincentives to labour market participation or encourage it, and other calls on women's time can detach them from the labour market (Rubery and Rafferty, 2013, p. 425).

Evidence shows that marriage and having children is good for men's employment and pay, while it has a negative impact on women (ONS, 2013b). However, there are now more households in relative poverty in Wales with household members in paid work than those in receipt of welfare transfers, and the majority of in-work poverty households are those with one main earner, or a main earner and a part-time worker (Kenway et al., 2013).[2]

Economic activity is a measure of the working-age population who are employed or unemployed but seeking work.[3] In 1994, Rees reported that women in Wales had the lowest economic activity rates in Britain, standing at 62.2 per cent and that men's economic activity rates were lower than the UK average, standing at 81 per cent (1994, p. 94). Time series analysis of Annual Population Survey data for Wales shows that in the subsequent twenty years, economic activity rates have fluctuated for both men and women but have remained consistently below average UK levels. Currently, men's economic activity rate is 5 per cent lower than the UK average, at 78 per cent (ONS, 2014a). Women's economic activity in Wales grew fairly consistently over the period 1994 to 2014, reaching 72 per cent in 2013, 10 per cent higher than in 1994, but stands currently at 69.4 per cent, which is 3 per cent lower than the UK average (ONS, 2014a).

With regard to economic inactivity (those not looking for work), Wales continues to have higher rates than the 'rest of the UK'. There has been a substantial change in the share of women who are economically inactive for 'reasons of looking after family and home'. This has declined from 18 per cent in 1992 to 10 per cent in 2010 (percentages are rounded up), which was 1.5 per cent less than the corresponding 'rest of UK' figure (Jones and Robinson, 2011, pp. 42–3).[4] However, Wales still has a disproportionately high percentage of men and women who are economically inactive due to being disabled (Disability Discrimination Act definition) and/or have a work-limiting long-term illness (Jones and Robinson, 2011, p. 70). From almost double the level for men in Wales, in comparison to 'rest of UK' in 2001 at 11.9 per cent, economic inactivity for this reason was around 8 per cent (rounded) for both men and women in 2010 in Wales, compared to 6 per cent for men and 5 per cent for women in the 'rest of UK' (Jones and Robinson, 2011, p. 42).

Table 9.1 illustrates the employment rate for men and women in Wales. This is the percentage of the working-age population who are employed. The data show that on this measure, Wales had a consistently lower employment rate relative to the UK over the period 2004–14.

Movement in the employment rate is not linear. Differences of age and gender are also worth noting, as young women in Wales are less likely to have low or no qualifications than men, but are more likely to be unemployed (Joll et al., 2011, p. 143). The employment rate gap between men and women in Wales was around 10 per cent between July 2004 and June 2008 (ONS, 2014b). Men's employment rate declined during the 2008/9 recession and continued to do so until 2012, while women's rate initially held steady.

Table 9.1. Employment rate UK and Wales, aged 16–64,
and by gender within Wales 2004–14

	All in UK	All in Wales	Men in Wales	Women in Wales
2004/5	72.5	69.1	74.3	64.0
2005/6	72.3	69.0	74.0	64.2
2006/7	72.5	69.0	74.3	63.8
2007/8	72.5	69.2	74.3	64.2
2008/9	71.3	67.2	71.3	63.3
2009/10	70.2	66.7	70.1	63.3
2010/11	70.1	66.2	69.7	62.8
2011/12	70.2	67.0	71.0	63.1
2012/13	71.0	67.7	71.6	63.8
2013/14	71.9	69.5	72.5	66.5

Source: ONS (2014b) Annual Population Survey, extrapolated from NOMIS
database 28 October 2014

Men were first to feel the impact of job losses in industries that they
dominate in the private sector. Unlike previous recessions, when
women may have been thought of as the 'reserve army of labour',
women initially enjoyed the 'protective effect' of working in the public
sector but when they did suffer jobs losses, they registered as
unemployed rather than revert to unpaid family work, becoming
economically inactive (Rubery and Rafferty, 2013). Involuntary part-
time working increased for women and men during and since the
recession, but women are now no more likely than men to be satisfied
with this arrangement (Rubery and Rafferty, 2013, p. 423). Welfare
policy is now said to 'help make work pay', meaning perverse
incentives for women to leave the labour market upon a partner's
unemployment have diminished (Rubery and Rafferty, 2013, p. 425).
In Wales, from the middle of 2009 to the middle of 2010 the
employment rate gap reduced to around 7 per cent, expanding again
when the policies of the Comprehensive Spending Review (Her
Majesty's Treasury, 2010) began to impact upon public sector
employment, where women predominate. Currently women's
employment rate in Wales is just 6 per cent lower than men's (ONS,
2014b).[5] Women's attachment to paid work is now a settled 'norm' and
has been influenced by changing industrial composition, the need for
household income and state support for working families (Rubery and

Rafferty, 2013). However, this does not tell us about where men and women work, the quality of that work and prospects for earnings.

Gender and changes in industrial composition

The legacies of deindustrialization in Wales are still apparent. Over the period from 1989 to 2009, Wales suffered the largest decline in Gross Value Added[6] per head relative to the UK as a whole, and the lowest rate of growth in GVA (4 per cent) when compared to the individual regions of the UK regions (Davies, 2011, p. 7). Wales demonstrates a lower proportion of economic activity in the private sector, a higher proportion of jobs requiring low qualifications, more prevalent gender segregation and lower average earnings compared to other parts of the UK (Felstead et al., 2013). West Wales and the valleys area of Wales were allocated a further £2 billion in European Social Funds in December 2014, the third round of structural funding, to support jobs and growth in the areas where GVA per head remains below 75 per cent of the average.

Women's entry into service jobs, predicated on part-time working patterns, cemented the already gendered composition of the labour market (Crompton, 1989; Crompton and Sanderson, 1990). In 2004, 89 per cent of women's employment was accounted for in tourism, retail/ wholesale, business services and public administration; in 2014, the figure was 91 per cent (ONS, 2014c). Agriculture, energy, manufacturing and construction are almost entirely comprised of male employees. These sectors accounted for 41 per cent of all men's employment in 2004, and 36 per cent in 2014 (ONS, 2014c). In 2004/5, women comprised 70 per cent of all public administration education and health workers (the majority working in the public sector). In 2014, women still comprised 70 per cent of health and education workers, despite the rise and fall of employment in those sectors over the ten-year period (ONS, 2014c).

Therefore, future changes in industrial composition will have significant impact on the gendering of employment. A more even gender distribution of quality jobs is vital to meet the aim of economic independence for women contained in the European Commission's gender equality strategy (EC, COM (2010) 491 final). This can be defined as an amount sufficient to run an independent household with at least one dependent (Siltanen, 1994). The EC strategy notably identifies the inclusion of women in the sectors selected for investment in the *Europe 2020: Jobs and Growth Strategy* (EC, 2010). This is in contrast to earlier EU regional development programmes where simply increasing women's labour market participation was envisaged (see Parken, 2010a). Increased participation in 'women's work', in low-skilled and low-paid part-time jobs is insufficient for economic independence.

However, both *Europe 2020* and the Welsh corollary, the *Economic Renewal Strategy* (WAG, 2010), have mainly focused on growth and investment in sectors dominated by men such as ICT, energy and environment, advanced materials and manufacturing, creative industries, life sciences and financial and professional services (WAG, 2010, p. 37). Further, in sectors that do show an overall gender balance, such as the financial sector in Wales, over half of men are employed in the top three occupational strata compared to one-third of women; 43 per cent of women in this sector work in administration (Parken et al., 2014, p. 26). Men also dominate the lead positions within universities, business and government in Wales (Parken and Rees, 2011), which are the institutions that form the tripartite axes of knowledge economy actors (Ekotwitz and Leydesdorff, 1997) within the *Europe 2020* strategy.

There are now many more highly qualified women in professional and associate technical and professional roles but they remain concentrated in education and health (Parken et al., 2014). Higher educational qualifications have not broken gendered associations within knowledge jobs. In July 2004, there were 21,000 science and technical associate professional jobs in Wales and men held 80 per cent of them. Ten years later the figure was 25,600 and men held 78 per cent of them (ONS, 2014e).

Despite more women attaining good-quality degrees (first or 2:1) than men, a higher percentage of women graduates work in lower-middle skilled jobs (teaching assistants, care and admin workers) (ONS, 2013b, pp. 14–15), and have taken a greater share of the expansion in these jobs in the past decade than men (Statistics Wales).[7]

Existing gender disparities have been transposed from the 'old' economy to the 'new' (Perrons, 2005). New economies are overlaid by stubborn patterns of gender segregation (Parken and Rees, 2011). These trends may continue, according to the *Working Futures* reports (UKCES, 2012a), which predict the industrial and occupational composition of the UK workforce to 2020.

Table 9.2. Changes in employment profile for Wales by sector, 1990–2020.
Percentage share of total employment

Industry Sector	1990	2000	2010	2020
Primary Sector and Utilities	6.5	4.1	3.3	3.3
Manufacturing	18.4	16.5	10.0	9
Construction	7.9	7.0	7.3	7.9
Trade, Accom, Transport	26.9	25.7	28.4	29.4
Business and other Services	16.7	19.2	20.8	22.0
Non-market services	23.7	27.4	30.3	28.3
All industries (000s)	1,259	1,246	1,330	1,401

Source: Working Futures, Table 6, Wales report (2012b), jobs not heads.

The Wales report predicts the further decline of manufacturing from almost a 20 per cent share of employment in 1990 to less than 10 per cent in 2020 (UKCES, 2012b; Felstead et al., 2013).

There was considerable decline in the share of employment in primary sector and utilities between 1990 and 2010, contrasted by growth in business and other services (BS), and trade, accommodation and transport (TAT) over the same time. TAT is forecast to provide the largest share of employment by 2020. Non-market services (the public sector), the largest single sector for employment in Wales since the late 1990s, is predicated to decline but still be the second largest source of employment in Wales. Reduction in public sector employment will have a significant impact on both professional and low-skilled women in Wales. However, women managers, professionals and associate professionals could take advantage of predicted growth in business services, if they are present in all the business areas and hierarchies within this sector.

Having considered the past and possible futures, I now turn to consider the current picture of gendered jobs and how this impacts on Welsh women in relation to quality of work, working patterns and pay.

Gender, occupations and working patterns in Wales

Gender imbalance in the distribution of jobs and working hours among men and women maintains gender pay disparities, more so than gender pay discrimination (EFLWC, 2008). Anti-discrimination legislation on equal pay, which requires comparators, can be ineffective when few men and women work in the same jobs and grades (Her Majesty's Government, 2010). We need to understand how work is valued and how the gender of job incumbents can impact on the value assigned to different types of jobs, and the working patterns on offer within them.

There are four distinct categories of gender segregation but they intersect and reinforce each other. This is why addressing gender pay disparities is so challenging: it requires changing the association of whole sectors or industries, jobs, authority, training, progression and skills with 'what men do' or 'what women do'.

The uneven distribution of jobs between men and women by sector (public, private, voluntary) and industry or business areas (energy, transport, finance, retail) is known as 'horizontal segregation by gender'. When men and women work in very different jobs and occupations, this is known as 'occupational segregation'. Where men and women work in the same occupations but at different levels of hierarchy, the term 'vertical segregation' is used, and when employment contracts and working patterns – permanent/temporary/fixed term, casual, and full- or part-time work – pertain to one gender more than the other, this is known as 'contract segregation by gender'.

The accepted convention for examining gender balance in jobs, occupations, on company boards or within decision-making bodies is a gender distribution of 60/40. Only three of the nine major occupational groupings in Wales have gender balance (SOC 1-digit): these are professionals, associate professional and technical, and elementary (Parken et al., 2014, p. 12).[8] Senior manager and officials, skilled trades, and process plant and machinery occupations are male dominated, comprised of 64 per cent, 91 per cent and 86 per cent of men respectively. Administration, personal services and sales occupations are female dominated, being comprised of 78 per cent, 83 per cent and 69 per cent of women respectively (Parken et al., 2014).

At the top end of the occupational structure, Rees's (1994) prediction of employment growth in quality jobs for women is borne out. Many women now hold the levers to access jobs where professional qualifications are required. There is now gender balance in the professional occupations overall, at 55 per cent men, 45 per cent women (SOC 1-digit) (Parken et al., 2014, p. 12). However, 75 per cent of all women professionals in Wales work in education, health and social care; consequently, only fifteen of forty-six professional occupations are gender balanced (SOC 4-digit). These include bioscientists and biochemists, medical practitioners, secondary school teachers, solicitors and lawyers, and public service administrative professionals. Gender segregation persists in many professional jobs:

> Men comprise 90 per cent+ of all civil engineers, mechanical engineers (100 per cent), electrical engineers, design and development engineers, IT strategy and planning professionals, software professionals, quantity surveyors, chartered surveyors, building inspectors, chemists, physicists, geologists. There are no professional occupations where women comprise 90 per cent or more of all workers. Women are between 80 per cent and 90 per cent of all primary and nursery education teachers, special needs education teachers, social workers, and librarians (Parken et al., 2014, p. 21).

Within associate professional and technical (APT) jobs only twenty-six of seventy-three are gender balanced (SOC 4-digit). These are jobs such as laboratory technicians, medical and dental technicians, artists, actors and entertainers, product clothing and related designers and journalists.

APT is the largest of the nine major occupational groupings (SOC 1) accounting for 14 per cent of all jobs in Wales. Nursing constitutes 15 per cent of all APT jobs, and 28 per cent of all APT work that women do. Nursing jobs are middle to high graded, mainly offered on a full-time basis and as such attract above-average median full-time annual earnings for women. Without nursing, the APT grouping would be male dominated, Wales's gender pay gap would be much larger and women would be without a key source of premium 'women's work' (Parken et al., 2014).

In management, which remains male dominated, with men holding 64 per cent of senior manager and officials posts, there is gender balance only among senior officials in special interest organizations, customer care managers, advertising and public relations managers, retail and wholesale managers, leisure and catering managers.[9]

As we travel down the occupational hierarchy, the number of gender-balanced jobs diminishes. Within the administration occupational grouping, which women dominate, just five jobs are in gender balance. These are executive officers in the civil service, stock control clerks, database assistants, market-research interviewers and communications operators. Men are the majority of administrators in male-dominated sectors such as transport and distribution. Women are 95 per cent+ of medical and legal secretaries, school secretaries, personal assistants and receptionists.[10]

At the bottom of the labour market hierarchy, elementary occupations are also gender balanced overall. These are jobs that require few formal qualifications or skills, such as traffic wardens, school crossing patrol, shelf fillers, labourers, postal workers, hospital porters, kitchen and catering assistants. Elementary jobs account for around 12 per cent of all jobs in Wales. Men and women have starkly opposing working patterns within elementary work: 73 per cent of women work on a part-time basis while 75 per cent of men work on a full-time basis (Parken et al., 2014, p. 47). They also work in highly gender-segregated jobs:

Men are 90 per cent of mobile machine drivers, forestry workers, labourers building and woodworking trades, stevedores, other goods handling and storage occupations, hospital porters, hotel porters, road sweepers, refuse and salvage workers, window cleaners.

Women are 90 per cent+ of school crossing patrol attendants, school mid day assistants. Men are 80–90 per cent of car park attendants, postal workers, security guards, fishing and agricultural labourers, industrial cleaning process operatives, labourers, process and plant workers. Women are 80–90 per cent of cleaners and domestics, dry cleaners.

(Parken et al., 2014, p. 47)

Men and women in the same job are legally required to earn the same hourly rate of pay whether working full- or part-time hours. However, the data demonstrates how job- and working-pattern segregation in combination effectively nullifies this legal right (Rubery and Grimshaw, 2015), where an opposite sex comparator is required to show discrimination.

Across the whole occupational strata, only 86 of 353 jobs (SOC 4-digit) where there was sufficient data to show gender composition and pay by working pattern showed gender balance (Parken et al., 2014). Around a fifth of employees and self-employed workers in Wales were incorporated within the gender-balanced jobs, meaning that working in gender-segregated jobs is the norm for 80 per cent of employed and self-employed people in Wales.

This finding is consistent with national skills surveys, repeated over time, which show that job segregation by gender is more persistent in Wales than in other parts of the UK, and that men and women are more likely to work in jobs mainly undertaken by members of their own sex (Felstead et al., 2013, p. 10). More women are in mixed occupations, while men are more likely than women to be in jobs exclusively undertaken by men (Felstead et al., 2013, p. 10).

Men are more likely to work in professional, associate professional, technical and skilled jobs, which are correlated with higher pay (ONS,

2013b, p. 10). Men hold 91 per cent of all the skilled jobs in Wales, and their gross median hourly pay is higher than in the sales, personal services and administration jobs where women cluster and which are associated with low pay (Parken et al., 2014, pp. 12–33). Since these jobs account for around 42 per cent of all of women's full-time work and 52 per cent of women's part-time work (Parken et al., 2014, p. 16), the reason that women are consistently more likely to be in low-paid jobs than men is clear (Jones and Robinson, 2011, p. 70), as is the persistence of gender pay gaps.

Pay, poverty and part-time work

In 2012, women held 80 per cent of all part-time jobs in Wales, with average annual earnings of £7,874 per annum (Parken et al., 2014). This is far below the low-earnings threshold, calculated at 60 per cent of annual median earnings for all employees, which stood at £14,046 (ONS, 2013a). Men held 64 per cent of all full-time jobs in 2012, with average full-time earnings of £22,291 (Parken et al., 2014).[11] Full-time work is correlated to higher-graded employment and career progression (Parken et al., 2014).

There is also a strong association between part-time hours and earning less than the National Minimum Wage (NMW), so that jobs held by women are much more likely to pay below the statutory minimum than men's (ONS, 2014d, p. 1). Pay gaps are lowest where there is overall occupational gender balance and low levels of part-time work for women, such as in the professions and associate professional and technical occupations (Parken et al., 2014).

Three-quarters of all women's part-time work takes place in administration, personal service, sales and elementary occupations (Parken et al., 2014). Young women joining the labour market in Wales will find that over 40 per cent of jobs in these occupations are offered on a part-time basis, leading us to question the assumption that working part time is always a choice (Parken et al., 2014; Parken, 2011). Part-time workers are an increasing proportion of the long-service workforce, that is, those workers who remain in the same jobs for ten or more years (Doogan, 2005). There are few training opportunities or routes out of such jobs (Beechey and Perkins, 1987; Callender and Metcalf, 1997; Felstead et al., 2013), meaning that women who start out in part-time work can find themselves 'stuck to the floor' of the employment structure over their working lives. Addressing the low skills associated with part-time jobs, through training, is, Felstead et al. (2013) suggests, key to addressing Wales's poor economic performance.

However, even full-time work, where confined to 'women's work' is no guarantee of decent earnings. Low pay attaches disproportionality to women in full-time work as well.

> The incidence of low weekly pay for full-time employees in the UK is 22 per cent, in Wales 28 per cent and for women full-time employees in Wales it is 38 per cent: a 'gender penalty' of 10 per cent. (Joll et al., 2011, p. 150)

Occupational clustering in caring or service work sees women bring skills to customer-facing roles that are assumed to be innate, and which are assigned a low economic rent when performed in the labour market (Rubery and Grimshaw, 2015). Their continued dominance of part-time employment in such jobs has changed little since the 1970s in the UK, suggesting that such supply-side policies, such as affordable childcare, are inefficient (Manning, 2010). The gender pay gap widens for women who have worked on a full-time basis after the age of thirty, when lack of such policies inhibits career progression (NEP, 2010, p. 417). Good quality, affordable childcare still does not meet demand in Wales (Family and Childcare Trust, 2014). And, although successive studies have shown that men aspire to undertake more childcare, relatively few do, citing that they would prefer flexible working to part-time hours in order to this (Ellison et al., 2009). Both flexible and part-time working patterns are much less available in the sectors and occupations that men dominate.

At the top end of the employment structure part-time working patterns are harder to secure. However, nearly a quarter (23 per cent) of women's part-time work in Wales takes place in the Top 3 occupations. Negotiating high-graded part-time work, where full-time work, and possibly long hours, is otherwise the occupational norm, depends upon women having specialist knowledge or skill. Women in high-graded work in health, law, engineering, ICT and science are working on a part-time basis in Wales, although still relatively few of them. For example, 2,279 health professionals work in this pattern but only 401 science professionals and 208 ICT professionals.[12]

The discussion here has demonstrated – twenty years on from Rees's review (1994) – that gender segregation, in all its forms and in combination, continues to reproduce gender inequalities in paid work. The monetized expression of such disparities is the persistence of gender pay gaps. Although gender pay gaps are lower in Wales in comparisons to UK averages, this is, sadly, a reflection of lower average earnings for men in Wales than in the UK, rather than greater gender equality. What then can Welsh policy do to make structural change in this regard?

Policy change

In 1994, Rees asked how Welsh education and childcare policies might assist women to meet competing demands for their labour from within an androcentric labour market and from men at home. She was foregrounding Gender Mainstreaming, which would dominate the equalities policy arena for the next decade (Rees, 1998). Four years later, the first Government of Wales Act 1998 contained a unique equality clause that required the Welsh Government to mainstream equality for all people in its duties and functions (§120). The Government of Wales Act 2006 (§77) strengthened this duty by placing responsibility for outcomes upon Welsh ministers.

A review of progress towards meeting the equality duty demonstrated a distinct approach to discussing and addressing equalities in Wales post-devolution, and noted that:

> Each of the first five proposed Assembly Measures deals explicitly with an equality-related topic (that is, an issue where there is a recognised need to adapt service provision, or increase the rights and/or resource allocation to historically marginalized or discriminated-against groups). (Chaney, 2009, p. 93).

Despite this, Chaney concluded that the first decade of devolution demonstrated 'declaratory' intent to act on inequalities but lacked clear policy outcomes, resulting in significant implementation gaps (2009, p. 13). In practice, the mainstreaming equality duty confers no additional rights and depends upon judicial review for raising complaint. Therefore, the requirements of the Public Sector Equality Duty (PSED) within the Equality Act 2010 and the underpinning Welsh specific equality duties, contained in the Equality Act 2010 (Statutory Duties) (Wales) Regulations 2011, are the actual drivers of efforts to 'advance equality' in Wales.

Under the Regulations, Welsh ministers were required to make their first full assessment of progress on equality since the introduction of the PSED by the end of December 2014, and biannually thereafter. The first review report drew heavily upon survey research previously commissioned by the Equality and Human Rights Commission (EHRC), which demonstrated a significant level of engagement with the PSED in Wales, no non-compliance and a number of actions demonstrating over-compliance, which are not evident in comparator reports for England (Mitchell et al., 2014). Of note is a range of inclusion actions undertaken to address employment pay differences across the dimensions of inequality, and which were not confined to vertical actions: for example, efforts to encourage reading among disadvantaged boys through initiatives such as *Premier League Reading Stars Cymru* (Welsh Government, 2014, p. 24).

There has been a long and creditable history of partnership working between the Welsh Government, the EHRC Wales (and in the former Equal Opportunities Commission) and the Wales Trades Union Congress (WTUC) to tackle pay inequalities between men and women (Parken et al., 2009). The 2011 Regulations afforded Welsh ministers the first opportunity to bring into law measures to address structural labour market inequalities, within the suite of specific equality duties that underpin action on the requirements of the PSED.

A research policy review and consultation exercise concluded that there was enthusiasm for a Welsh-specific equality duty on equal pay, and recommended that public sector organizations in Wales should undertake an analysis of gender in employment through considering the combined impact of job, hours, grade, contract type and working pattern (Parken et al., 2009). The Equality Act 2010 (Statutory Duties) (Wales) Regulations 2011 contain a requirement for public sector organizations in Wales with over 150 employees to have an equal pay objective, or evidence why one is not required, report pay gaps annually and create an action plan to address gender pay gaps. This requirement intends that employers analyse the correlation between gender segregation and gender pay gaps in their organization and take action.

Aware of the possibility of an implementation gap, the Welsh Government funded the 'Women Adding Value to the Economy' (WAVE) partnership project, through European Social Funds. WAVE at Cardiff University worked collaboratively with public sector employers to analyse their workforce and pay information, interpret results and act on the evidence (Parken, 2015). This was a gender mainstreaming project, demonstrating the intent of Welsh Government policy to address structural issues, as well as evidencing a recognition that structural change requires research, capacity building and practical application to 'bring alive' duties to promote equality. The 'equal pay duty' aims to effect lasting improvement in the position of women in paid work in Wales, one organization at a time.

Conclusion

The past twenty years have seen momentous change for women in paid work, particularly for those who have been able to use 'the qualifications lever' to enter professional and associate professional roles, albeit mainly in health and education or within niches in business services and law. However, this 'opportunity bargain' is no guarantee of future success in a period of mass higher education and standardization within middle- to higher-skilled jobs (Brown, 2013), when women graduates are already more likely to be in jobs with lower-skills requirements than their qualifications should lever (ONS, 2013b). At the other end of the labour market women are finding it increasingly hard to 'make work pay' given their over concentration in low-skilled, low-paid, part-time work.

Welsh policy recognizes the gendering of labour markets and the unequal division of labour through such instruments as the 'equal pay duty'. Although the Welsh Government cannot address labour market segmentation in isolation, it is attempting to ensure that individual organizations address the reproduction of gender inequalities within their employment structures. The Welsh Government must also ensure that investment priorities are not concentrated only in the sectors and occupations where women are not (Parken and Rees, 2011). It must challenge the maintenance of a full-time working norm as the default route to progression, so that women can participate, remain and progress within employment. It must further challenge the use of low-skilled low-hours jobs as the default form of flexible working.

Notes

[1] Disabled meaning as defined within the Disability Discrimination Act 2005, now Equality Act 2010 and have a work life-limiting illness (LLI). Data gaps remain in large-scale national datasets for the parameters of sexual orientation and transgender. These reports took 'additive approach' to intersectionality combined with a 'soft class analysis' (Walby et al., 2012), and provided insights into the compound impact of belonging to several disadvantaged groups.

[2] Relative poverty here means below the low-pay threshold, that is earning less than 60 per cent of Annual Median Gross Earnings.

[3] Economically active is defined as being in paid work or being unemployed but actively seeking work and able to start work immediately (International Labour Organisation official definition).

[4] 'Rest of UK' includes the English regions, Scotland and Wales and excludes London and south-east, which is so qualitatively different in terms of employment and earnings to the rest of the UK it skews simple Wales/UK comparisons.

[5] ONS (2014b), *Time Series*, 2004–14, current quarterly figure quoted is for the period June–August 2014, downloaded from NOMIS, 28 November 2014.

[6] Gross Value Added (GVA) measures the value of economic output per head of population.

[7] For an extended discussion of the gendered knowledge economy, innovation and investment in Wales see Parken and Rees (2011).

[8] Data for this examination of occupational segregation was originally collated for the 'Women Adding Value to the Economy' (WAVE) research project (ESF, part-funded by the Welsh Government), which considered the impact of occupational segregation on gender pay gaps in Wales (Parken et al., 2014). ONS, Annual Population Survey, 'Special License'. Occupation, gender, working pattern and pay data were pooled, weighted and averaged for the years 2004–10, and for the years 2004–8 for gender and occupation within different industry sectors. Unadjusted pay gaps are reported. The dataset is 'pooled' Annual Population Survey results for the years 2004–10 inclusive, and includes employment and self-employment. Wales is a small population sample area and even the 'Welsh boost' to the Labour Force Survey cannot provide sufficient data in one year's survey at the fine level required to examine occupations by gender, working patterns and pay. The collation and averaging of seven years of data provides a reliable source of information to compare the 1994 picture, and also has the effect of 'flattening out' any single year-on-year anomalies.

[9] ONS, Annual Population Survey, 'Special License'. Occupation, gender, working pattern and pay data were pooled, weighted and averaged for the years 2004–10, and for the years 2004–8 for gender and occupation within different industry sectors. Unadjusted pay gaps are reported.

[10] ONS, Annual Population Survey, 'Special License'. Occupation, gender, working pattern and pay data were pooled, weighted and averaged for the years 2004–10, and for the years 2004–8 for gender and occupation within different industry sectors. Unadjusted pay gaps are reported.

[11] Pay is gross value and adjusted to CPI (2012=100) represents employee only.

[12] ONS, Annual Population Survey, 'Special License' (as above).

References

Acker, J., 'Gendering Organisational Theory', in A. Mills and P. Tancred (eds), *Gendering Organisational Analysis* (London: Sage, 1992).

Adkins, L., *Gendered Work: Sexuality, Family and the Labour Market* (Milton Keynes: The Open University Press, 1995).

Beechey, V. and Perkins, T., *A Matter of Hours, Part-Time Work and the Labour Market* (Cambridge: Polity Press, 1987).

Brown, P., 'Education, Opportunity and the Prospects for Social Mobility', *British Journal of the Sociology of Education*, 34/5–6 (2013), 678–700.

Butler, J., *Gender Trouble: Feminism and the Subversion of Identity* (New York and London: Routledge, 1990).

Callender, C. and Metcalf, H., *Women and Training*, Department for Education and Employment Research Report RR35 (London: DfEE, 1997).

Chaney, P., *Equal Opportunities and Human Rights: The First Decade of Devolution* (Manchester: Equality and Human Rights Commission, 2009).

Cockburn, C., 'The gendering of jobs', in S. Walby (ed.), *Gender Segregation at Work* (Milton Keynes: The Open University Press, 1988).

Crompton, R., 'Women in banking: continuity and change since the Second World War', *Work, Employment & Society*, 3/2 (1989), 141–56.

—— and Sanderson, K., *Gendered Jobs and Social Change* (London: Unwin Hayman, 1990).

Davies, R., Joll, C. and Parken, A., 'Inequalities in Wales: The Policy, Economic and Political Context', in R. Davies, S. Drinkwater, C. Joll, M. Jones, H. Lloyd-Williams, G. Makepeace, M. Parhi, A. Parken, C. Robinson, C. Taylor and V. Wass (eds), *An Anatomy of Economic Inequality in Wales*, a report prepared on behalf of the Wales Equality and Human Rights Commission (Cardiff: EHRC, 2011), pp. 1–13.

Doogan, K., 'Long-term Employment and the Restructuring of the Labour Market in Europe', *Time and Society*, 14/65 (2005), 65–87.

Ellison, G., Baker, A. and Kulasuriya, T., *Work and Care: A Study of Modern Parents*, Research Report 15 (London: Equality and Human Rights Commission, 2009).

Etzkowitz, H. and Leydesdorff, L. A., *Universities and the Global Knowledge Economy: A Triple Helix of University-Industry-Government* (London: Continuum International, 1997).

European Commission (EC), *EUROPE 2020: A Strategy for Smart, Sustainable and Inclusive Growth*, COM (2010) 2020, Brussels, 3.3.2010.

European Foundation for Improvement in Living and Working Conditions (EFLWC), *Mind the Gap – Women's and Men's Quality of Work and Employment* (Office for Luxembourg: Official Publications of the European Communities, 2008), *www.eurofound.europa.eu/pubdocs/2008/39/en/1/ ef0839en.pdf* (accessed 18 November 2015).

Family and Childcare Trust, 'Annual Childcare Cost Survey', *www.Familyandchildcaretrust.org* (accessed 24 December 2014).

Felstead, A. and Gallie, D., 'For Better or Worse? Non-standard Jobs and High Involvement Work Systems', *The International Journal of Human Resource Management*, 15/7 (2004), 1293–316.

——, Davies, R. and Jones, S., *Skills and the Quality of Work in Wales 2006–2012, Main Report, Report for the UK Employment and Skills Council* (Cardiff: WISERD, 2013).

Gheradi, S., *Gender, Symbolism and Organizational Culture* (London: Sage, 1995).

Hakim, C., 'The Myth of Rising Female Employment', *Work, Employment and Society*, 7/1 (1993), 97–120.

——, 'Five Feminist Myths about Women's Employment', *British Journal of Sociology*, 46/3 (1995), 429–55.

Her Majesty's Government, *Equality Act 2010: Chapter 15* (London: Stationery Office, 2010).

Her Majesty's Treasury, 'Comprehensive Spending Review 2010', Cm 7942, October 2010 (London: The Stationery Office, 2010).

Hills, J., Brewer, M., Jenkins, S., Lister, R., Lupton, R., Machin, S., Mills, C., Modood, T., Rees, T. and Riddell, S., *An Anatomy of Economic Inequality in the UK: Report of the National Equality Panel* (London: Government Equalities Office, 2010).

Joll, C., Parken, A. and Wass, V., 'The positions of different groups in Wales: a cross-cutting summary and conclusions', in R. Davies, S. Drinkwater, C. Joll, M. Jones, H. Lloyd-Williams, G. Makepeace, M. Parhi, A. Parken, C. Robinson, C. Taylor and V. Wass (eds), *An Anatomy of Economic Inequality in Wales*, a report prepared on behalf of the Wales Equality and Human Rights Commission (Cardiff: EHRC, 2011), pp. 131–54.

Jones, M. and Robinson, C., 'Employment in Wales', in R. Davies, S. Drinkwater, C. Joll, M. Jones, H. Lloyd-Williams, G. Makepeace, M. Parhi, A. Parken, C. Robinson, C. Taylor and V. Wass (2011), *An Anatomy of Economic Inequality in Wales*, a report prepared on behalf of the Wales Equality and Human Rights Commission (Cardiff: EHRC, 2011), pp. 41–70.

Kenway, P. and New Policy Institute research team, *Monitoring Poverty and Social Exclusion in Wales* (London: Joseph Rowntree Foundation, 2013).

Leidner, R., 'Serving Hamburgers and Selling Insurance', *Gender and Society*, 5/2 (1991), 154–77.

McDowell, L., *Capital Culture: Gender at Work in the City* (London: Routledge, 1997).

Manning, A., 'Forty Years After the Equal Pay Act, What Prospects for Gender Equality?', presentation to conference, Royal Statistical Society, London, 16 November 2010.

Mitchell, M., Beninger, K., Rhamin, N. and Morell, G., *Review of the Public Sector Equality Duty (PSED) in Wales*, NatCen research report for the Equality and Human Rights Commission (Wales) (Cardiff: EHRC, 2014).

National Equality Panel (NEP), *Report of the National Equality Panel: Executive Summary* (London: Centre for Analysis of Social Exclusion and Government Equalities Office, 2010).

Office for National Statistics (ONS), *Annual Survey of Hours and Earnings* (London: ONS, 2013a).

——, *Full Report – Women in the Labour Market* (Newport: ONS, 2013b).

——, *Economic Activity Rate, Wales, Annual Population Survey Time Series Analysis for 1990–2014*, data extrapolated from NOMIS database, 1 November 2014 (Newport: ONS, 2014a).

——, *Employment Rates Wales*, Annual Population Survey, Time Series Analysis, data extrapolated from NOMIS database, 28 October 2014 (Newport: ONS 2014b).

——, *Employees by Gender within Occupations and Sectors in Wales, Time Series Analysis for July 2004–June 2014*, data extrapolated from NOMIS database, 26 October 2014 (Newport: ONS, 2014c).

——, 'Statistical Bulletin', *Low Pay*, April 2014, 19 November 2014 (Newport: UK Statistics Agency, 2014d).

——, *Occupations in Wales by Gender, Time Series Analysis for July 2004–June 2014*, data extrapolated from NOMIS database, 26 October 2014 (Newport: ONS, 2014e).

Osborn, M., Rees, T., Bosch, M., Ebeling, H., Hermann, C., Hilden, J., McLaren, A., Palomba, R., Peltonen, L., Vela, C., Weis, D., Wold, A., Mason, J. and Wennerås, C., *Science Policies in the European Union: Promoting Excellence Through Mainstreaming Gender Equality*, Report from the ETAN Network on Women and Science (Luxembourg: Office for Official Publications of the European Communities, 2000).

Parken, A., 'Gender Mainstreaming: "Outing" Heterosexism in the Workplace' (unpublished PhD thesis, University of Wales, Cardiff, 2003).

——, 'Gender, Knowledge Dynamics and Regional Policy', in H. Halkier, J. Manniche, M. Dahlstrom and L. Smid-Olsen (eds), *Knowledge Dynamics, Regional Development and Public Policy*, published on behalf of the EURODITE project sponsored by the Sixth Framework Programme of the European Union (Denmark: University of Aalborg Press, 2010a), pp. 86–98.

——, 'A Multi-strand Approach to Promoting Equality and Human Rights in Policymaking', *Policy and Politics*, 38/1 (2010b), 79–99.

——, *Research Review: Employer Case Studies*, Research Report for the WAVE Programme (Cardiff: Cardiff University, 2015).

——, Pocher, E. and Davies, R., *Working Patterns in Wales: Gender, Occupations and Pay*, Research Report for the WAVE programme (Cardiff: Cardiff University, 2014).

—— and Rees, T., 'Economic Renewal and the Gendered Knowledge Economy in Wales', *Contemporary Wales*, 24 (2011), 113–34.

——, —— and Baumgardt, A., *Options for an Equal Pay Duty in Wales, Research Report for the Welsh Assembly Government* (Cardiff: Welsh Assembly Government, 2009).

Pateman, C., *The Sexual Contract* (Cambridge: Polity Press, 1988).

Perrons, D., 'Gender Mainstreaming and Gender Equality in the New (Market) Economy: An Analysis of Contradictions', *Social Politics: International Studies in Gender State and Society*, 12/3 (2005), 389–411.

Pfau-Effinger, B., 'Gender Cultures and the Gender Arrangement – A Theoretical Framework for Cross-National Gender Research', *Innovation: The European Journal of Social Sciences*, 11/2 (1998), 147–66.

Rees, T., 'Women and paid work in Wales', in J. Aaron, T. Rees, S. Betts and M. Vincentelli (eds), *Our Sisters' Land: The Changing Identities of Women in Wales* (Cardiff: University of Wales Press, 1994).

——, *Mainstreaming Equality in the European Union* (London: Routledge, 1998).

——, *Women and Work: Twenty-Five Years of Gender Equality in Wales* (Cardiff: University of Wales Press, 1999).

Rubery, J. and Rafferty, A., 'Women and Recession Revisited', *Work Employment Society*, 27/3 (2013), 414–32.

—— and Grimshaw, D., 'The Forty Year Pursuit of Equal Pay: A Case of Constantly Moving Goalposts', *Cambridge Journal of Economics*, 39 (2015), 319–43.

Siltanen, J., *Locating Gender: Occupational Segregation, Wages and Domestic Responsibilities* (London: University College of London Press, 1994).

——, 'Full Wages and Component Wages', in S. Jackson and S. Scott (eds), *Gender: A Sociological Reader* (London: Routledge, 2002), pp. 133–5.

Statistics Wales, 'Statistics on Job Quality in Wales: Statistical Article', 27 October (Cardiff: Welsh Assembly Government, 2007).

UK Commission for Employment and Skills (UKCES), *Working Futures 2012–2022, Evidence Report 83* (London: UKCES, 2012a).

——, *Working Futures Report for Wales, October 2012* (London: UKCES, 2012b).

Verloo, M., *Gender Mainstreaming: Practice and Prospects*, Council of Europe, EG (99) 13 (1999).

Walby, S., *Gender Inequality and the Future of Work*, research report for the Equal Opportunities Commission (Manchester: Equal Opportunities Commission, 2007).

——, Armstrong, J. and Strid, S., 'Intersectionality and the quality of equality architecture', *Social Politics*, 19/4 (2012), 446–81.

Welsh Assembly Government (WAG), *Economic Renewal: A New Direction* (Cardiff: Department for Economy and Transport, Welsh Assembly Government, 2010).

Welsh Government, *Welsh Ministers Report on Equality 2014* (Cardiff: Welsh Government, 2014).

West, C. and Zimmerman, D., 'The social construction of gender', *Gender and Society*, 1/2 (1987), 125–51.

195

III

Welsh Public Life, Social Policy, Class and Inequality

Politricks *by Jamie Feeney aka Sapien*

Yeah ya see they don't think like me
My soul is gold and I yearn to be
*   free*
I can challenge and breakdown
*   every single MP*
And tell them why we don't agree
*   with their policies*
Cos their funds on constant
*   deflation*
Health care gone privatisation
New promises old legislation
It's not a solution it's a dictation
Look at the real problems we're
*   facing*
Young offenders need education
Motivation, participation not
*   incarceration or a year on*
*   probation*
Plus the addicts need consultation
Rehabilitation, a new occupation
A bit of understanding,
*   consideration*
Not sedation to avoid temptation
What about the homelessness and
*   starvation*

Heard the food banks taking
*   donations*
Sports cars cruise past the bus
*   station*
Nevertheless you won't rest for your
*   wages*
To the gap between rich and poor
Contrast from a tramp to an
*   entrepreneur*
If he made the money treat him
*   different than before*
They say money makes the world go
*   round and of course*
You're not thinking of the next man
On road like the wheels of your
*   Porsche*
Where's equality when you can't
*   afford*
The same things that the next man's
*   bought*
Taxpayer's money gets spent on
*   porn*
While the next man's looking for
*   something to pawn*
But apparently we got the right to
*   vote*

*No surprise it's a low turnout at the
  polls.
Born too late to explore the earth
Born too early to explore the galaxy
Born just in time to explore my
  mind
I wasn't born just to work for a
  salary
Grow old and die after raising a
  family
My son will know a system that's
  more than planetary
Built in an image a reflection of
  vanity
Social expectation insanity
They don't focus on the local views
So we're looking at the global news
Conspiracy theories make more
  sense than the truth
That's why they're so popular with
  the youth
A revolution uniting the nation
Urban development Los
  Angelisation
Still looking at the capital gain
Let's build a metropolis on this
  terrain*

*Suburbs, towns, cities merge into
  plains
Solar energy, wind power and
  change
Environmental like wind and rain
Same old record like a vinyl, on the
  turntable
Now the turbines are turning the
  tables
Clean, free energy is stable
This place is our grave, cos it was
  our cradle
Assembly members, if I was asked
  to name one I wouldn't
  remember, Why?
Cos they wanna close down the
  centre
And then the kids would have
  no-where to venture
And I, dream of a future where the
  government try
To do right by the people, just living
  their lives
But we're stuck in the system,
  funding's cut by the knife*

Music and media webcontent is hosted on the following websites:
www.molgroup.org.uk/ourchangingland and
https://www.youtube.com/watch?v=KOrPYVXq32I.

Clocking Out, Hoover, Merthyr Tydfil – by Ian Homer

10

Class, Poverty and Politics in Devolved Wales

DAVE ADAMSON

Introduction

This chapter revisits a range of research I conducted in the 1990s into the changing class structure evident in Wales, including the discussions in my 2008 article 'Still Living on the Edge', which was published in *Contemporary Wales*. The period 1981–90 witnessed a spasm of rapid socio-economic change in Wales. The industrial base of production, which had characterized the previous 100 years, was effectively decimated by a complex combination of government policy, globalization and changing patterns of consumption in society. The result was the transition from an 'organised' capitalism (Lash and Urry, 1987) to a post-industrial society marked by rising levels of poverty and economic inactivity and associated patterns of social dislocation in previously cohesive working-class communities (Adamson, 2001).

My work was concerned initially to understand the 'fracturing' of a traditional working class in Wales and subsequently to fully map the patterns of poverty and social exclusion that resulted from the rapid process of economic decline, which was especially evident in the south Wales valleys. These patterns of change were also experienced in other areas of the UK and Europe and the research was guided by a dynamic literature on social class, which moved from structuralism to post-structuralism to post-modernism as social theorists wrestled with a significant restructuring of capitalism as both an economic and social order.

With the benefit of hindsight of some twenty-five years it is now apparent that these changes were less located in the politics of the UK and more connected to an increasing globalization of the economy and an international ascendancy of neo-liberal economic practice that has increasingly marginalized and deregulated labour. More importantly, the research took place against a backdrop of the post-war settlement of improved working conditions, higher household incomes and an ever-widening welfare provision. On reflection, this was a temporary hiatus in a 200-year trend of widening inequalities under capitalism (Piketty, 2014); and the redistributive policies evident from 1945 to 1975 were fragile and easily reversed with considerable implications for the social structure evident today.

We can also now understand that there were considerable structural weaknesses in the Welsh economy in which Welsh coal and steel were not internationally competitive and in which subsequent diversification of the economy would be transitory and fragile as international capital searched for ever lower costs of production within a globalized economy. The consequence has been a stubborn refusal of the Welsh economy to achieve growth and it remains around 75 per cent efficient compared to the wider UK when measured by Gross Domestic Product (GDP) or Gross Value Added (GVA) based assessments of economic performance. Within Wales, regional disparities add to the picture of poor economic performance with the Gwent valleys only achieving 57.2 per cent GVA of the UK average in 2012. Only Cardiff and the Vale of Glamorgan achieve near the UK rate at 99.7 per cent (Stats Wales, 2014a).

These combined factors have a significant impact on the contemporary structure of Welsh society. The following sections will revisit and reflect on my earlier work and assess the extent to which the analysis of the 1990s has relevance for contemporary Wales. The discussion will also consider to what extent a conceptual revision is required to reflect current conditions, and offer some tentative recommendations to reverse the current trends that continue to position Wales as a nation characterized by pervasive inequalities. However, these recommendations are made with a consideration of the inability to do more than ameliorate the experience of poverty within the current Welsh socio-political structure.

Looking back

My research was grounded in the contemporary social science perspectives of the period (Meiksins-Wood, 1986; Bourdieu, 1984; Goldethorpe, 1980: Hindess, 1987; Poulantzas, 1975, 1978), which argued that class structures in post-war capitalism had become more complex and differentiated. These conceptualizations argued that there was a need to move beyond conventional Marxist class analysis, which could be simplistically represented as a division between a proletariat and a bourgeoisie. Often posed at the time as a distinction between Marxist and Weberian analysis, there was a shared concern to map the increasingly nuanced relationship that social groups had to capital. It was a relationship that had become more mediated and negotiated through a range of social institutions and more intricate patterns of ownership and control of the means of production.

In sociology, class analysis reached a peak at this time with a range of concerns about social structure, social mobility, class consciousness, social class patterns of consumption and the political manifestations of class identity. Crompton (2008) identifies three strands in class analysis: a macro-level interest in large-scale occupational class surveys, accounts of the historical developments of social classes and interest in the consumption patterns of class formations. There was also an emerging view that class was waning in significance, politically and culturally, and that sociology must also concern itself with alternative structures of power and inequality, especially those of race and gender. These interests were to develop significantly to lead ultimately to a decline of class analysis, only occasionally lifted by renewed interest. More recently class analysis has been concerned with widening inequalities in British society and a general lack of social mobility (Savage et al., 2013).

However, in the period dealt with here, social class was probably the core concern of sociology. My research attempted to locate Wales, and the sociology of Wales, centrally in this diverse literature. Heavily influenced by Marxist, post-Marxist and neo-Marxist theorists, I was particularly concerned to identify and understand changes in working-class socio-cultural and political practices. The work of Poulantzas (1975, 1978) was influential and identified the concept of a fracturing of traditional social-class patterns. It was this approach that appeared to me best placed to describe and analyse the changes in Welsh society that could be observed at the time.

Consequently, I identified a fracturing of a historical monolithic industrial working class into three separate fractions to create a 'tri-partite' class structure emerging in modern Wales (Adamson, 2001). Whilst recognizing the historical differentiation within the working class, the research identified an emerging, more exaggerated separation, which influenced social practices, cultural consumption and political behaviours. In keeping with the wider theories of the time, this was not conceived of as the emergence of new classes. Fundamental relationships to capital and its ownership and control were unchanged but were mediated through different employment and managerial patterns. Nor did I recognize the emergence of an 'underclass' (Adamson, 1996) in Wales with consciously elective patterns of behaviour grounded in lone parenthood, economic inactivity and welfare dependency (Murray, 1989).

Instead the three identified working-class fractions remained bound to a subordinate relationship to capital with little economic power or control over the relations of production in which they were located. It was rather that the experience of those relations was differentiated by ideologically and culturally driven patterns of perception and behaviour. This approach distanced the work from more economistic and deterministic conceptions of the relationship between capital and labour and introduced cultural elements into the understanding of class behaviours. The three class fractions were the traditional working class, the new working class and the marginalized working class.

The traditional working class

This class fraction was identified as the element of the population either still employed in traditional manual occupations or with recent histori-cal connections to these occupations. Despite the decline of coal and steel production in the 1980s, many allied industries and heavy manu-facturing activities survived in Wales and manufacturing remains an important element of the Welsh economy to this day at 21 per cent of GVA (Stats Wales, 2014b). Furthermore, those elements of the work-force forced into economic inactivity by redundancy from the traditional industries retained their political praxis and cultural patterns of consumption (Adamson, 2001). The traditional working class engaged with Labour Party voting in the main, were supportive of trade union-ism and demonstrated generally collectivist behaviours. In this way, the traditional patterns of working-class life survived, visibly, and to some extent they still dominate to this day in areas like the south Wales valleys.

The new working class

It was also possible to identify, within the diversifying economy, new forms of economic activity that created a more differentiated work-force. In particular, activities associated with regional relocation of major state administrative agencies such as the Driver and Vehicle Licensing Agency (DVLA) and Passport Office, the development of a financial services sector and a burgeoning retail sector created a large number of jobs that could be perceived of as 'white collar'. Although later recognized as a 'proletarianisation' of white-collar professional and technical services rather than an 'embourgeoisement' of working-class roles, these locations in the workforce created a different relationship with capital, which could be perceived as more 'middle-class' in popular culture and social class identification (Adamson, 2001). Following Bourdieu (1984), I identified changing cultural and consumption practices with lifestyle choices more associated with the middle class. This included physical movement to places of work and residence along the M4 corridor as well as changing political allegiances that favoured Plaid Cymru in areas previously regarded as Labour strongholds.

The marginalized working class

It was also evident that there was an increasingly marginal class fraction emerging with a long-term disconnection from the economy and effectively excluded from the emerging labour market of the 1980s onwards. Primarily, the labour shed by traditional industries had declined into what would become long-term disaffection and disengagement. Additionally, annually throughout the 1990s, cohorts of school leavers joined the economically inactive population. They left education with poor skills and without prospect of anything other than unemployment or precarious employment in deregulated work with low wages. Casualized conditions of service were the norm and they had little prospect of permanent employment, let alone career security and development. In large part, a generation of these individuals joined the ranks of an increasingly socially excluded section of Welsh society. Nowhere was this more visible than on the marginalized housing estates of the south Wales valleys, where this fraction of the working class became residualized in social housing. High levels of crime, substance misuse, alcohol misuse, lone parenthood, school avoidance and general economic inactivity became a stereotype for many south Wales communities, a stereotype with a very strong foundation in the social reality of life on our large estates.

A review

Having outlined the major elements of the research findings of the 1990s, I will now review to what extent is as an accurate assessment of the class structure of the Welsh social formation and what, if any, insights developed at that time remain salient for an understanding of contemporary Welsh society. To achieve this, I will draw on recent class analysis and empirical investigation, employing some of the findings of the Great British Class Survey of 2012 (Savage et al., 2013). The survey employed a web-based questionnaire administered through the BBC which acquired 161,400 respondents. Following concerns over bias within this sample, it was supplemented by a representative sample survey of a further 1,026 respondents. The methodology sought to include elements of class identity deriving from access to economic, social and cultural capital (Savage et al., 2013) in a more sophisticated understanding of socio-cultural influences on class identity than was available to me in the 1990s.

In reviewing the essential framework of work in the 1990s, I would suggest that the tri-partite class structure identified in the 1990s was a reasonably accurate portrayal of divisions opening in the structure of the Welsh working class. It was also correctly identified as the consequence of de-industrialization and a transition to a post-industrial economy and society. In relation to specific components of the analysis it can perhaps be better considered as a snapshot located in a specific process of change that continues to evolve. My work at the time lent it a sense of permanence that I would not now recognize and would rather identify as more dynamic and less static. At the time, I envisaged a consolidation of the traditional working class and an expansion of the new middle class. I also assumed that the marginalized working class would be reintegrated into these primary fractions through appropriate social and economic policy.

Historically, class structures have been relatively permanent and subject to slow patterns of change within any specific mode of production. Whilst the broad parameters determined by relations of production have remained largely unchanged within capitalism, the period since the 1980s has seen much more fluid socio-cultural patterns of class behaviours and cultures. A more succinct and detailed understanding is required of how different relationships to the means of production have emerged within classes. This leads to an identification of patterns of change that shift more rapidly than envisaged in the 1980s and 1990s. The findings of the Great British Class Survey (GBCS) (Savage et al., 2013) point to the saliency of the class fractions that I identified in the 1990s but also to the continued fragmentation of the class structure since that time.

In relation to specific fractions within the tri-partite model the following observations can be made. The traditional working class is generally recognized to have diminished numerically and in cultural and political significance (Savage et al., 2013). Simply by population attrition, those employed in the latter days of the dominant Welsh traditional working-class labour market have declined in number. Furthermore, the continued decline of traditional occupational roles in industrial and manufacturing settings has ensured that there has been no replenishment of this class fraction. Savage et al. suggest that this class represents 14 per cent of the population at the UK level and has little economic, social or cultural capital. With a household income of £13,000 per year in 2011 it is likely that this group is significant in the rise of 'in-work' poverty, particularly in Wales where the 'production' classification still contributes to 21 per cent of GVA (Stats Wales, 2014b).

The new working class is still clearly recognizable within Wales and has stabilized to be a core element of the class structure. Employment in routine clerical work, public services, the financial services sector, transport and in retail and leisure services has continued to develop and now provides significant employment opportunities, with a combined figure of 36 per cent of GVA (Stats Wales, 2014b). To some extent, this class has been severely affected by the great financial crisis and its leisure and consumption patterns can no longer be supported by cheap and easily available credit. Its lifestyle is dependent on 'moderate' (Savage et al., 2013, p. 237) household income and accrues only 'small amounts of savings'.

However, the new working class score well on the emerging cultural capital of sport, music and leisure cultures and are well connected socially. They originate in non-middle-class families and the group has relatively few graduates. The GBCS estimated the group to constitute 15 per cent of the population. The survey also identifies a further grouping of 'emergent service workers' who in my analysis of the 1990s would also have been part of the new working class. For Savage et al., this is a group with modest incomes of £21,000 with high levels of emerging social capital. It is also socially connected but with contacts with only moderate status scores. Savage et al. (2013, p. 246) see these classes as 'the children of the traditional working-class', which is entirely in keeping with the conclusions I drew in the 1990s.

The traditional working class and the new working class I identified in the 1990s as fractions of the working class remain evident in Wales. However, their political and social visibility in Wales has tended to be overshadowed by the necessary political and social policy focus on the poverty of the marginalized working class. Consequently, much of the remaining analysis will concern itself with the increasing scale and depth of poverty of that working-class fraction in Wales and the Welsh Government's response to this pervasive inequality.

The marginalized working class and poverty in Wales

Writing in the 1990s it was possible to see the emergence of this class fraction as a temporary hiatus in the emergence of a post-industrial Wales. It was reasonable to expect that with the correct policies and full political commitment to change, the tide of rising poverty would be turned. Writing in the 1990s, it was all too easy to see the 'new poverty' as a temporary symptom of industrial restructuring. It was hoped that this issue would eventually be resolved by economic diversification, reskilling of the workforce and ultimately a change of government, which would introduce policies that were more relevant to the post-industrial regions of the UK.

Writing in 1996, I identified a crisis that at the time was not being addressed by any political party or state agency in Wales: 'There is a crisis deep in the heart of Welsh society but no one speaks of it. There is a crisis which, if unresolved will waste the lives of a substantial proportion of a generation of Welsh people' (Adamson, 1996, p. 5). However, I did not envisage the continuation of a situation that would impact three generations; a social landscape in which poverty would become normalized as the dominant social experience for nearly a quarter of the Welsh population and almost a third of our children. In hindsight this was a naive and simplistic assumption given that for many of the communities concerned no attempt was made to address the fundamental lack of employment that had created the marginalized working class in the first place.

The election of a Labour government in 1997 with a clear commitment to poverty eradication significantly contributed to my optimism of the 1990s. I was also involved by 2001 in the drafting of Welsh policy in the form of Communities First to echo the UK Strategy for Neighbourhood Renewal with its New Deal for Communities that targeted the most deprived communities for specific support. In Wales, Communities First focused on 132 initial communities with an innovative approach to community-led regeneration. This approach stemmed from a new understanding of poverty as the consequence of a pattern of social exclusion.

Borrowing from European models of citizenship, poverty was seen as a consequence of sections of the population becoming excluded from their fundamental ability to participate as full citizens. For the French, this was a failure of the state rather than of the individual, in contrast to the Anglo-Saxon view of poverty as the fault of the poor. In conventional welfare models poverty was resolved through redistributive taxation and policies that effectively took money from the better-off sections of society and gave it to those experiencing poverty. In this model poverty was seen as simply a lack of financial resource.

In theories of social exclusion poverty is seen as a set of negative relationships to wider society experienced by the poor. Patterns of social exclusion result in poor health performance, low educational attainment and negative patterns of collective behaviour at a neighbourhood level. The policies to tackle social exclusion are therefore not redistributive but rather based on the need to change those negative relationships. Consequently, attempts were made to reverse social exclusion by the development of spatially targeted programmes of community development to improve collective and individual capacity to engage with society and particularly access employment opportunities. It was argued that by challenging the cultural patterns of behaviour that had emerged in our poorest communities, a reintegration of 'disaffected' people would eradicate poverty.

However, despite nearly fifteen years of such policies in Wales, little has changed for the poor (Adamson, 2008). According to the Joseph

Rowntree Foundation (2013), currently 23 per cent of the population live in low-income households, defined as below 60 per cent of median income, after housing costs. More worryingly 31 per cent of children in Wales live in such households. Whilst there has been little change in the level of poverty since around 2000 there has been some shift in the pattern of those experiencing poverty. Pensioner poverty has reduced to around 12 per cent of pensioners compared to 19 per cent in 2003. Correspondingly, working-age poverty now stands at 58 per cent compared to 50 per cent in 2003. Most fundamentally, 'in-work' poverty in Wales is now the largest category with 51 per cent of those experiencing poverty compared to ten years ago when benefit-related poverty was the most significant cause. However, there are significant regional variations in this relationship and in the south Wales valleys worklessness remains the primary cause of poverty.

These statistics translate into a poverty of social experience for a significant proportion of people in Wales. In 2012–13, a third of the population were 'struggling from time to time' to pay bills and 12 per cent experienced a 'constant struggle' (Welsh Government, 2013a). Food poverty has risen as a significant element of the experience of poverty in Wales where use of food banks is proportionally higher than other UK regions with 711,000 food contributions for a population of 3 million compared to Scotland with 639,000 contributions for a population of 5 million (Cooper et al., 2014). The same report identifies that increased food-bank provision is not the driver of a 120 per cent increase in food-bank use in Wales during 2013 and 2014. Generally, there is recognition that welfare reform has been the significant driver of food poverty with some 31 per cent of food-bank referrals resulting from benefit delays.

Welfare reform also significantly threatens major rises in the level of poverty with the Welsh Government estimating that current reforms will remove over £900,000 per year from the Welsh economy in 2015–16. This constitutes an average loss of income of £500 per working-age adult in Wales (Welsh Government, 2013b). Importantly, this loss is not evenly distributed and areas with high-benefit dependency will experience greater losses. In reality, it is our already poorest communities that will experience the greatest loss of personal income with an identifiable 'multiplier' effect on the local economy to add further to the poor economic performance in key areas of Wales.

In the Great British Class Survey this group is referred to as the 'precariat', a term borrowed from Standing (2011). With household income of only £8,000 and negligible saving (Savage et al., 2013) this group scores low on social, cultural and economic capital. It is largely located in old industrial areas and represented by 'the unemployed, van drivers, cleaners, carpenters, care workers, cashiers and postal workers' (p. 243).

In Wales, economic inactivity contributes significantly to the permanence of this class fraction and its spatial concentration in the south Wales valleys, and some of our city peripheral estates, has presented a long-term policy challenge for the Welsh Government. The following section will examine how this has shaped much of devolved policy since 1999, and reflect on the outcomes and limitations of these policies in the Welsh context.

Poverty, politics and policy

In the work I conducted in the 1990s, I was also concerned with the impact of the emerging tri-partite class structure on Welsh politics. I suggested at the time that for the new working class, a departure from the Labour-dominated politics of the traditional working class was possible. As one element of emerging consumption patterns, I argued that the new patterns of home ownership, a physical movement to the coastal belt and M4 corridor, and changing voting patterns were all demonstrative of a new working class distinguishing itself from the traditional working class through patterns of consumption of physical, cultural and political goods (Bourdieu, 1984).

In a general trend, over ten years Labour lost control of local authorities in Wales with a decline from sixteen of the twenty-two local authorities in 1998 to controlling only two, Neath Port Talbot and Rhondda Cynon Taf, by 2008. There is no clear alternative dominant party in this shift, with Liberal Democrat, Plaid and Conservative gains leading to a majority of councils with 'no overall control' by 2008 (IWA, 2014). I interpreted the initial loss of key local authorities to Plaid Cymru and Liberal Democrats as indicative of a destabilization of the Labour vote deriving from changing class identities. In retrospect, and when factoring in both general elections and elections to the Welsh Assembly, we can see that there is no clear trend and that this shift is indicative of a more generally fluid UK and Welsh political scene. Just as coalition was the outcome for the 2010 UK General Election this was foreshadowed in the 2007 election to the Welsh Assembly. Plaid Cymru gained at the expense of Labour, robbing them of an overall majority. Following failed negotiations for coalition with the Liberal Democrat and Conservative parties, Plaid entered the One Wales Coalition with Labour. However, Labour regained seats in 2011 allowing it to form a government with exactly half of the seats.

Perhaps the major connection between class fracturing and political change in Wales has been the falling electoral turnout at General Elections – down to 64.7 per cent in 2010 from a high of 84.8 per cent in 1950. More worryingly, turnout for Welsh Government elections has been as low as 38 per cent in 2003, only rallying slightly to 42.2 per cent in 2011 (UK Political Info, 2014). These figures suggest a wider disinterest in politics that is reflected elsewhere in the UK and indicates a growing disengagement from party politics and the electoral system. Without further research in the Welsh context, it is only possible to conjecture that this reflects rising levels of poverty that reinforce the general tendency of low-income sections of the population to disengage from the political and democratic process.

This in itself becomes an element of the wider pattern of social exclusion evident for the marginalized working class in Wales (Electoral Commission, 2005). Consequently, I conclude that the major political shifts I anticipated as arising from the emergence of a class fracturing in Wales during the 1980s and 1990s have not materialized, and that political fluctuations have been more influenced by wider UK party political processes. Only the rise of poverty and an associated political disaffection can be identified with changes in the class structure, with what has become an embedded and permanent marginalized working class.

If politics has only been partly influenced by the rise of poverty in Wales, the policies pursued by Welsh Government have in contrast been heavily influenced by the extent of poverty. It is clear that the direction of policy implemented by Welsh Government has been significantly skewed by the need to directly tackle the consequences of poverty in the health, education, housing and employment policy domains. By the time of its first administration in 1999 poverty was the central challenge facing the newly elected ministers. A range of initial policy documents addressed this fact including *Better Wales.com* (WAG, 2000); *Wales: A Better Country* (WAG, 2002) and *Wales: A Learning Country* (WAG, 2003).

Consistently, since that period, anti-poverty initiatives have been a core component of the programmes of subsequent administrations. A complex policy platform has developed addressing related poverty issues in Wales and in general terms has attracted cross party support, particularly for the central programme, Communities First. Currently, the three core anti-poverty policies are Communities First, Families First and Flying Start. These collectively recognize the communal, family and early-years patterns of reproduction of poverty, and attempt to break the dominance of the cultural experiences of poverty in Wales.

These policies form the heart of the current *Tackling Poverty Action Plan* (Welsh Government, 2012). Prior to the cabinet reshuffle of September 2014, there was a minister and deputy minister charged with tackling poverty in Wales, indicating the centrality of the issue to the Welsh Government. Poverty is also regarded as a whole government issue in the current administration's *Programme for Government* (Welsh Government, 2011), with the current *Tackling Poverty Action Plan* and its updates (Welsh Government, 2012 and 2014) providing the overarching framework across departments and integrating the monitoring of impact of a range of Welsh Government policies. Additionally, Welsh Government has engaged with local authorities through the creation of Anti-Poverty Champions where each local authority nominates a senior officer and an elected member to coordinate local authority anti-poverty actions. Ministers have also been supported by a panel of external experts convened as the Tackling Poverty External Advisory Group, chaired by Professor David Egan, a leading expert in educational inequalities. These range of policies and supporting structures indicate a key intention on the part of Welsh Government to address the critical levels of poverty evident in Wales.

Welsh Government also shares the UK Government's legally enshrined requirement to eradicate poverty by 2020, a target no commentator with any knowledge of the issue believes is possible to achieve. As well as the impact of welfare reform in Wales already discussed, it is evident that the primary policy levers are not in the hands of the Welsh Government. Taxation, welfare policy and minimum wage levels are the primary means of addressing financial poverty and these are currently non-devolved issues. However, routes out of poverty are also influenced by educational qualifications, skills levels and economic policy, and these are within the remit of Welsh Government.

It is not possible to review the range of policies in any detail within the scope of this chapter. I have examined Communities First elsewhere (Adamson, 2010a; Adamson and Bromiley, 2013) and there are additional commentaries (WAO, 2009) that suggest an overall failure of that specific programme to change the poverty rate in Wales. Whilst this is clearly evident, it is also the case that programmes such as Communities First, Flying Start and Families First generally target individual, family and community experiences of poverty and the interventions they marshal are not in themselves capable of reducing poverty measured as a financial characteristic. Rather, they address what I have termed elsewhere the 'lived experience of poverty' (Adamson, 2010b) in trying to improve the skills and capacity to deal with poverty and enable families to improve their quality of life and the future life chances of their children. In this they can be seen as tackling social exclusion, which results from financially defined poverty. However, this suggests that in the quest to eradicate poverty they are ameliorative and cannot tackle the fundamental causes of poverty in Wales.

In recognition of the perceived failure of such programmes and the stubborn resistance of financial poverty to respond to the host of policies developed in Wales, in 2013 with Dr Mark Lang, I conducted a major study of the town of Tredegar. We explored what actions were necessary to achieve social, economic and environmental sustainability by 2030. This included the objective of eradicating or significantly reducing the incidence of poverty. We developed the 'Deep Place' (Adamson and Lang, 2014) methodology to establish a detailed mapping of issues and opportunities and engaged with a wide range of local and academic expertise to identify a range of action points, which were based on successful interventions here and elsewhere in Europe and North America.

Our fundamental conclusion was that whilst Welsh Government had a wide range of policies to tackle housing, health, educational and transport inequalities these did not address the 'cause of the causes of poverty'. Borrowing this approach from Marmot (2010), we concluded that the root of the pattern of poverty evident in places like Tredegar lies in a poor economic performance at community level that reduces personal productivity, creates significant levels of worklessness and establishes a cultural acceptance of poverty by residents and all the agencies that deliver services to the locality. Fundamentally, we argued for a revitalization of the local economy to provide work opportunities, which could match the local skill range and capabilities of a population separated from the labour market for nearly thirty years.

Much of this approach was informed by the work of the Centre for Research on Socio-cultural Change (CRESC) based at the Manchester

University Business School. This work suggests that governments 'frame' the economy in a very specific way, influenced by neo-liberal economic approaches that enshrine short-term profitability and GDP growth (Johal et al., 2014). This prompts governments to support economic development in the high technology, fashionable economic sectors. This 'framing' of the economy favours sectors such as pharmaceuticals, aerospace and the automotive industries. Consequently, there is little investment in what is termed the 'foundational economy' associated with meeting the 'mundane' needs of the general population. Bentham et al. (2013) argue that all sections of the population require food, energy, education, health care, transport and housing. This foundational economy employs about 30 per cent of the population and draws around 30 per cent of household expenditure. Attention to and promotion of the foundational economy could provide major opportunity for local employment growth.

In applying this model to Tredegar we identified food production, energy conservation and generation, care provision and remote working and trading as potential sectors that would provide opportunities for growth of the local economy and the employment of local populations. The sectors identified by Welsh Government for economic development have some potential to support the foundational economy. The original six sectors announced in the 2010 *Economic Renewal* document (Welsh Government, 2010) and supplemented by an additional three sectors in 2011 include energy and environment, food and farming, tourism and construction, all with potential for developing the foundational economy in some of the most disadvantaged regions of Wales. However, the major emphasis remains on ICT, advanced materials and manufacturing, life sciences, and financial and professional services.

Furthermore, policy is set within a framework of large-scale infrastructural development, making Wales a more attractive location for foreign direct investment and an export-based model of growth achievement. This approach to economic development is clearly an essential component of the modernization of the Welsh economy but it will not address poverty through the development of appropriately skilled and rewarded work opportunities for the marginalized working class. Developments derived from this model tend to be highly skilled, located on the development corridors of the M4 and A55 and do not reach into the communities where poverty is now endemic.

Consequently, a 'reframing' of economic policy is required, which specifically targets the foundational economy and the populations that require integration into the labour market as the only long-term solution for their poverty. In the Deep Place report (Adamson and Lang, 2014) we also identify the fundamental challenges of poor health and the low educational and skills outcomes of the local population. These are additional challenges that must be adequately addressed if communities like Tredegar are to achieve a reasonable quality of life and play a productive and sustainable role in the Welsh economy. In short we need an economic policy that directly engages with the marginalized working class.

Conclusions

In reviewing work that was initiated over twenty years ago, it is sobering to conclude that the phenomenon of what was then termed the 'new poverty' has become embedded as the key feature of Welsh society. Spatially concentrated in the south Wales coalfield region, the major shifts in economic patterns of production and employment experienced in the 1980s continue to influence contemporary Welsh society. In reality, many communities in Wales have never recovered from the mid-1980s recession and the disruption to communal and family patterns of social cohesion experienced at that time have become normalized as the dominant social experience for a significant part of the Welsh population.

The extent of poverty, and its, now, endemic characteristics, have posed the most fundamental difficulties for developing effective social policy in Wales and continue to condition the programmes developed by successive administrations in Welsh Government. The distortion of the social policy agenda in Wales by the need to address poverty is particularly evident in the domains of education and health provision. By all recognized measures, Wales trails significantly in both health and educational outcomes, largely as a consequence of poverty. The long-term experience of poverty has led to low aspirations becoming the norm in attitudes to personal health and educational attainment and the consequences are posing a significant challenge to the very survival of the health service (Longley, 2013) and ensure that subsequent cohorts of school leavers are unable to participate effectively in the economy.

Reversing this pattern has now become a task that requires a Beveridge scale programme of state intervention and cultural change that is almost impossible to imagine in the current climate of neo-liberal economic orthodoxy, austerity measures and welfare erosion. At the UK level welfare provision has become delegitimized in popular and political culture and empathy with the poorest sections of the population has significantly diminished (Park et al., 2012). For the poor themselves there is often a cultural acceptance of poverty as the norm and no expectation that their personal situation will change. This suggests that poverty is now established as a permanent feature of British and Welsh society without the prospect of serious political commitment to its eradication from any major political party. In this, the voice for social justice evident in the Scottish campaign for independence is being ignored by the Westminster parties and despite the good intentions of Welsh Government, without major policy change at the UK level, the best that can be achieved in Wales is a limited amelioration of the effects of poverty.

References

Adamson, D., *Living on the Edge. Poverty and Deprivation in Wales* (Llandysul: Gomer Press, 1996).

——, 'Social segregation in a working-class community: economic and social change in the south Wales coalfield', in G. Van Guys, H. De Witte and P. Pasture (eds), *Can Class Still Unite? The Differentiated Work Force, Class Solidarity and Trade Unions* (Aldershot: Ashgate, 2001), pp. 101–28.

——, 'Still Living on the Edge', *Contemporary Wales*, 21 (2008), 47–66.

——, 'Community Empowerment: Identifying the Barriers To "Purposeful" Citizen Participation', *International Journal of Sociology and Social Policy*, 30/3 and 4 (2010a), 114–26.

——, *The Impact of Devolution: Area-based Regeneration Policies in the UK* (York: Joseph Rowntree Foundation, 2010b).

—— and Bromiley R., 'Community Empowerment. Learning from Practice in Community Regeneration', *International Journal of Public Sector Management*, 26/3 (2013), 190–202.

—— and Lang, M., *Toward a Deep Place Approach to Equitable and Sustainable Places* (Merthyr Tydfil: Centre for Regeneration Excellence Wales (CREW), 2014).

Bentham, J., Bowman, A., de la Cuesta, M., Engelen, E., Erturk, I., Folkman, P., Froud, J., Johal, S., Law, J., Leaver, A., Moran, M. and Williams, K., *Manifesto for the Foundational Economy* (Manchester: CRESC, 2013).

Bourdieu, P., *Distinction. A Social Critique of the Judgment of Taste* (London: Routledge, Kegan Paul, 1984).

Crompton, R., *Class and Stratification* (3rd edn; Cambridge: Polity, 2008).

Cooper, N., Purcell, S. and Jackson, R., *Below the Breadline: The Relentless Rise of Food Poverty in Britain* (Oxford: Church Action on Poverty, Oxfam and Trussell Trust, 2014).

Electoral Commission, *Social Exclusion and Political Engagement: Research Report* (London: Electoral Commission, 2005).

Goldethorpe, J., *Social Mobility and Class Structure in Modern Britain* (Oxford: Clarendon Press, 1980).

Hindess, B., *Politics and Class Analysis* (Oxford: Blackwell, 1987).

Institute of Welsh Affairs (IWA), *Wales Factfile: Welsh Democracy* (2014), *www. clickonwales.org/wp-content/uploads/13_Factfile_Democracy_6.pdf* (accessed 20 September 2014).

Johal, S., Law, J. and Williams, K., *From Publics to Congregations? GDP and its Others*, CRESC Working Paper Series no. 136 (Manchester: CRESC, 2014).

Joseph Rowntree Foundation, *Monitoring Poverty and Social Exclusion in Wales 2013* (York: Joseph Rowntree Foundation, 2013).

Lash, S. and Urry, J., *The End of Organized Capitalism* (Cambridge: Polity Press, 1987).

Longley, M., 'Demand and Budget Cuts will Force Health Change', *Agenda* (winter 2013), 25.

Marmot, M., *Fair Society, Healthy Lives. The Marmot Review. Strategic Review of Health Inequalities in England post-2010* (London: UCL, 2010).

Meiksins-Wood, E., *The Retreat from Class: A New 'True' Socialism* (London: Verso, 1986).

Murray, C. 'The emerging British underclass', in C. Murray, *Charles Murray and the Underclass* (London: Institute of Economic Affairs, Health and Welfare Unit, 1989).

Park, A., Clery, E., Curtis, J., Phillips, M. and Utting D. (eds), *British Social Attitudes: The 29th Report* (London: NatCen Social Research, 2012).

Piketty, T., *Capital in the Twenty-First Century*, trans. A. Goldhammer (Harvard: Harvard University Press, 2014).

Poulantzas, N., *Classes in Contemporary Capitalism* (London: New Left Books, 1975).

——, *Political Power and Social Classes* (London: New Left Books, 1978).

Lash, S. and Urry, J., *The End of Organised Capitalism* (Cambridge: Policy Press, 1987).

Savage, M., Devine, F., Cunningham, N., Taylor, M., Li, Y., Hjellbrekke, J., Le Roux, B., Friedman, S. and Miles, A., 'A New Model of Social Class? Findings from the BBC's Great British Class Survey Experiment', *Sociology*, 47/2 (2013), 219–50.

Standing, G., *The Precariat: The New Dangerous Class* (London: Bloomsberg Academic, 2011).

Stats Wales, *Gross Value Added (UK=100) by Welsh NUTS3 Areas and Year* (2014a),*https://statswales.wales.gov.uk/Catalogue/Business-Economy-and-Labour-*

Market/Regional-Accounts/Gross-Value-Added-GDP/gva-by-welshnuts3areas-year (accessed 18 November 2015).

——, *Gross Value Added by area and industry* (2014b), *https://statswales.wales. gov.uk/Catalogue/Business-Economy-and-Labour-Market/Regional-Acc ounts/Gross-Value-Added-GDP/latestgva-by-area-industry and us* (accessed 18 November 2015).

UK Political Info (2014), *www.ukpolitical.info* (accessed 20 September 2014).

Wales Audit Office (WAO), *Communities First* (Cardiff: WAO, 2009).

Welsh Assembly Government (WAG), *Better Wales.com* (Cardiff: WAG, 2000).

——, *Wales: A Better Country* (Cardiff: WAG, 2002).

——, *Wales: A Learning Country* (Cardiff: WAG, 2003).

Welsh Government, *Economic Renewal: A New Direction* (Cardiff: Welsh Government, 2010).

——, *Programme for Government* (Cardiff: Welsh Government, 2011).

——, *Tackling Poverty Action Plan* (Cardiff: Welsh Government, 2012).

——, *National Survey for Wales, 2012–13: Financial Inclusion* (Cardiff: Welsh Government, 2013a).

——, *Analysing the impact of the UK Government's welfare reforms in Wales. Stage 3 analysis. Part 2. Impacts on local authority areas* (Cardiff: Welsh Government, 2013b).

——, *Building Resilient Communities: Taking Forward the Tackling Poverty Action Plan, Annual Report 2014* (Cardiff: Welsh Government, 2014).

Don't Attack Iraq – by Ian Homer

11

Women and Policy-making: Devolution, Civil Society and Political Representation

PAUL CHANEY

Introduction

This discussion revisits a chapter, 'Inclusive Government for Excluded Groups', which Sandra Betts, John Borland and I wrote for an edited collection *New Governance: New Democracy? Post-Devolution Wales* (Chaney, Hall and Pithouse, 2001). The chapter was written in the first months of the National Assembly. It discussed the potential implications of devolution for women's political representation in Wales, and was integral to the volume's reflection on the concept of 'inclusiveness'. Referred to at the time as 'the guiding concept that has been widely regarded as the key to the Assembly's future success' (Betts et al., 2001, p. 48), inclusiveness was an elastic term that had many meanings. It was variously a code for cross-party campaigning, as well as a cryptic reference to the proposed use of proportional representation in Assembly elections (anathema to many Labour and Conservative Party activists) (Chaney and Fevre, 2001). Yet it was principally employed as a unifying device to say that devolved politics would be different to the past. Not least it would deliver positive change by addressing the long-standing marginalization experienced by women and other social groups and identities.

Interviewed in 1999, many of the women quoted in the original chapter spoke of their high expectations for the new National Assembly. They expressed excitement and looked forward to significant change (see also Feld, 2000). For example, the representative of one leading women's umbrella organization said, 'it will be very exciting. I'm sure that because there are so many people, so many women that have been elected, it will reflect a lot of our concerns.' Similar optimism was echoed by the Women's Officer of a trade union who had 'a high expectation that it [the Assembly] could drive the agenda in a very positive way'; and the representative of a prominent voluntary group felt that 'it is going to give us a much larger voice ... I think it's very positive'. Here, almost a decade-and-a half on, this chapter reflects on developments since the Assembly opened its doors with reference to the nature and quality of women's political engagement, as well as the issues and challenges associated with representation and devolved policy work. Following an outline of the methodology, attention centres on political representation with reference to the political parties, the National Assembly, Welsh Government and public life. The chapter ends with the views of civil society organizations.

Methodology

The first part of the discussion is based on a series of studies conducted over the past fifteen years as well as secondary data sources including Assembly proceedings, policy documents and government reports. The second is based on seventy-five interviews undertaken in 2013–15 with managers of a purposive sample of third-sector organizations. Unlike 2001, these were not solely with 'women's organizations' but, further to the ethos of mainstreaming, they relate to a broad range of NGOs as it was decided to take views on gender equality from across the sector.

Political representation

Political parties

The number of women elected to the first National Assembly was much lauded. Forty per cent of AMs was a vast improvement on Wales's lamentable record of electing women MPs: to date, it is still the case that just thirteen women MPs have represented Welsh constituencies since the Acts of 'Union' in the early sixteenth century. The subsequent attainment of gender parity in the second Assembly was a high point, one celebrated as a world first (see Chaney 2003, 2006). There was a modest drop to 47 per cent following the 2007 elections. This striking and, viewed from the perspective of the 1980s and 1990s, unlikely progress was largely the result of positive action measures in candidate selection by Welsh Labour and Plaid Cymru (Chaney et al., 2007).

However, a sharp decline was widely anticipated for the fourth elections in 2011. As McAllister and Cole (2014, p. 184) note, such concerns were based on

> the rescinding of affirmative or positive action used in the first two elections by Labour and Plaid Cymru; the number of women standing down at this election (particularly Labour AMs who had been selected through the party's highly successful, but controversial, 'twinning' policy in 1999 and subsequently benefitting from incumbency); and the high proportion of women contesting marginal seats.

Ultimately, the decline in the number of women AMs (down to twenty-five or 42 per cent) was not as bad as feared (-5 percentage points). This was largely a function of Labour's electoral success, which prevented the loss of women previously selected using positive action measures. It was also helped by the Welsh Conservatives fielding more women candidates than in the past.

For Welsh Labour, as the bitter internal party disputes in Blaenau Gwent and the Cynon Valley attest, the use of all-women shortlists remains a divisive and contested issue. In March 2014 the party conference voted to use positive action measures in forthcoming elections including the decision to field women candidates in half of its winnable seats at the 2017 Welsh council elections and use all-women shortlists in the 2015 general election. In contrast Plaid Cymru decided that local parties will decide the candidates for council, Assembly and parliamentary elections; however, a gender balance will be required for the top two positions on its Assembly regional list. The Welsh Liberal Democrats have rejected all-women shortlists (but have also ruled out all-male shortlists) for Westminster and Assembly elections. The Welsh Conservatives have no mechanisms to increase the number of women selected. Overall, this combination of strategies means that there is a real prospect that the number of women AMs may fall following the 2016 elections.

However, whilst the fears about the 2011 elections were largely unrealized, evidence of systemic inequality can be seen in the number of women election candidates. Worryingly, in the 2011 Welsh general election under a third (30 per cent) were women; there were just 78 compared to 184 men (Brooks and ap Gareth, 2013, p. 8). This is a key concern and suggests that insufficient numbers of women are putting themselves forward as candidates and, notwithstanding gender equality rhetoric from all party leaders, internal selection procedures and party practices are not facilitating equal representation.

The National Assembly

There is mixed evidence on women's political representation in Wales's new national legislature. On a positive note, analysis of the 327 plenary debates held during the first term of the National Assembly provides evidence of how the 'critical mass' of women AMs elected in 1999 acted to promote substantive representation; in other words, the situation whereby women's priorities are reflected in policy and law-making (Chaney, 2006). The analysis affirms this relationship as 'probabilistic' rather than 'deterministic'. The gender-disaggregated incidence of selected key terms in political debate during the first Assembly reveals a significant difference between male and female parliamentarians, with as noted, women exhibiting a greater propensity to engage in debate on 'women's issues'. They account for between two-thirds to three-quarters of all interventions using the key terms analysed, namely inter alia, childcare, domestic abuse and equal pay.[1]

This is significant in a number of respects; not least because it provides empirical evidence of the difference that women parliamentarians make. It also underlines that the presence of women in the Assembly shapes the policy and legislative agenda. This is reinforced by the fact that women AMs had a significantly greater propensity than male AMs to *initiate* debate on the gender equality; and such cases comprised approximately two-thirds to three-quarters of all instances when such terms featured in plenary debate. This matters because it shows women AMs taking the lead in shaping the political agenda to advance substantive representation, and their presence is necessary to ensure such matters are addressed. The data also illustrate the role played by feminist activists elected to the first Assembly – key individuals drawn from a range of civil society organizations. These 'critical actors' intervene in debate much more frequently than other female colleagues and account for between, approximately, one-third and one-half of all women's interventions on the issues in plenary debates.

Feminist institutionalist theory (Kenny, 2007) underlines that the design of political institutions matters. Existing work (Chaney et al., 2007) has charted how measures such as the outlawing of sexist language and family-friendly working hours in the Assembly's Standing Orders, and the cross-party Standing Committee on Equality of Opportunity have been valuable in advancing women's representation. Thus, the data on the Equality Committee show how women AMs have used it to generally good effect to both scrutinize government policies and advance women's representation (Chaney, 2008). Analysis of the transcripts of committee proceedings during the second Assembly shows female AMs predominate in intervening on key topics in order to advance the representation of women, accounting for 84 per cent of the topics analysed.

This is significant in two important regards. It again underlines the need for equal representation for it demonstrates that women are more likely to shape the political agenda in order to advance women's interests. It also shows the value of institutional mechanisms such as the Equality Committee in advancing substantive representation. In addition, the data show how the committee acted as an important nexus between AMs and those outside the Assembly. Thus, when female and male advisors (or 'expert witnesses') to the committee are compared, the former accounted for 71 per cent of the references to the gender-equality related terms in the committee transcripts (Chaney, 2008), thereby underlining that women's engagement with the legislature is integral to the promotion of substantive representation.

However, there are also some concerns related to women's role in the policy and scrutiny work of the Assembly. A key example is the demise of the Equality Committee, in March 2011, when it was subsumed into the Communities, Equality and Local Government Committee. This means less committee time dedicated to equalities matters than before. Moreover, data reveal how, over the first three Assemblies to 2011, women constituted a minority of expert witnesses called to committees (Rumbul, 2013). Thus, they accounted for just a quarter (25.2 per cent) of expert witnesses from civil society organizations called before 387 meetings of seven committees held during the first Assembly. In the second Assembly (2003–7) the proportion increased to just under a third (31.8 per cent);[2] whilst in the third (2007–11) it remained at a similar level (32.7 per cent). When the first and third Assemblies are compared the number of women expert witnesses rose by just over a third (35 percentage points).

Such an increase reflects Assembly Commission Outreach Teams' engagement with representative and community groups to facilitate input into assembly business. This is one of a series of such initiatives seen over past years aimed at boosting women's engagement through affirmative action. Other examples include 'Step up Cymru!'[3] The Women in Public Life Development Scheme, and Women Making a Difference. The latter is a programme that has also been central in providing women with opportunities to engage with public life by offering a range of courses, mentoring and role shadowing. It has proven impact and has led to positions for women in public life such as community councillors and public appointments. While these measures are invaluable, their modest size and resources are unequal to the scale of structural and cultural transformation needed. When the different sectors are compared women constitute a higher percentage of expert witnesses from third-sector organizations (40 per cent) compared to those from public bodies (33 per cent in the third Assembly – up from 23 per cent 1999–2003) and the private sector (17 per cent). Yet for each sector it remains the case that it is men that predominate in engaging with Assembly committees.

Analysis of the Assembly's proceeding shows how women AMs use the breadth of institutional mechanisms to promote women's representation. For example, Written Assembly Questions (WAQs) are tabled by opposition and backbench AMs and are a procedural mechanism to scrutinize the actions of Welsh ministers. Analysis of 2,467 WAQs asked during the second Assembly 2003–7 reveals that women AMs had a markedly greater propensity than their male counterparts to ask questions about 'equal pay, domestic abuse, women's health and childcare' (or 74 per cent of the total) (Chaney, 2008, p. 279).

Given its iconic status, a symbol of the putative 'new politics', it was particularly important that the new legislature led by example as an employer. In this regard the Assembly Commission has made good progress in securing gender balance in staffing. In contrast to the Welsh Office, women make up just over a half of all employees (51.1 per cent of the workforce) and, in 2012–13, exactly half of the senior management team were women. In addition, they constituted 50.9 per cent of the top three grades and 61.4 per cent of management grades (NAfW, 2013, p. 34).

Welsh Government

During the early years of devolution successive Assembly – and later Welsh Government – administrations were strong on rhetoric about mainstreaming gender and other modes of equality into the work of government. However, previous studies have identified a disjuncture between this espousal of gender equality and policy outcomes (Chaney, 2010, 2013). Problems included the setting of imprecise policy objectives and generalized goals that precluded meaningful assessment. Moreover, comprehensive examination of the work of government departments and policy outputs found attention to gender equality to be highly variable across portfolios (Chaney, 2011). In turn, this was the product of an under-resourced equality unit within the bureaucracy, one that lacked the institutional power to transform policy-making.

Since 2011, there has been an improvement. One key difference seen over the past three years is the setting of clear and legally enforceable policy goals. Thus, gender features in the Welsh Government's Equality Objectives, a statutory requirement under the Equality Act 2010 (Statutory Duties) (Wales) Regulations 2011. Examples include: 'to work with partners to identify and address the causes of the gender, ethnicity and disability pay and employment differences' (Objective 2); 'to reduce the incidence of all forms of violence against women, domestic abuse, "honour" based violence, hate crime, bullying and elder abuse' (Objective 4); and to 'improve the engagement and participation of under-represented groups in public appointments' (Objective 7).

There is also evidence of a more systematic attention to developing the evidence base and improving equality information held by the Welsh Government. Compared to past practice there are now enhanced monitoring and review processes in place including greater use of Equality Impact Assessments. According to a recent statutory assessment by the compliance authority, the Equality and Human Rights Commission Wales, this shift has led to 'progress on outcomes'. It noted that 'there were good examples of progress being made in relation to age, sex, race, disability and sexual orientation' (Mitchell et al., 2014, p. 8). According to the EHRC review 'a great deal of progress had already been achieved'. Cited examples included: 'organisations demonstrat[ing] steps they had taken to review and address the gender pay gap' and 'colleges and universities [... making] progress in a number of areas including ... addressing gender stereotyped subject choices, gender segregated career paths and the consequences for seniority and pay' (Mitchell et al., 2014, p. 32).

However, such progress needs to be seen in the context of the formidable scale of the prevailing policy challenge. Women and girls in

Wales continue to experience deep-set patterns and processes of inequality and discrimination. For example, they are twice as likely as men to be victims of sexual violence, or of non-sexual violence by their partner or family; they are by far the most likely to be victims of rape (90 per cent of offences were committed against females); and with regard to fear of crime, more women feel unsafe than men (8 per cent of 16–59-year-old women compared with 1 per cent of men), and 20 per cent of older women feel unsafe. Moreover, women continue to experience significant segregation within the Welsh labour market. They are concentrated into health, education and administrative work and are more likely to report being discriminated against regarding promotion than men. In addition, women are more likely to live in low-income households than men (this is principally because most lone parents, a group with a high risk of low income, are women) (EHRC, 2011).

Notwithstanding such challenges another aspect of political representation that has seen significant progress as a result of devolution is women's presence as ministers in successive Welsh Government cabinets.[4] The number of women ministers has increased from 40 per cent in 1999, to a world first with gender parity – and then a majority – in the cabinet between 2000 and 2007. It is a pattern broadly mirrored by junior ministerial posts for the number of women rises from a zero-base in 1999, peaks at three-quarters 2009–11 and falls to a third thereafter (Brooks and ap Gareth, 2013, p. 9). This is significant for ministerial posts afford women power to challenge male norms and shape the policy agenda. Analysis shows how this operates in plenary debates. Data covering the first Assembly show that women predominated in ministerial interjections on 'women's issues', typically accounting for two-thirds to three-quarters of all such interventions (Chaney, 2006, p. 699). Similar evidence of women ministers acting to advance gender equality can be found in analysis of the papers and minutes of the cabinet meetings held during the first Assembly (Chaney, 2005). These record women ministers intervening in cabinet discussions in order to promote women's interests across the breadth of policy portfolios.

At the outset of devolution many in the political classes repeatedly stated the need to avoid replicating the male-dominated institutional culture of the Welsh Office (Chaney et al., 2000), the territorial ministry that served Wales from 1964 to 1999. Whilst it is clear that there has been some progress in this regard, it is also the case that gender disparities remain. For example, of the Welsh Government's 5,560 strong workforce, women constitute a majority (58 per cent). Yet, they make up less than half of the senior civil service (42.9 per cent) and Executive Band 1 and 2 posts (38 and 44.8 per cent, respectively), whereas they constitute almost two-thirds (62.9 per cent) of the lowest grade Team Support roles (Welsh Government, 2014a, p.18).

Current data also indicate that more needs to be done with regard to equalities training for, of the 5,560 employees, 1,900 women and 1,190 men – just 55.6 per cent of the workforce – have attended core training (Welsh Government, 2014b, p.4). This is notwithstanding the fact that just months after the Assembly was founded, in April 2000, the Assembly's Equality Committee published its 'Baseline Equality Audit'. It stated: 'Training: It was considered by almost all Divisions that there is a need for greater equality awareness training within the Assembly ... It was suggested that innovative ways of meeting these requirements *should be looked at as a matter of urgency'* (NAfW, 2000, p. 3; emphasis added). Fifteen years on it remains an issue that has yet to be fully addressed. The latest Welsh Government Equality Strategy states:

> we recognise that reporting on training completed from our core offerings does not go far enough. We are in the process of developing an individual record for each employee that will be aligned to the performance management cycle which will give details of training applied for (successfully or otherwise) and completed by protected characteristic. The new platform will be in place to allow for a full reporting cycle from 2014–15. (Welsh Government, 2014b, p. 31)

Public life

Halfway through the second decade of the twenty-first century women continue to be marginalized and under-represented in many aspects of public life in Wales. For example, only one of the country's twenty-two council leaders is a woman. In charting a modest rise in the number of women elected to local government from 18.2 per cent in 1999 to 26.3 per cent in 2012, the Electoral Reform Society (2012, p. 1) paints a bleak picture:

> At this slow rate of progress women will not have an equal voice in Welsh local authorities until 2076. Decisions about the future of key services and council tax levels will continue to be made with too few women around the table. At the current rate of progress a girl born today will have to wait until retirement before she will have an equal say in how her local council is run.

Elsewhere fifteen years of devolved governance has signally failed to address gender inequality in many other aspects of Welsh public life. The litany includes: no women amongst Wales's four police and crime commissioners (with women making up just 13 per cent of candidates for such posts); and no females in charge of the country's three fire and rescue authorities (in two authorities women constitute just 21 per cent of members and they make up a quarter in the other). In local health boards women total just 14 per cent of chairs and 43.1 per cent of board members. They constitute 40 per cent of Wales's public commissioners, for example, the older people's, children's and Welsh language. Furthermore, just 10 per cent of chief executives of Welsh Government-sponsored bodies are female – and under a third (31 per cent) of board members. Women are also under-represented in education. They make up a fifth of university vice-chancellors, 24 per cent of heads of further education colleges and 32 per cent of secondary school head teachers. Furthermore, just a quarter of Wales TUC executive committee members are women – the same proportion as are chief constables in Wales. The malaise is not confined to the public sector. A survey of the top fifty Welsh companies found only two women in the most senior position (EHRC, 2012).

Civil society

Interviewed in 2013–14 there were mixed views from civil society organizations on the nature and extent of women's political engagement in Wales following devolution. For some there was a degree of cynicism. The manager of a women's NGO said 'they dine out on us. Every time they [AMs] want to be seen as acting for women they parade us in the Senedd or somewhere.' There was also evident frustration coupled with fears that any gains made over the past fifteen years might be reversed. For example, a women chief executive of a third-sector organization said, 'we haven't made as much progress as we'd hoped. I'm really concerned with the effects of the current austerity measures on women that we are going to be travelling backwards.' Others were more optimistic, yet acknowledged that progress also required a change in social attitudes and norms:

> I sense a growing interest in this area [gender equality] but we've still got a massive cultural change to make – in our collective psyche we've got that thing about men earn first and care second, women care first and earn second – we've still got to really challenge that.

Some interviewees echoed a concern expressed by women in the original interviews in 1999–2000. They alluded to a wariness and reluctance on the part of some women to engage in policy work for it was seen as too 'political'. For example, the manager with one women's organization observed:

> for some reason that commitment and enthusiasm [for devolution] hasn't translated into a really strong engagement ... I was really interested when I joined the organisation but there are a lot of women that are not terribly comfortable with that [policy work/political engagement] and I actually heard someone say 'we are not a feminist organisation' – and I thought 'what?!' How can you say we are not a feminist organisation?'

Another noted a lack of confidence or assertiveness: 'there are lots of women who are involved in policy development, lots who are brilliant, but it's still that thing about women not pushing themselves forward and not wanting to put themselves in the firing line'.

There was further continuity with the original interviews for respondents again identified one of the biggest challenges as securing adequate resources to facilitate engagement. However, in contrast to 1999–2000, the key difference today was meeting this challenge during a time of austerity. One said,

> it's about how you cover all the policy areas and the law[-making] side now as well, with fewer and fewer people because with organisations like ours it's often the case if you've got to make cuts it's the policy people [policy officers and researchers] that are the first to go.

Some interviewees referred to the need for women's NGOs to work harder to better use the political opportunities presented by devolved governance: 'whether we have – or are "pushing the envelope" as it were is something we all have to ask ourselves – I don't think that we have [done so] as much as we should or could have ... it's got to come from us'. Another noted, 'I don't really get a sense of organisations reacting as perhaps they should have as if they properly understood devolution'. Others spoke of greater access to government following devolution, something that presented more lobbying opportunities than at Westminster. One said, 'I say to our colleagues in London "look we can probably get stuff delivered here, we can get calls delivered here that can then become drivers for change in England"'. Several inter-viewees also spoke of what they saw as a strong desire by women in civil society to engage in the policy work of the Assembly and Welsh Government. One said: 'I think they *really do* want a voice in it. I think double amputees really want a voice for women – they do. I think the transgender women do, they really do – *they all do, we all do.*'

A number of interviewees saw the first two Assemblies as a high point in relation to gender equality. They noted how the rapid development of the National Assembly and move to a parliamentary mode of working had slowed or reversed progress. For example, one noted:

> politics has become more male, certainly the cabinet has become male-dominated ... is that just a gentle shift? Will it move back? We have moved from an Assembly that was consensual – now we have law-making powers, a government and opposition – it's more oppositional – is that part of the reason why we've had the shift [back towards male-dominated politics]?

Others reflected on what was seen as a failure to deliver the early post-devolution rhetoric on mainstreaming equality. They alluded to how gender equality was effectively 'siloed': 'I feel that equalities is very much in a section, in a box and not across everything as it should be.'

For some, there was cynicism about Welsh Government policy consultations. For example,

> we used to respond to them all [calls for consultation responses] we're much more selective now. It is something that comes up at our executive [meet-ings] again and again ... do they listen? Does it make a blind bit of difference what we say? ... I think members are right to question this ... it is hard to point to a bit [of policy] and say 'we did that – they listened'.

Others questioned the representativeness of policy consultations and whether they were anything but an executive exercise:

> the people who give the responses are the people who are like the chief executives or the policy officers for those organisations. How much real consulting do they do? I think they take it on hearsay – 'this is our policy and this is what we want to get through to you' ... I don't think they are roll-ing real women out in front of ministers saying this is the story, this is how it is.

Another noted: 'if you are not consulting [your membership] it's your opinion – *not* the people you are representing and that's quite different. Is that right?' Comments about consultation fatigue and NGOs' policy capacity echoed the original interviews. One interviewee reflected the wider view: 'in my day job it's hard enough to get funded to do the job I'm doing, I can't sit there for a week and a half doing this research and producing their papers'.

Others referred to the fall in the number of women AMs in 2011 and current debates about parties' use of positive action as a 'wake-up call', one that underlined the need for continuing activism. Thus, a woman policy officer said:

> I think there's quite a battle to come ... lessons have been learned, you can't be complacent, you've got to have positive action ... there's been a waking up amongst those that want fair play and want gender balance because if we don't do something now goodness knows what it's going to be like.

Others were quick to state that the largely liberal approach to gender equality seen over the past decade-and-a-half had not delivered. A number called for a more radical stance. One said,

> it is time for quotas! [Previously] I thought we can educate these women, we can empower these women – it'll be fab – we'll have loads of women at all these levels [but] No! – So, why don't we start being brave? So if thirty per cent [of women] is the critical mass let's say we want thirty per cent – or [if this is not achieved], you leave those places empty because if you can't fill them with women *don't* fill them with another man ... somewhere along the line we've got to start making some positive change.

Yet others were less certain. One said,

> I have some sympathy with that [quotas for women in public life] but there are other ways that we have not exhausted yet – like informal approaches. Finding out who the good women are, sounding them out, encourage them to apply for posts. It's not favouritism, it's common sense ... make sure you get the best people.

Some interviewees lamented about what they saw as a loss of momentum. One said: 'there's new blood coming into the Assembly but then again with the [Welsh Government cabinet] reshuffle [c.2013] no women came through in that – and the make-up of the cabinet we are so far away from [where we were] ten years ago'. The political parties came in for significant criticism from interviewees. For example, one said 'they have got to change. While we leave it to a voluntary code of conduct they can play all these stupid games, and mind-sets and try and convince us they are putting women forward – they're not!' Others referred to what they saw as missed opportunities: 'there is a lot more that the Welsh Government could demand of the organisations that they fund through [public] procurement'.

Interviewees were asked to identify areas of progress and challenges related to the impact of devolution on women's political representation. Amongst the positive aspects one noted: 'we've got a woman party leader in Plaid Cymru and the Liberal Democrats so we've got more equality in relation to political leadership in the Bay ... I guess it's progress in relation to the visibility of women in some public roles'. Others referred to (albeit) belated attention to domestic abuse: 'we have a fantastic piece of legislation coming up in the Violence Against Women [Domestic Abuse and Sexual Violence (Wales)] Bill and this is a real opportunity to drive forward education policy'.

However, many interviewees found it easier to identify policy challenges. One said, 'the obvious one is that the gender pay gap still exists in the public sector in Wales and we didn't deal with it in "the [pre-2008] time of plenty"'. Another noted 'nobody's using the [legal] equality duties [under the Equality Act, 2010] properly at the moment across the range of sectors – you know, organisations should be setting equality objectives now [under the Welsh PSED], I'm thinking we should be using these more as drivers [of gender equality]'. Another interviewee reflected the views of many:

> there are still huge challenges, challenges about roles that are seen as stereo-typically female – or male roles – and the current austerity climate that we are going to face for many years to come is going to further increase the gap between men and women – and between the highest and lowest paid which is going to impact adversely on women.

Another alluded to the view that the extension of equalities law across a greater number of protected characteristics has diluted the focus on gender with adverse consequences:

> I fully embraced the development of the Equality and Human Rights Commission but I remember listening to the debates around the potential loss of focus across all protected characteristics and I think that some women might say 'long live the Equal Opportunities Commission' – its [impact has] been questionable.

Another identified challenges shared by many interviewees:

> it's women in the economy. Giving women the opportunity to do what they want to by vastly improving childcare provision [and] the costs of childcare provision ... it's reaching out – and this is such a challenge because things can become so elitist but it's reaching out as much as possible to as many women.

Discussion

Centuries of gender inequality and sex discrimination were never likely to be overturned in a decade-and-a-half. Yet such was the excitement and expectations of those interviewed back in 1999–2000 that even the most sceptical and cautious interviewees acknowledged the potential for progress. The swift gains made in the number of women AMs through the use of positive action measures by Welsh Labour and Plaid Cymru reinforced already heightened expectations. Weighed against these initial hopes, progress in women's political representation, in both public life and policy-making, has been disappointing in three key respects – depth, breadth and permanency. Although there are gaps in the information base, extant data confirm the endurance of long-established patterns and processes of inequality faced by women across many social and economic aspects of life. Thus 'depth' refers to the fact that whilst the past fifteen years has seen some progress, it has fallen short of achieving gender parity and eliminating inequality. Allied to this, 'breadth' refers to variability across policy areas and issues: some have seen greater progress whereas others have registered little change. 'Permanency' refers to the fact that, as interviewees alluded to, the gains made to date are vulnerable to reversal, notably in the face of current austerity and spending cuts.

A number of factors explain the limited advances made in women's representation. First, as noted, there has been an overemphasis on the number of women elected to the Assembly. By international comparison, this has been high, and for a few years, world beating. However, the disproportionate attention given to this aspect of governance has given the false impression that devolution has transformed gender relations in Wales. This is far from the case. The gains in the number of women AMs have been based on a flawed mechanism – positive action. This exaggerates progress. Worse, it fails to address the underlying structural and cultural dimensions to gender inequality – and, as the 2011 election (and, most likely 2016 ballot) attest, once it is removed, things tend to revert to type and old male-dominated practices reassert themselves. A further break on progress has been the limited resources, expertise and capacity of a chronically under-sized legislature (typically there are just 45–50 AMs outside the executive). As if this was not bad enough, during its crucial developmental phase the Assembly's powers were not only limited but ill-defined and the whole institution underwent the, wholly necessary but diverting, distraction of a major redesign on parliamentary lines (in place of the corporate body). All in less than a decade.

Notwithstanding this, there are some positive aspects. Devolution has seen the development of a range of legal instruments, institutional mechanisms and policy-making procedures with the potential to advance the substantive representation of women and promote gender equality. These were largely absent during the Welsh Office era. Compared to the early years of devolution the policy tools available to ministers today are stronger and more sophisticated. Will these deliver greater progress over the next decade? That depends upon effective monitoring and compliance, and a 'step-change' in equalities training in the Welsh Government bureaucracy and wider public sector. It is also conditional on extending political engagement; and for women (and men) in civil society to lobby and pressure AMs into introducing further reform. It also requires two further, more elusive commodities, determination and imagination.

Acknowledgements

The author wishes to acknowledge grant funding under Economic and Social Research Council Award No. ES/L009099/1.

Notes

[1] It is acknowledged these are not exclusively policy issues that apply to women. Rather, their use in the earlier analysis is consistent with Norris and Lovenduski's (2001) notion of women's issues as being defined through a process of politicization that acknowledges that such issues may be disproportionately affected by prevailing patterns and processes of gender inequality – such that they may be regarded as 'women's issues'.

[2] 297 meetings of 6 committees.

[3] A partnership scheme aimed at widening democratic participation launched by the presiding officer in 2009 involving thirty-three participants from under-represented groups given the chance to shadow local councillors and Assembly Members over six months.

[4] Or equivalent executive capacity during the years of the NAfW as a corporate body.

References

Betts, S., Borland, J. and Chaney, P., 'Inclusive government for excluded groups', in P. Chaney, T. Hall and A. Pithouse (eds), *New Governance: New Democracy? Post-Devolution Wales* (Cardiff: University of Wales Press, 2001).

Brooks, S. and ap Gareth, P., *Welsh Power Report: Women in Public Life* (Cardiff: Electoral Reform Society Wales, 2013).

Chaney, P., 'Increased Rights and Representation: Women and the Post-Devolution Equality Agenda in Wales', in A. Dobrowolsky and V. Hart (eds), *Women Making Constitutions: New Politics and Comparative Perspectives* (Basingstoke: Palgrave, 2003).

——, 'Women's Political Participation in the Welsh Assembly', in J. Aaron and C. Williams (eds), *Postcolonial Wales* (Cardiff: University of Wales Press, 2005), pp. 114–33.

——, 'Constitutional Reform and Women's Political Representation', in M. Sawer, M. Tremblay and L. Trimble (eds), *Representing Women in Parliament* (London and New York: Routledge, 2006).

——, 'Devolved Governance and the Substantive Representation of Women: The Second Term of the National Assembly for Wales, 2003–07', *Parliamentary Affairs*, 61/2 (2008), 87–102.

——, 'Delivery or Déjà vu? Gender Mainstreaming and Public Policy', in N. Charles and C. A. Davies (eds), *Gender and Social Justice* (Cardiff: University of Wales Press, 2010).

——, *Equality and Public Policy* (Cardiff: University of Wales Press, 2011).

——, 'New Legislative Settings and the Application of the Participative-Democratic Model of Mainstreaming Equality in Public Policy Making: Evidence from the UK's Devolution Programme', *Policy Studies*, 33/5 (2013), 455–76.

—— and Fevre, R., 'Ron Davies and the Cult of "Inclusiveness": Devolution and Participation in Wales', *Contemporary Wales*, 14 (2001), 21–49.

——, Hall, T. and Dicks, B., 'Inclusive Governance? The Case of "Minority" and Voluntary Sector Groups and the National Assembly for Wales', *Contemporary Wales*, 13 (2000), 203–29.

——, Mackay, F. and McAllister, L., *Women, Politics and Constitutional Change* (Cardiff: University of Wales Press, 2007).

Electoral Reform Society, *Women and Local Government* (Cardiff: Electoral Reform Society, 2012).

Equality and Human Rights Commission (EHRC), *How Fair is Wales?* (Cardiff: EHRC, 2011).

——, *Who Runs Wales?* (Cardiff: EHRC, 2012).

Feld, V., 'A New Start in Wales: How Devolution is Making a Difference', in A. Coote (ed.), *New Gender Agenda: Why Women Still Want More* (London: Institute of Public Policy Research, 2000).

Kenny, M., 'Gender, Institutions and Power: A Critical Review', *Politics*, 27/2 (2007), 91–100.

McAllister, L. and Cole, M., 'The 2011 Welsh General Election: An Analysis of the Latest Staging Post in the Maturing of Welsh Politics', *Parliamentary Affairs*, 67 (2014), 172–90.

Mitchell, M., Beninger, K., Rahim, N. and Morrell, G., *Review of the Public Sector Equality Duty (PSED) in Wales* (Cardiff: Equality and Human Rights Commission, 2014).

National Assembly for Wales (NAfW), *Equal Opportunity Baseline Survey* (Cardiff: NAfW, 2000).

——, Assembly Commission, *Annual Equality Report April 2012 – March 2013* (Cardiff: NAfW, 2013).

Norris, P. and Lovenduski, J., *Blair's Babes: Critical Mass Theory, Gender, and Legislative Life* (Cambridge, MA: John F. Kennedy School of Government Harvard University, Faculty Research Working Papers Series, 2001).

Rumbul, R., 'Unpublished data analysis – women's participation in selected National Assembly Committees 1999–2011' (2013).

Welsh Government, *Welsh Government Employer Equality Report 2012–2013* (Cardiff: Welsh Government, 2014a).

——, *Strategic Equality Plan and Objectives 2012–2016* (Cardiff: Welsh Government, 2014b).

Dr Who – by Nathan Bond

12

The Transformation of the Media in Wales: Technology and Democracy

HUGH MACKAY

Introduction

This chapter revisits a paper authored by myself and Tony Powell that was published in *Contemporary Wales* in 1996, entitled 'Wales and its Media: Production, Consumption and Regulation'. It reviews and updates that account, reflecting on how the field has changed in the intervening two decades. The 1996 paper was the first comprehensive overview of the breadth of the mass media in Wales.[1] It included a brief historical overview, going back to the earliest days of each mass medium, presenting data on the production, consumption and regulation of the mass media in Wales, pulling together facts and figures about who owns, produces, listens to and views the press, radio and television in Wales.

It introduced this data in a theoretically informed way, bringing to bear some of the core concerns of those who study the media, and of policy-makers – the fragmentation of viewing, increasing concentration of ownership, the decline of public service broadcasting, the persistence of the local in the face of globalization, transnational media flows, the compression of time and space and the significance of digital technology. This chapter, like that paper, highlights the key issues and trends, updating that account of two decades ago.

Looking back, the explosion of academic research on the media in Wales is remarkable. The first published research on the mass media in Wales was a journal article on newspapers and the Stamp Acts (Rees, 1960) and later an insider's history of BBC Wales (Lucas, 1981). The first work on the contemporary mass media was published in 1983 when two chapters appeared on reporting the referendum (Osmond, 1983; Jones, 1983). This was followed by David Bevan's research on media elites in Wales, published in 1984, a study that remains prescient today (Bevan, 1984). We now have a vast field of published research, including work on *Gavin and Stacey*, *Dr Who*, *Coal House*, heritage cinema, ITV Wales, broadcasting policy in Wales. This corpus of literature has been pulled together on the website of *Cyfrwng*, the umbrella body of researchers of the media in Wales, practitioners and policy-makers, which was founded in 2004 and publishes a journal and convenes conferences. The field has grown enormously, some coordination is emerging and connections are being strengthened between researchers, practitioners and policy-makers.

The key areas outlined in the 1996 paper – production, consumption and regulation – are represented in subsequent research; as are many others, notably theatre and film, but also media forms, analyses of the content of various programmes and genres. Unsurprisingly, it is television that has received the most attention. It remains the case that studies of production and ownership are not common, this is not an area that academics have covered well, often relying on the reports of Royal Commissions for up-to-date data on patterns and trends. Indeed there has been little data on who owns what of the media in Wales or the number of Welsh journalists. The major exception to this is the recent IWA report, which constitutes a remarkably comprehensive and useful source of this data (IWA 2015).

This chapter updates the 1996, examining the press, radio, television and the Internet. The chapter concludes with some reflections on three major issues which have emerged in the field since 1996. In broad terms, the 1996 account remains relevant, many of the contours have not changed a great deal: the media landscape is fragmenting with the growth of multi-channel television and the Internet; the significance of public service broadcasting is declining; newspaper circulations are falling; and the newspaper market remains dominated by papers produced in London.

However, three striking changes in the intervening period are discussed in the conclusion of this chapter. One is the arrival of the National Assembly for Wales and the Welsh Government, which has enhanced concern about the communications environment in Wales. Obviously this is a very different situation from prior to the 'Yes' vote on devolution in 1997. This concern is about the inability of people in Wales to talk with one another, in some sort of public sphere (Habermas, 1989), and of Assembly members and the government to communicate with people across Wales. Whilst the worth of the notion of the public sphere is debated (Downey and Fenton, 2003), it is useful for considering the 'fit' between a communications system and notions of citizenship and democracy. This moves us into the realm of media regulation, regarding which there is increasing interest and concern in Wales.

The second notable change is the outcome of the phenomenal growth of digital technology in the past twenty years, which has significantly affected the press and broadcasting. The Internet, although still in its infancy as a communications technology, had hardly appeared in 1996. History illustrates that the uses to which new communications technologies are put, the form in which they stabilize, have never been apparent in their earliest years. For example, the telephone started as a broadcasting system, and only later became one-to-one (Marvin, 1988); whilst radio began as one-to-one (ship-to-shore) but became a broadcasting system (Williams, 1974). However, twenty or so years after the arrival of the Internet as a part of the media landscape in Wales, and although remembering Raymond Williams's (1974) concern with the long durée, we can begin to make sense of how it has transformed the communications environment.

The third issue raised in the conclusion of this chapter is that digital technology has changed not just the mass media, but how we do social research, and the sort of data that can be gathered on the mass media. The instantaneity of access to information and its volume are huge changes. Furthermore, with analytical tools we can measure new aspects of communication, and thus understand more fully the significance of the media. These are enormous changes to have occurred in such a short time span.

The press

One of our arguments in 1996 was that very little of the press in Wales is Welsh-owned. This remains the case, indeed, some of the little that was Welsh-owned in 1996 has since become owned by a company based in England: Cambrian News, publisher of the weekly of that name and of *Y Cymro* and the monthly *Y Dydd*, was acquired in 1998 by the Tindle Newspapers, a large UK family-owned publisher of over 200 weekly newspapers, based in Surrey. The loss of Welsh ownership of the press, whilst it may be insignificant for content and for the public sphere, is significant for the export of profit and control.

As well as the reduction of indigenous ownership, there has been an accelerating series of corporate takeovers and mergers, demonstrating how very local newspapers are parts of larger corporations and their strategies. For example, in 2012, Local World acquired Northcliffe Media (which includes Swansea's *Evening Post*) from Daily Mail and General Trust. In 1999 Trinity International (owner of *Wales Online, The Western Mail, South Wales Echo* and the *Daily Post*) merged with the Mirror Group to become Trinity Mirror. Most recently there was major consolidation of these two groups in October 2015, when Local World was acquired by Trinity Mirror. In 1998, United Provincial Newspapers (publishers of the *South Wales Argus, Penarth Times*, seventeen dailies including Glasgow's *Herald* and over a hundred weeklies) was split in two, with the southern UK part sold to Southnews, which became Newscom and was acquired in 2000 by Gannet, a USA newspaper publisher. And in 1998 Tindle Newspapers bought Cambrian News; since then Tindle has acquired other weekly titles in Wales.

At the same time as a concentration of ownership, several newspapers in Wales have been closed, largely because of falling sales and declining advertising revenues (the latter following the former). For example, Trinity Mirror closed three freesheets, *Abergele & St Asaph Visitor* and the *Barry Post* in 2008 and the *Wrexham Chronicle* in 2009; and Media Wales, owned by Trinity Mirror, closed two paid-for titles in south Wales in 2009, the *Neath Guardian* and the *Port Talbot Guardian*.

Perhaps the greatest issue since 1996 has been declining circulations, which have been happening since about 1980. Newspaper circulations have nearly halved since 1996. In the UK, the seventy-five regional daily and Sunday newspapers lost an average of 13.5 per cent year-on-year in the first half of 2014 (Ponsford, 2014). The figures for the year ending December 2014 for four key newspapers in Wales are shown in table 12.1.

In this context, the notion today of an 'all Wales newspaper' – which we discussed in 1996 – is much less feasible than it was even then. The circulation of the *Western Mail* has declined from about 60,000 in 1996 to under 19,000 by August 2014. Of this, only about 5 per cent (under 1,000 copies) are sold in north Wales.

One very serious consequence has been a dramatic reduction in the number of journalists in Wales (as elsewhere in the UK), and in their salaries, in real terms. At Media Wales (owner of the *Western Mail,*

South Wales Echo, Celtic Weekly Newspapers (with seven titles) and *Wales Online*), there were 700 journalists in 1999 but only 196 in 2012 (Williams, 2013).

In this dire context, it is remarkable that a number of new and locally owned newspapers have been launched. The *Pembrokeshire Herald* was launched in Milford Haven in 2013 – despite the area being covered by *The Western Telegraph* in nearby Haverfordwest. It has established a niche in serious investigative journalism, much of it regarding local authority corruption. Owned by a Milford Haven company which also runs an online radio station and a free local magazine, the *Pembrokeshire Herald* had a circulation of 8,000 by July 2014 and a part-time editorial staff of seven.

The *Caerphilly Observer* started as an online newspaper in 2009, and in 2013 launched a paper edition. Funded in part by a grant from the local authority, it prints 10,000 copies and has a growing staff and readership (Gurner, 2014). The third newspaper launched in Wales is the *Port Talbot Magnet*. Supported by a grant from the Carnegie Trust, it is published by a co-operative social enterprise. It is a free sheet (with a website) – the first paper edition was published in September 2013 – and they try to produce one edition a month. Such ventures involve new business models and a highly committed workforce. They demonstrate the opposite of the growth of distant ownership and control, namely local control. They do, however, involve professionals working very hard and paying themselves very badly, and it is questionable whether these models are sustainable.

There are two other factors that mean that the story is not simply one of decline. One is that, to a certain extent, the fall in circulations over the decades has been off-set by the growth of freesheets. This is something that was happening by 1996, when we reported that the circulation of freesheets in the UK had doubled (to 33 million) in the

Table 12.1. Change in circulation, Trinity Mirror newspapers in Wales, 2013–14

Title	Dec. 2013	Dec. 2014	% Change
South Wales Echo	24,261	20,433	-15.8%
Daily Post	27,126	25,422	-6.3%
Western Mail	22,854	19,283	-15.6%
Wales on Sunday	19,131	16,238	-15.1%

Source: Sharman (2015)

period 1981–95. Subsequently, circulations rather stalled, hence the closure of Cardiff's *Echo Extra*, and some freesheets becoming paid-for, for example the *Bangor Mail* in 2011. In the weeklies market there are now twenty paid-for titles in Wales and only seven freesheets. Some free titles, however, have thrived. The *Metro*, launched in the UK in 1999, arrived in Cardiff in 2006 and by 2013 had a circulation of 26,650 in south Wales. Whatever their fortunes, freesheets are thin on news and journalists, since they do not have to attract readers who will want to buy the newspaper, relying instead on advertising revenue (Franklin, 1998).

The main reason why discussion of declining circulations can be misleading is the phenomenal growth of newspapers' websites, which simply did not exist in 1996. In other words, traditional newspaper and other media organizations are major players online. Table 12.2 illustrates the losses of print and the gains of online readers or users of some of the main newspapers in Wales.

Thus we can see that readers overall are increasing, despite newspaper circulations falling. The online figures are still growing fast: in the first six months of 2014 those of the *South Wales Evening Post* increased 61.5 per cent to 828,486 and *Wales Online* increased 58 per cent to 2,122,895 (Sweney, 2014).

Finally, it is worth reviewing what has changed regarding the state of the Welsh-language press in Wales. *Y Dydd*, a monthly in Dolgellau, was sold by its local owners and bought by Cambrian News, part of Tindle Newspapers, in 2003; and in 2007 Tindle acquired *Y Cymro* (and Radio Ceredigion) from North Wales Newspapers. *Y Cymro* is a national weekly, the only Welsh-language one, and in 2006 it had a circulation of 4,000 (ap Dyfrig et al., 2006); since 2007 it has been available online.

Golwg was founded in 1988 as a Welsh-language news and current affairs weekly. Its circulation peaked around 1998 at about 5,200 per

Table 12.2. Print losses and online gains, selected newspapers in Wales, 2012–13

Title	Print loss	Online gain	Net gain
South Wales Evening Post	2,835	6,676	4,841
Western Mail + Echo + Wales on Sunday	7,493	9,155	1,662
Daily Post	2,264	2,289	25

Source: Haggett (2013)

week and was down to about 2,800 in 2011, when it employed seven journalists. A fifth of its revenue is from grants, which have come from the Welsh Books Council and the Arts Council of Wales (Iorwerth, 2011). In 2009, *Golwg360* was launched. By 2011 it was publishing thirty stories a day and receiving 5,000 visitors (Schiavone, 2011). *BBC Cymru Wales* and *Golwg360* are the main websites for Welsh-language news. Thus, the Welsh-language sector of the press is holding up, and has in general made a successful transition to online.

Radio

It seems remarkable that such an old technology as radio has not only survived but maintained its cultural significance with the arrival of the Internet. Since 1996 it has experienced two significant changes, the shift from analogue to DAB (with 42 per cent of households in Wales owning a DAB radio in 2014, an increase of fifteen percentage points over 2013).

In broad terms, radio in Wales has performed well in the period since 1996 and continues to do so – in terms of the number and variety of stations, hours of broadcasts and listeners. The exception to this broad picture is Welsh-language radio, which has seen a significant decline in audience and broadcast hours. In 2013–14 Radio Wales had a weekly reach of 468,000 (up from 409,000 in 1996) and 144,000 for Radio Cymru (the Welsh language station; down from 177,000 in 1996) (BBC, 2014). The weekly reach is the number of people who listen for at least five minutes a day. So Radio Cymru saw a 19 per cent fall in listeners in the period 1996–2014, whilst Radio Wales experienced a 14 per cent increase. Subsequently, however, in the period October 2014– March 2015, Radio Wales has experienced some decline, down to 426,000 listeners, whilst Radio Cymru's weekly listening increased to 126,000.

This decline in the Radio Cymru audience is caused by a variety of factors: potential listeners do not see the programmes as attractive as used to be the case; the growth of households where Welsh is spoken but not by all members of the household; the increasing heterogeneity of Welsh speakers, as the language has shifted from Y Fro Gymraeg to the capital city; the increasing variety of Welsh-language competence among Welsh speakers; the off-putting effect on the more traditional audience of efforts by the station to sound more relevant to younger and more cosmopolitan listeners; and the growing diversity of alternative media channels.

Commercial radio in Wales continues to enjoy substantial audiences, on a diet of broadcasting that is not particularly Welsh or local. Of all the UK nations, the share of listening hours for local commercial radio is lowest in Wales, at 23 per cent. Commercial radio overall accounted for 35 per cent of the total share of listening hours in Wales, lower than the other nations and six percentage points below the UK average. Conversely, listening to BBC local radio (Radio Wales and Radio Cymru) is higher in Wales than in Scotland, England or the UK as a whole.

The names and owners of commercial radio in Wales have all changed since 1996. Today there are three main commercial groups: Global Media (running the 'Capital' stations, several of them formerly Heart and before that Real); Town and Country (operating Nation Radio across south Wales, Bridge FM in Bridgend, Nation Hits in Swansea, Scarlet FM in Llanelli, Radio Carmarthenshire, Radio Pembrokeshire and Radio Ceredigion); and UTV (operating Swansea Sound, Real Radio and The Wave). Additionally, there has been the development of community radio stations. Ten of these have been licensed in Wales by Ofcom and are broadcasting.

One issue with commercial radio has been the amount it broadcasts in the Welsh language. Several stations (including Capital Cymru and Scarlet FM) have Welsh-language obligations in their licences, in varying amounts. Controversy has focused on another station with Welsh-language obligations, Radio Carmarthenshire. In 2004, a few weeks after the station's launch, about a dozen activists from Cymdeithas yr Iaith Gymraeg (the Welsh Language Society) occupied the studios in Narberth to protest about the amount of Welsh-language programming being broadcast. A majority of the population of Carmarthenshire was Welsh-speaking, whilst only about 5 per cent of the radio output was in Welsh. There were scuffles, injuries and arrests. Following complaints, Ofcom investigated the matter and issued a warning to Radio Carmarthenshire for failing to conform to the conditions of its licence. It stated that it was particularly concerned at the complete absence of Welsh-language music from the evening show, in clear breach of the undertaking to provide a two-hour youth programme on weekday evenings, which would include music by Welsh-language artists. This omission connects with an argument made in chapter 3, that it is important to provide young people with social opportunities in the medium of Welsh, outside school and work (see Geraint, this volume).

Television

A major change for television since 1996 has been funding cuts for all of the major broadcasters. There are two reasons for this, the growth of multi-channel television and public sector budget cuts. The former has meant that the audience for public service broadcasters is smaller. They remain the most-watched channels, but the numerous other channels, although none of them has a huge audience, have together eroded the market for the older, public service broadcasters (PSB). This has meant falling advertising revenue for ITV (which has been caused too by the growth of the Internet); and a reduction in the legitimacy of the arguments that the BBC can make for public funding. This is a step change in the shift from seeing viewers as consumers rather than citizens, and in the shift from the Reithian notion of giving the audience what is good for them, to providing what they want. This is the context for the Charter Review process in 2015–16, at the end of which many expect the BBC to have a rather different shape and size than has been the case in the past.

Whilst the average hours of daily viewing by all individuals have fallen only a little, the audience of the five main PSB channels (excluding the smaller, additional channels or these broadcasters) has declined since 2004. ITV's share has decreased the most, from 23 to 15 per cent, followed by Channel 4 (from 10 to 5 per cent). BBC One's and BBC Two's shares declined by four percentage points and Channel 5's share declined the least, by three percentage points. In 2009, the numerous other channels combined overtook the most-watched channel (BBC One), in terms of average weekly reach (Ofcom, 2014b). In Wales, television viewing is relatively high, 4.4 hours a day, compared with a UK average of 3.9 hours. For 53 per cent of the population in Wales, television is their main source of local (in this context, Welsh) news (Ofcom, 2014b).

In October 2010, it was announced that the BBC licence fee would be frozen until 2016, and that the BBC would pick up the cost of funding the BBC World Service and BBC Monitoring (which until April 2014 were funded by the Foreign and Commonwealth Office), and much of the funding of S4C. Together this led to 20 per cent cuts at the BBC, leading to reduced output hours and audiences, large job losses and the closure of BBC3 broadcasting (it is to continue online). There has been a reduction in public support for the BBC (BBC Cymru Wales, 2014), in the context of the growth of multi-channel television, the Jimmy Saville and other scandals, and concern about the pay and number of senior managers. This is fuelled by commercial media organizations that are always seeking new sources of business and profit.

As well as producing programmes for itself, BBC Cymru Wales produces (as it has since 1982) over ten hours of broadcasting per week for S4C – including *Newyddion* and *Pobol y Cwm* – funded by the licence fee. BBC Wales also provides factual and especially drama programming to the BBC's UK network (including *Doctor Who*, *Atlantis*, *Sherlock*, *Hinterland* and *Crimewatch*). BBC Wales's television output (hours of origination) in English decreased from 698 hours in 2011–12 to 614 hours in 2012–13, and 603 hours in 2013–14. Its output on S4C also reduced again in 2013–14.

BBC Cymru Wales's output for the network, however, increased by about 3 per cent in terms of hours. About 7 per cent of BBC network television expenditure is spent in Wales (which has 4.8 per cent of the UK population). BBC Wales has approximately 1,300 employees, mostly in Cardiff but also at its centres in Swansea, Carmarthen, Aberystwyth, Bangor and Wrexham. In Cardiff, the drama production centre at Roath Lock, Cardiff Bay was opened in 2011, and in 2014 it was announced that a new headquarters next to Cardiff central rail station is to open in 2018, replacing the current headquarters in Llandaff.

In the case of S4C, its budget was reduced by 36 per cent in real terms in the period 2010–14, largely to enable the Department for Culture, Media and Sport (DCMS) to meet its budget cut for the public spending review. Since April 2013, 90 per cent of S4C's funding (£76 million) has come from the licence fee, with 8 per cent (£6.787m) funded by DCMS until March 2016. This happened at the same time as serious governance problems, and the departure within six months of one another in 2010 of the S4C authority chair, the chief executive and the head of commissioning. Obviously, funding S4C with the licence fee and increasing its links with the BBC reduces media plurality, the number of voices that can be heard. There is increasing collaboration between the two broadcasters, with S4C programmes now available on iPlayer and possibly sharing facilities in Cardiff after the move of S4C's headquarters to Carmarthen by 2018. One outcome of cuts to S4C's budget has been a reduction in production costs and audiences. The average cost per hour of S4C's commissioned content has fallen from £52,700 in 2009 to £31,100 in 2013–14, while the cost per hour of all S4C broadcasts fell from £16,400 to £10,800 (S4C, 2014b).

More people are watching S4C programmes for longer, 6.5 million in 2013–14, up from 5.3 million in 2012; and they are viewing for an average of eight hours a week, an increase of one hour on the previous year. However, there was a drop of 17 per cent in S4C's peak-time audience, and the number of Welsh speakers watching S4C in an average week fell from 216,000 to 194,000 (S4C, 2014b).

ITV too has faced a declining audience. In pre-multi-channel days, it produced local (Welsh) programming as a quid pro quo for access to the broadcasting spectrum, which was scarce and hence valuable. With multi-channel, the value of the spectrum has fallen and ITV has successively renegotiated its public service obligations, in the knowledge of all parties that one option is to return the licence. ITV Cymru Wales has been separated from ITV in the west of England, and now constitutes a separate Channel 3 licence. Its local (national) news in Wales has been better protected than local news in the English regions. Its new licence requires delivery of five and a half hours per week of Welsh programming, of which four hours are news. *Wales This Week*, its flagship news programme, achieves a peak-time audience of about 200,000. In 2013, ITV Wales launched *Newsweek Wales*, a weekly news programme on Sunday mornings, and a new factual series *Coast & Country*. However, ITV's spend in the UK as a whole on all output declined by 5 per cent (£202 million) over the period 2008–13 (compared with a 10 per cent (£391m) reduction in BBC spending).

However, analogue switch-off has resolved one problem faced by broadcasters in Wales in 1996. A significant issue then was people in Wales choosing to receive transmissions from England, by pointing their aerials to transmitters in England, mainly to receive Channel 4 and Channel Five. With the switch-off of analogue television, which took place in Wales in 2009, this is no longer necessary. People in Wales now enjoy access to hundreds of channels, whether by satellite (Sky), cable (Virgin) or digital terrestrial (Freeview), and viewers throughout the UK can now access Welsh channels and stations. S4C has 174,000 viewers outside Wales every week, totalling 4.76m over the year (2013–14), strengthening its audience significantly and serving the demand of the Welsh-speaking diaspora.

Online

The mass take-up of the Internet is perhaps the most significant change to the media landscape, in Wales as elsewhere, since 1996. In the *Contemporary Wales* article we devoted about as much space to teletext as to the Internet (teletext closed its service on ITV, Channel 4 and Five in 2010; the BBC closed Ceefax, its teletext service, in 2012, as a part of analogue switch-off). Teletext has largely been superseded by the Web.

In 1996, about 5 per cent of the UK population had Internet access, all of them via 'dial-up' rather than 'always-on'. Today, things are very different: 80 per cent of households in Wales have access to the Internet (Q4, 2014), which has been increasing in recent years by five percentage points per year. Fifty-two per cent have access to the Internet by mobile, and 45 per cent have a tablet computer. This proliferation of devices on which the Internet is used is both cause and indicator of its use being more embedded in everyday life, of Internet use taking place in more ways and locations in and out of the home than was the case in earlier days, when (in the few places it was to be found) it was confined to a PC fixed in one place.

The infrastructure continues to be upgraded, with Welsh Government, European (ERDF) and BT financial support. The plan is for 96 per cent of homes and businesses to have access to high-speed (or superfast) broadband by 2016; the figure for Wales is currently 58 per cent, compared with a UK average of 78 per cent (Ofcom, 2014b). The take-up of broadband in Wales is below the UK average: the proportion of adults with a fixed or mobile broadband connection (71 per cent) is six percentage points lower than the UK average (77 per cent). Within this overall figure, broadband access is higher in urban areas than rural areas, higher in particular age groups and in higher-income households.

As was the case when radio and then television arrived, it does not simply replace pre-existing media, but adds to and makes more complex the media landscape. Unlike previous new media, however, the Internet can be seen as absorbing all hitherto mass-media technologies and forms – print, radio and television. Unsurprisingly, many of the major players on the Internet are 'old media' organizations – newspapers and television stations.

Until 1997, of all the newspapers in Wales, only the *Daily Post* had a website. S4C, the BBC and HTV all opened their websites that year. Today, website users constitute a significant part of the audience for these newspapers and stations, as detailed earlier in this chapter in relation to the press.

This is a remarkable rate of growth, from zero in 1996. Additionally, the use of online viewing services has increased dramatically in recent years. Taking S4C, for example, online viewing sessions (which includes Clic, iPlayer, YouView and TVCatchup) were about 1.1 million in 2009 and 5.2 million in 2013–14. Online viewing on mobile devices increased from 72,000 in 2011 to 1.1 million in 2013–14 (S4C, 2014b).

One of the most interesting things about the Internet, of course, is that it allows multiple voices, it facilitates the voice of ordinary and diverse people, in ways that are unfiltered by conventional media organizations. A multiplicity of voices, many of them in the Welsh language, are to be found on blogs and numerous other forms of social media, including Facebook and Twitter. The *Penarth Daily News*, for example, has provided since 2013 thoroughly researched and well-written articles, together with some excellent photographs, that together rival the weekly *Penarth Times*. Compared with even a local weekly, many blogs have a personal and informal style, leaving the reader well aware of the values, predispositions or character of the author. This makes for more idiosyncratic and diverse content, although with (in many cases) lower professional standards of verification and accuracy. However, as highlighted by the Leveson inquiry, one should not overstate the professionalism of all journalists; many blogs are about lifestyle rather than news, where practices of journalism are different, and many are highly professional.

This burgeoning of private publishing has enhanced the diversity of the public sphere enormously. Blogs are commonly combined with opportunities for readers, or visitors, to post comments, making them relatively interactive compared with the traditional media, where access is highly circumscribed. They also allow immediacy: responses to an event or an idea can be posted quickly, in contrast with the timescales of traditional media production. They are, of course, multimedia, commonly including video as well as still images and text. Some blogs

Table 12.3. Welsh broadcasters' website users
(weekly unique users, thousands), 2013–14

BBC Cymru Wales English-language sites	3,650
BBC Wales Welsh-language sites	40
S4C	224

have become resources, and sources, for mainstream journalists; others are produced by mainstream journalists to extend and amplify their impact and influence.

Conclusion

Reflecting on our study after twenty years, three major changes stand out: the democratic deficit in Wales, technological change, and research data and methods.

Today there is much greater concern about 'the democratic deficit', the role that is and might be played by the media in relation to citizenship and democracy, and specifically connecting people in Wales with the work of the government and Assembly.

Arguably, the Welsh Government has insufficient influence over the funding and governance of the media organizations, given their centrality to the cultural life of Wales. This raises questions about media regulation and governance, about the structures that are appropriate, given the significance of the media for democracy. The Assembly's interest was indicated when in 2013 two conferences were convened by the presiding officer on how traditional and new media can better communicate the public policies that are emerging from the Assembly.

Broadcasting, communications, film and media regulation remain reserved matters for the Westminster Government. The Welsh language and economic development, both areas closely connected with the media, are devolved matters. The government has a cultural strategy but the Assembly has the power to comment on reserved matters in which it has an interest – and has shown itself particularly concerned with the media in this regard. For example, in 2008 the Assembly constituted a broadcasting committee to investigate and report on the future of public service broadcasting in Wales; and in 2011–12 a task and finish group of the Communities, Equality and Local Government Committee was established on the future outlook for the media in Wales.

The crisis at S4C and the reduction in DCMS grant for that body was a critical point for debate about Assembly powers in this area. Since 1996, the governance structure of the BBC and S4C has changed significantly, and a new regulator, Ofcom, has arrived. With devolution, and in the passage of the Communications Act 2003 (in Westminster) in particular, there has been debate about the role of the Welsh Government in relation to media policy.

The BBC Board of Governors was replaced with the BBC Trust in 2007. With the same number of members – twelve – the trust has a national trustee for Wales (currently Elan Clos Stephens). The national trustee is appointed by the Queen in Council, on the recommendation of the Minister for the DCMS, though a senior Welsh Government official is involved in the process. In addition, and chaired by the trustee for Wales, is the Audience Council Wales, which is intended to work on behalf of BBC audiences in Wales. Its twelve members are appointed by the BBC Trust. Its purpose is two-fold: 'to scrutinise the BBC's performance on behalf of audiences living in Wales, and to advise the Trust on issues relating to BBC audiences and services at a Wales level'; and 'to undertake a continuing assessment of BBC programmes and services in Wales and the extent to which the BBC's network output and other activities reflect the diversity of the UK and its nations, regions and communities'. It is likely that BBC governance changes fundamentally following the process of Charter Review that is underway.

Thus the Welsh Government has no formal role in the governance of the BBC, nor is the BBC in any sense accountable to the Assembly; however, on occasions the director of BBC Cymru Wales and the trustee for Wales have made presentations to the Assembly, answered questions and contributed their expertise to the development of Assembly and government inquiries. On the one hand, this follows the proper separation of the BBC from the government. On the other hand, it is Westminster that is responsible for the Charter Review and setting the terms of the BBC licence. The Welsh Government plays no part in this periodic political intervention in the BBC. Yet today the BBC is responsible for most of the budget of S4C.

Ofcom, the regulator of communications, was established in 2003, replacing the Independent Television Commission, the Radio Authority Oftel and various other bodies in the light of convergence. It has a small board, and beneath this has the content board and the communications consumer panel, both of which have representatives from Wales (and the other nations). These people are also members of the Advisory Committee for Wales, which has seven members, and which exists to advise Ofcom about the interests of people in Wales regarding communications. Ofcom has an office in Wales to connect Ofcom with Wales and vice versa, facilitating Ofcom relationships and consultations with stakeholders in Wales. Whilst 'the team makes sure it has its finger on the pulse and is acutely aware of the needs of industry, consumers and citizens in Wales' (Ofcom, 2015), arguably, given the importance of media plurality and telecommunications infrastructure for Wales, there should be a more formal mechanism for the Assembly to engage with the work of Ofcom.

Members of the S4C Authority are appointed by the Secretary for State for Culture, Media and Sport following consultation with the Wales Office, Welsh Government and the BBC Trust. This governance structure meant that there was no Welsh Government (or S4C) involvement in the negotiations between the DCMS and the BBC over fundamental changes to the funding and accountability of S4C in 2010 (IWA, n.d.). These negotiations concluded with a partnership that was agreed in January 2013, which was intended to ensure 'the editorial, managerial and operational independence of S4C'.

Discussion of Welsh Government intervention in the press has generally been confined to funding or subsidy. Some argue that the government should subsidize the press, as occurs in some other small European nations – though this raises concerns about political interference or distortion of the market. However, the government funds Welsh journals and books, for example, through the Welsh Books Council and the University of Wales Press, so one could argue that it should not exclude newspapers. Use of procurement (in the form of promotional and advertising material) is another possible source of government funding for the press in Wales; the £1m that Welsh local authorities spend on free newspapers is another possible source of finance (BBC, 2012).

From the earliest days of the BBC there was awareness in Wales of the significance of broadcasting for the Welsh nation (Davies, 1994). In many ways (as was acknowledged by the minister recently in the context of the arrival of local television) the BBC has served Wales well. Despite the growing public support for devolution, and for increasing the powers of the Assembly, there are few today who call for dismembering the BBC, for setting up a Wales Broadcasting Corporation – as did Gwynfor Evans in 1944 (Barlow et al., 2005) and as did some in Scotland in debates about *Newsnight Scotland* and the *Scottish Six O'clock News*. Anthony King's (2008, 2012) revisit of his damning indictment of the Anglocentrism of the BBC makes for positive reading, and the increasing commitment of the BBC and S4C to increase production outside London and in the nations is a positive sign. The fragmentation of the media, and the reduction in the scale and significance of public service broadcasting, however, pose challenges for the Assembly and government. Addressing the challenge involves achieving the right balance between consumer choice and serving our needs and interests as citizens.

The Silk Commission, the cross-party commission on devolution, which issued Part II of its report in March 2014, was quite clear that the regulation of broadcasting should stay in Westminster. In this it reflected the view of the Welsh Government and of 60 per cent of those it polled in Wales. It did, however, recommend involving the Welsh Government in the appointment of the Wales representative on the BBC Trust; reformulating the trust's Audience Council Wales as a Welsh broadcasting trust, responsible for policy, content and resources for all services delivered solely in Wales; transferring DCMS's S4C funding to the Welsh Government; and having a Welsh representative on the Ofcom board. It felt it was wrong for the management at BBC Wales to be accountable only to the BBC Trust regarding its activity in Wales.

The second major change is the development of new technology and devices. There was almost no use of the Internet in 1996. Today, 80 per cent of households have access. Consumers have demonstrated a willingness to pay for this new technology but costs for producers have increased as platforms have proliferated. In the process, the media landscape has fragmented, in that more of us are accessing different rather than the same material, and we are doing so at different times. The common viewing experience that characterized the broadcast era is breaking down.

Flexibility and choice is enhanced by recording and other technologies that allow catch-up television viewing (in the form of PVRs, iPlayer and similar services), but has contributed to the decline of a temporally common viewing experience. The numbers owning a DVR increased from 29.2 per cent in 2008 to 71.2 per cent in 2013, and younger people are more likely to watch time-shifted television and iPlayer. On S4C, 12 per cent of viewing is non-linear and the channel had almost 4 million online viewing sessions in 2013–14 (S4C, 2014a).

Most interesting perhaps is the growth of social media, where news and information is less filtered than it was, sources are more numerous and more personal, the time between an event and the circulation of news has become compressed, and representations and content may well be more diverse. Social media have shaped the practices of mainstream media, as journalists develop new practices (seeking breaking news on Twitter and using crowd sourcing and citizen journalists). Crucially, the one-to-many of the press and broadcasting is being complemented by new patterns of networking, and new forms of mediated intimacy. Trusted friends and sources, sometimes engaged concurrently in meshing activities on multiple devices, can be more important than the fourth estate as a form of validation or verification (Dutton, 2009). Correspondingly, the authority of journalists and media organizations is challenged. Social media involve a distinct culture, format, style and temporality, things which do not fit easily with 'old media' organizations and practices.

The third and final major change in the past twenty years, largely driven by technological change in the form of the Internet, is in the data that is available, the means of doing research and the new possibilities that have emerged with the growth of real-time and accessible data.

Data is more accessible now than it was twenty years ago. In 1996, to gather the data we had to telephone or write to the marketing department of each newspaper and even finding the names of all the newspapers was itself a major task; it can now be undertaken by checking *Britishpapers.co.uk*. More than the speed of locating information is its volume. Ofcom's research reports provide volumes of data on so many dimensions of telecommunications that were simply not available twenty years ago. This is very good news for knowledge, accountability and democratic engagement, as well as for conducting social research.

There is, of course, a huge difference between public and private sector organizations in this regard. Relatively little information is available on ITV or newspaper organizations, beyond that which they have to provide for various regulatory purposes or to inform potential advertisers – so we know much less about their practices. The arrival of the Welsh Government and Assembly have led to an explosion of searchable and accessible information about Wales – the capacity to find information and make sense of what is happening are much greater than they were. This is a product of technology, but also of the nature of these public bodies, their commitment to providing information and engaging citizens.

The government, of course, could do more. For some time media researchers (many of them under the auspices of Cyfrwng) and others (notably the IWA) have been urging the Welsh Government to collate, on a regular basis and in a standardized form, data on the media in Wales – the number of journalists, the number of newspapers, their circulations and so on. Such data would be extremely useful for policy-makers as well as researchers. Online searchable resources are not, of course, confined to the Welsh Government and Ofcom. 'Welsh newspapers online' at the National Library of Wales is a remarkable development, allowing full text searches of Welsh newspaper content. The National Screen and Sound Archive at the National Library is another rich resource.

At the same time, new media beg new forms of investigation. How do or should we be counting online television viewing? Do such categories as newspapers, radio and television have any significance anymore? These activities have to some extent converged on the Internet, rather than being discrete – and now are commonly practised simultaneously, as devices are meshed. Does, indeed, the notion of 'mass media' have the significance today that it did prior to the explosion of media devices and activities?

Thus the data that has become available links with the changes this chapter has reported. The BBC and others tend to count a click on a website (a page impression) or a unique user as equivalent to a listener or viewer (which is measured in terms of a particular length of time and/or frequency). But what is the meaning of a click? What does such activity mean in terms of engagement, or style of interaction? Might we develop typologies of web use, in the same way as there has been debate about styles of television viewing? In the same way as radio stabilized in the 1930s as it became a mass medium, one can perhaps identify stabilizing web genres and styles of web use.

Finally, it is worth mentioning the availability of new research tools, with the arrival of social media. In some respects social media analytics allow us to measure old things in new ways. At the same time, they allow the measurement of new things, which were either absent or could not be measured in the past. For example, by looking at 'likes' and retweets, or tracking the use of particular terms, one can map the network across which a given reference is being communicated on social media. Some dimensions of the impact of a message can thus be tracked – and in real time.

Thus the new media technologies that have shaped so many of the changes that this chapter reports are themselves facilitating dramatically improved access to data and new possibilities for social research.

Notes

1 Though a more limited chapter had been published by Hume (1986). Subsequently, Barlow et al. (2005) became the most comprehensive review of the field and the recent IWA report is the most comprehensive contribution (IWA, 2015).

References

Barlow, D., Mitchell, P. and O'Malley, T., *The Media in Wales. Voices of a Small Nation* (Cardiff: University of Wales Press, 2005).

Bevan, D., 'The Mobilization of Cultural Minorities: The Case of Sianel Pedwar Cymru', *Media, Culture & Society*, 6 (1984), 103–17.

BBC, '£1m council newspapers: Welsh Government to review code' (2011), *www.bbc.co.uk/news/uk-wales-19036367* (accessed 20 January 2015).

——, *Management Review 2013/14* (BBC, 2014).

Davies, J., *Broadcasting and the BBC in Wales* (Cardiff: University of Wales Press, 1994).

Downey, J. and Fenton, N., 'New Media, Counter Publicity and the Public Sphere', *New Media & Society*, 5/2 (2003), 185–202.

Dutton, W., 'The Fifth Estate Emerging through the Network of Networks', *Prometheus*, 27/1 (2009), 1–15.

ap Dyfrig, R., Gruffydd Jones, E. H. and Jones, G., *The Welsh Language in the Media*, Mercator Media Monographs, 1 (Aberystwyth: Mercator, 2006).

Franklin, B., 'No news isn't good news: the development of local free newspapers', in B. Franklin and D. Murphy (eds), *Making the Local News: Local Journalism in Context* (London: Routledge, 1998).

Gurner, R., 'Caerphilly Observer: our highlights so far', post on Centre for Community Journalism blog, 8 September (2014), *www.communityjournalism.co.uk/blog/2014/09/08/caerphilly-observer-our-highlights-so-far/* (accessed 15 January 2015).

Habermas, J., *The Structural Transformation of the Public Sphere* (Cambridge: Cambridge University Press, 1989).

Haggett, M., 'Changing consumption patterns of Welsh news', *ClickonWales*, 7 September (2013), *www.clickonwales.org/2013/09/changing-consumption-patterns-of-welsh-news/* (accessed 15 January 2015).

Hume, I., 'Mass media and society in the 1980s', in I. Hume and R. Pryce (eds), *The Welsh and Their Country* (Llandysul: Gomer, 1986).

Institute of Welsh Affairs (IWA), *IWA Wales Media Audit* (Cardiff: IWA, 2015).

Institute for Welsh Affairs (IWA) Media Policy Group, 'Devolution and the media', in J. Osmond and S. Upton (eds), *A Stable, Sustainable Settlement for Wales* (Cardiff: The UK Changing Union Partnership, 2013), pp. 122–34, *www.clickonwales.org/wp-content/uploads/ChangingUnion_Complete11.pdf* (accessed 20 January 2015).

Iorwerth, D., 'Evidence from Golwg for the National Assembly for Wales Task and Finish Group on the future outlook for the media in Wales' (2011), *www.senedd.assembly.wales/documents/s4722/Consultation%20Response%20-%20Media%2036%20-%20Golwg%20360.pdf* (accessed 20 January 2015).

Jones, H. P., 'The referendum and the Welsh language press', in D. Foulkes et al., *The Welsh Veto* (Cardiff: University of Wales Press, 1983).

King, A., *The BBC Trust Impartiality Report: BBC Network News and Current Affairs Coverage of the Four UK Nations* (London: BBC Trust, 2008).

——, 'The Changing Face of the British Constitution: Reporting the Nations', Royal Television Society Wales Annual Lecture, October (2012), Cardiff Bay, *www.youtube.com/watch?v=ODySS91SKVg&feature=youtu.be* (accessed 6 June 2015).

Lucas, R., *The Voice of a Nation?* (Llandysul: Gomer, 1981).

Mackay, H. and Powell, A., 'Wales and its Media: Production, Consumption and Regulation', *Contemporary Wales*, 9 (1996), 8–39.

Marvin, C., *When Old Technologies Were New. Thinking About Communications in the Late Nineteenth Century* (Oxford: Oxford University Press, 1988).

National Library of Wales, *Wales' Community Newspapers*, *www.llgc.org.uk/index.php?id=communitynewspapers&0=* (accessed 16 January 2015).

Ofcom, *PSB Annual Report 2014* (London: Ofcom, 2014a).

——, *The Communications Market 2014* (London: Ofcom, 2014b).

——, *www.ofcom.org.uk/about/how-ofcom-is-run/nations-and-regions/ofcom-in-wales/* (2015) (accessed 20 January 2015).

Osmond, J., 'The referendum and the English language press', in D. Foulkes et al., *The Welsh Veto* (Cardiff: University of Wales Press, 1983).

Ponsford, D., 'UK regional dailies/Sundays lose print sales at 13.5 per cent year on year with Newsquest biggest fallers', *UK Press Gazette*, 27 August (2014), *www.pressgazette.co.uk/uk-dailies-loses-sales-135-cent-year-year-price-rises-make-newsquest-titles-biggest-fallers* (accessed 15 January 2015).

Rees, R. D., 'South Wales and Monmouthshire Newspapers under the Stamp Acts', *Welsh History Review*, 1 (1960), 301–24.

S4C, *The Future of Welsh Language Television* (Cardiff: S4C, 2014a).

——, *Annual Report* (Cardiff: S4C, 2014b).

Schiavone, O., 'Evidence from Golwg for the National Assembly for Wales Task and Finish Group on the future outlook for the media in Wales' (2011), *www.senedd.assembly.wales/documents/s4722/Consultation%20Response%20-%20Media%2036%20-%20Golwg%20360.pdf* (accessed 20 January 2015).

Sharman, D., 'Trinity Mirror dailies post year-on-year circulation drops', *HoldTheFrontPage*, 12 January (2015), *www.holdthefrontpage.co.uk/2015/news/year-on-year-decline-at-all-trinity-mirror-dailies/* (accessed 15 January 2015).

Sweney, M., 'Newsquest and Local World enjoy surge in online readership', *Guardian*, 27 August (2014), *www.theguardian.com/media/2014/aug/27/newsquest-local-world-south-wales-evening-post-johnston-press* (accessed 15 January 2015).

Williams, A., 'Stop Press? The crisis in Welsh newspapers, and what to do about it', *Cyfrwng: Media Wales Journal*, 10 (2013), 71–80, *http://orca.cf.ac.uk/49504/1/Andy%20Williams,%20Cardiff%20University%20School%20of%20Journalism,%20Media,.pdf* (accessed 15 January 2015).

Williams, R., *Television. Technology and Cultural Form* (London: Fontana, 1974).

No Way to Powys Pylons – by Ian Homer

13

Wind Energy: Revisiting
the Debate in Wales

KAREN PARKHILL AND RICHARD COWELL

Introduction

In 1994, Merylyn McKenzie Hedger, in her article 'Wind Energy: the Debate in Wales', assessed the emerging controversy surrounding the exploitation of wind power. At the time, wind energy was still relatively novel but growing more rapidly in Wales than in other parts of the UK, and McKenzie Hedger charted how the concentration of development in the Welsh uplands was causing a range of concerns.

At the centre of her detailed and prescient account is an analysis of the actors supporting and opposing wind energy. Support for the technology brought together developers and manufacturers of wind technologies, as well as farmers, landowners and (some) rural communities, seeing economic advantages in wind for supporting fragile hill farming economies. Opposition included local residents living near potential wind farm sites along with statutory countryside and nature conservation agency, the Countryside Council for Wales (CCW), concerned with 'the industrialization in the hills' (McKenzie Hedger, 1994, p.7). Environmental NGOs were split on the issue, between those promoting wind energy as preferable to energy futures based on fossil fuels or nuclear power, such as FoE Cymru, and groups more concerned with landscape, such as the Campaign for the Protection of Rural Wales (CPRW).

More than two decades have elapsed since McKenzie Hedger's contribution, and it is timely to revisit her observations. Two points of 'then and now' comparison stand out. The first is that although onshore wind energy has continued to expand in Wales, the rate of expansion has been slow, with the 'wind rush' presented by McKenzie Hedger as imminently engulfing rural Wales not appearing in the way anticipated. Indeed, growth rates for wind energy in Wales have been slower than the majority of the UK. By 2013, England was leading the way with wind energy installation, onshore and offshore, at 5154 megawatts (MW), with Scotland on 4701MW, Northern Ireland on 579MW and Wales on 771MW (DECC, 2014). If the lower level of installation in Wales might be expected from a smaller territory, the slow rate of increase would not (see figure 13.1). This slowness is all the more remarkable given the intensifying attention to climate change and renewable energy since 1994. Whereas McKenzie Hedger set her account against the then modest UK target of obtaining 1000 megawatts (MW) of new renewable energy capacity by 2000, targets embedded in the European Union Renewable Energy Directive (2009/28/EC) require the UK to obtain 15 per cent of its energy (and probably therefore 30 per cent of its electricity) from renewables by 2020. This is but a stepping-stone towards the UK Government's target to reduce GHG emissions by 80 per cent by 2050, likely to require the complete decarbonization of electricity generation.

The second point of comparison may explain the first: the persistence of opposition to wind energy development. In one particularly spectacular protest, on 11 May 2011, 'mid-Wales came to Cardiff', as approximately 1,500 people gathered on the steps of the National Assembly for Wales building, the Senedd, protesting against proposals to build numerous large wind farms and high-voltage grid lines across tracts of rural Wales (Mason and Milbourne, 2014). It became a divisive electoral issue in mid Wales, especially Montgomeryshire, as anti-wind politicians – mainly from the Conservatives – unseated the incumbents at county council, Assembly and national government levels.

Importantly, McKenzie Hedger saw the institutional context as shaping and exacerbating the conflict: pointing to a system of financial support that encouraged the rapid exploitation of the windiest upland sites, and a planning system that exerted little purchase on a disorderly, 'unregulated' pattern of development (1994, p. 139). It should be significant, therefore, that the institutional context has since changed remarkably, with the creation in 1998 of new elected government institutions for Wales: the National Assembly for Wales and the Welsh Government. What gives devolution further pertinence is that McKenzie Hedger concluded her article by reviewing potential

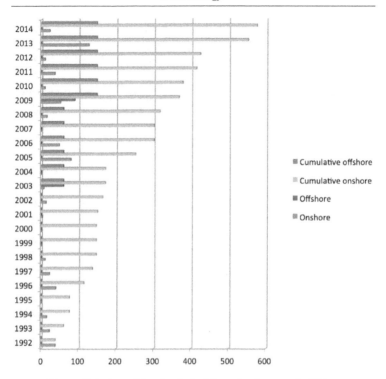

Figure 13.1: Annual levels of wind-farm development in Wales
(volumes in megawatts, MW)
Source: *www.renewableuk.com/en/renewable-energy/wind-energy/uk-wind-energy-database/* (accessed 19 May 2015), with Cowell et al. (2012) to ensure annual additions to capacity reflected net additional capacity of repowering.

solutions to the mounting controversy: the various calls for a more strategic planning approach to wind energy, and her own suggestion that further expansion should be preceded by a review of the wind energy development to date, and incorporate wide-ranging strategic environmental assessment of alternative future energy options. Welsh governments have indeed intervened to impart strategic direction on wind energy development in Wales, allowing us to consider the effects.

In our chapter, we reflect on and update the analysis by McKenzie Hedger, but also pursue themes that bind renewable energy development conflicts more centrally to the focus of *Our Changing Land*. Although McKenzie Hedger delineated processes unfolding *in* Wales, she was largely agnostic about whether the Welshness of the social context had any distinctive effects on, or was specifically affected by, the emerging wind farm conflict. This remains an under-examined issue and there is scope to explore how stances on the wind energy conflict intersect with the politics of place and civic dimensions of nationalism (Freeden, 1998).

We draw on a number of pieces of research conducted by one or other of us over the last ten years, as well as a relatively small but significant set of studies completed by others based on attitudes to wind energy in Wales (Woods, 2003; Haggett, 2008; Devine-Wright and Howes, 2010; Mason and Milbourne, 2014). Parkhill draws upon research projects where attitudes to wind have been a key focus (Parkhill, 2007; Butler et al., 2013; Demski et al., 2013a, 2013b; Parkhill et al., 2013). Cowell draws upon analyses of the emergence, effects and contestation of spatial planning guidance for onshore wind energy in Wales (Cowell 2007, 2010; Power and Cowell, 2012) and studies of the effects of devolution within the UK on the delivery of renewable energy (Cowell et al., 2015; Strachan et al., 2015).

In the next section, we examine how far devolution has changed the institutional arrangements for renewable energy development in Wales. Thereafter, we assess a body of research that has burgeoned since McKenzie Hedger was writing, on public attitudes to wind energy, onshore and offshore. We also use documentary data to examine how, in the light of ongoing wind farm conflicts, different organizations have reacted to the prospect of more energy-related powers being devolved to the Welsh Government, and what that says about the evolution of Wales as a focus for civic identification. We end with reflections on the relevance of McKenzie Hedger's original conclusions.

Governing wind energy in Wales

At its creation in 1998, the Welsh Government inherited a situation surrounding wind energy widely seen as dysfunctional. High rates of planning application refusal had slowed development, prompting industry representatives to 'see no evidence of a welcome for renewable energy in Wales' (ENDS, 2002). By 2002, the proportion of electricity supplied from renewable sources in the UK had stumbled upwards to a mere 2.2 per cent, and the Assembly Government was caught up in mounting political anxieties about delivering rising renewable energy targets as well as climate change commitments. The response reflected the new institution's desire to 'do things differently' from Westminster. Planning policy was an area of devolved responsibility, and the Welsh Government moved to review previous, pre-devolution policies. In the case of renewable energy, the review process initially was given a collaborative format (Stevenson, 2009): convening a working group with members from the energy industry, the conservation sector (state bodies and NGOs) and local government.

After three years of formulation, the result was new planning policy guidance for renewable energy in Wales – *Technical Advice Note 8: Renewable Energy* (WAG, 2005), or 'TAN8' for short – of which a key feature was the creation of new spatial planning guidance for onshore wind (Cowell, 2007). This sought to steer the development of larger wind farms (those over 25MW) to seven 'Strategic Search Areas' (see figure 13.2). These areas had been identified as preferable in landscape terms – being free of specific constraints such as national parks – while having sufficient wind resource. The Strategic Search Areas (SSAs) also gave effect to the Welsh Government's preference to concentrate wind farm development in certain areas of Wales rather than allowing turbines to scatter across the countryside. The advice of TAN8 is that planning authorities should give a presumption in favour of development to large wind farms within the SSAs, but TAN8 also allowed them to be more restrictive to wind farms outside them. TAN8 had an energy target dimension as well as a spatial dimension: each SSA was allocated a share of the Welsh Government's own target to install 800MW of new onshore wind energy in Wales by 2010, designed to ensure that Wales contributed proportionately to steadily rising UK targets for renewables.

The creation of TAN8 can be read as a response to the demands, conveyed by McKenzie Hedger, for a more strategic approach to onshore wind energy development. As a governance device, it radiates a certain symbolic power: new Welsh governing institutions had produced the first 'all Wales view' of wind energy, invoking in its apparent cartographic comprehensiveness the sense that Welsh policy matters in determining where turbines will be acceptable. In TAN8, the Welsh Government might also have hoped that it had found a way of mediating the conflicting interests described by McKenzie Hedger: by steering the *locations* of wind farm development, the expansion of the sector could be reconciled with societal concerns about the impacts.

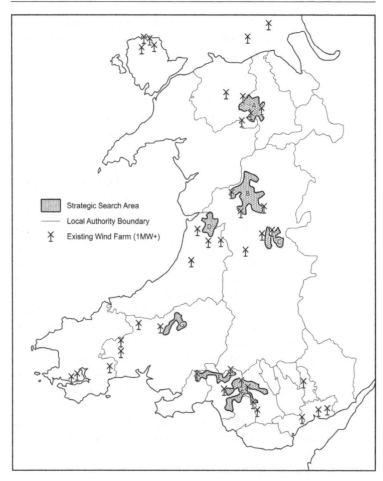

Figure 13.2: Strategic search areas for large-scale onshore wind development
Source: after WAG 2005, depicting operational wind farms of at least 1MW
installed capacity, as of 30 April 2015.

As of 2015, wind energy in Wales was still the subject of intense conflict and, moreover, the Welsh Government and its strategic approach had become the focus of much dispute. Why was this so? One line of explanation would point to 'classic' procedural weaknesses in government policy-making (Irwin, 2006). Although the Welsh Government began formulating TAN8 with the ambitions of using multi-stakeholder collaboration, in practice this proved fraught. There was consensus on some wind farm siting principles – that nationally designed landscapes and European wildlife sites should be avoided – but not on others, such as the status of 'wild land'. Disagreements stymied progress, the multi-stakeholder approach was placed in abeyance and the more detailed processes of policy formulation, including mapping the strategic search areas, was conducted by consultants working for the Welsh Government. Once completed, a draft policy was released for consultation. The draft policy attracted 1,700 responses, many of them critical (Cowell, 2007), and the mode of policy formulation allowed TAN8 to readily be presented as a top-down imposition of wind energy development, and one that emphasized onshore wind to the detriment of alternative energy pathways.

Such explanations imply that if only TAN8 had been formulated through a wider, more inclusive and comprehensive process it would have been more positively received. However, another explanation is that TAN8 reveals a chronic weakness in the capacity of states to govern across their territory and align the heterogeneous elements required to deliver certain outcomes. By dint of being constructed from the centre (Scott, 1998), the process of drawing up the zones emphasized the factors that were clearly and unambiguously mappable but could not 'see' the myriad, complex connections between different social communities, landscapes and the wider environment (Cowell, 2010), such as alternative economic activities within the SSAs, exploiting the 'relatively unspoiled landscape' for informal recreation and tourism (see, for example, the written response to the TAN8 consultation exercise from the Pentir Pumlumon Tourism Association, September 2004). As specific wind farm projects came forward, they encountered site-specific issues not included in the drawing up of the SSAs, such as risks from peat soil erosion, oxidization and carbon release, at the upland Mynydd-y-Gwair in Glamorgan. It is questionable whether including more stakeholders in drawing up strategic plans could ever foreclose the complexity of siting (Nadai, 2007) and places (Devine-Wright, 2009).

Moreover, whatever its claims to offer an all-Wales spatial view, TAN8 could not – simply by guiding development locations – order and control all of the elements that needed to come together in making wind farms. On the technological-development side, various factors converged to rapidly up-scale the size of wind farm projects. Wind turbines increased in capacity and therefore height, from the 300–400 kilowatt machines in place as McKenzie Hedger was writing, to a

1.5MW norm at the time TAN8 was being drawn up, with some schemes constructed during 2015 using 3MW turbines. The notionally supportive policy context of the SSAs stimulated developer interest and this, coupled with the larger turbines, encouraged the submission of bigger projects. The Pen-y-Cymoedd scheme in south Wales, commissioned in 2015, has a capacity of 228MW, ten times that of the largest Welsh wind farm in 1994. In effect, TAN8 precipitated the 'wind rush' heralded by McKenzie Hedger, but more than a decade later. The Welsh Government opportunistically embraced these trends, by raising its policy goals for onshore wind beyond the 800MW in TAN8 to levels that assumed 2000MW would come on stream by 2015–17 (WAG, 2010). However, the larger turbines were to be much more visible, begging questions about the landscape judgements that had underpinned TAN8. This growth in scale also exposed weaknesses in how TAN8 had treated available grid capacity to export the energy.

If anything, the symbolic power of TAN8 further exposed the Welsh Government's limited actual powers in the energy sphere. Energy policy was not an area of devolved competence and, although the Welsh Government could control planning policy, it did not in fact hold the power to determine the largest wind energy applications. All applications for electricity-generating stations over 50MW, in England and Wales, are determined by Westminster, where decision-makers are not bound to give pre-eminence to TAN8 in deciding whether applications are in acceptable locations (DECC, 2011). Many of the 'TAN8 wind farms' exceeded 50MW. Decisions on market support systems for encouraging renewable energy also lay with Westminster. This is important because the design of these systems affects the form of renewable energy development. The successor support system to the Non Fossil-Fuel Obligation (NFFO) was the Renewable Obligation, which supported renewables through the sale by renewable energy producers of certificates (Renewable Obligation Certificates or ROCs) to energy suppliers who are obliged to source a certain percentage of supplies from renewable sources. Although more successful than NFFO in stimulating investment in renewable energy, the complexities and risks of the ROC system made it more readily adopted by larger, international companies (Woodman and Mitchell, 2011). Thus, while McKenzie Hedger describes an emerging trend of major engineering companies moving into wind energy development, this trend intensified, such that much of the capacity coming forward by 2014 was in the hands of major international utilities, with new entrants remaining marginal. Smaller-scale, community-centred energy projects had a place in Wales since the 1990s, such as projects led by the well-established Centre for Alternative Technology at Machynlleth, but expansion has proved slow, and it was not until June 2012 that Community Energy Wales was formed, to represent this part of the sector (Strachan et al., 2015).

Despite this complex dispersion of power, by 2014 many of the 'battle lines' drawn around wind energy in Wales were focused on the powers and actions of the Welsh Government. TAN8 has been consistently supported by successive Welsh governments, and by key conservation bodies with an interest both in protecting special sites and fostering low-carbon forms of energy, such as CCW and the Royal Society for the Protection of Birds. The energy industry was initially hotly opposed because it regarded spatial zoning policies as restrictive, but became a grudging supporter: 'we've got so much invested with it now we have to support it'; if TAN8 is 'dumped', then 'nothing is going to happen'.[1] To that extent, strategic policy has created some mutuality of interest. However, there remained much opposition to wind energy in Wales with much of the ire directed towards TAN8. A particularly galvanizing factor has been the proposals by National Grid in 2011 for a new 400kV high-voltage line through mid Wales, to connect prospective wind energy output coming from the SSAs. The grid projects both spread conflict to areas that previously might have felt themselves unaffected by the wind farms themselves, and intensified opposition. As in the early 1990s, opposition is constituted by residents and communities near SSAs and potential grid routes, along with other longer-standing groups, critical of wind power since early 1990s, like CPRW.

An important dynamic that has unfolded since 1994 is the way in which new opposition groups have formed and up-scaled, as illustrated by two groups in particular. In the mid-1990s, opposition to the local impacts of individual wind farm projects in mid Wales led to the formation of opposition groups and an expansion of critique to the nature of financial support for the sector: for some, 'this was just a con; this was never going to save the world'.[2] These local groups coalesced into the wider Conservation of Upland Montgomeryshire but: 'after TAN8 when the (SSA) boundaries ... crossed the old county boundaries, it became appropriate that the most sensible thing to do ... was to become an organisation for Powys'. Thus the Conservation of Upland Powys was formed. Much more recently, one of the proposed routes for the mid Wales grid sparked the formation of a community-level group – Meifod Against Pylons – which expanded and coalesced to become Montgomeryshire Against Pylons, to present a more united front against all potential routes. As one of the founders explained, they had been little engaged by the preceding debates about wind energy, but they quickly shifted attention to TAN8 as the driver for the grid investment. In terms of strategy, both groups have acted in other arenas, individually and as part of wider anti-wind networks, to challenge UK renewable energy policy as it applies to wind, and acted on electoral processes in mid Wales.

As of 2015, while there was a considerable volume of wind energy investment in Wales lodged in the planning system, outcomes were highly uncertain. Numerous applications had gone to public inquiry but decisions had yet to be issued. Schemes in the SSAs of south Wales had tended to receive consent, and constituted most of the new onshore capacity in Wales added since 2005. In mid Wales, where the fate of wind farms was linked to new grid investments, development had been most intensely resisted. Moreover, opposition in mid Wales was one element in a wider destabilization of political support for onshore wind, making common cause with opposition in many parts of rural England. This had led to the 2010–15 Conservative-dominated coalition government to begin scaling back financial support for onshore wind and, in England, legitimize local planning authorities in taking a more restrictive stance. The Conservatives (and UK Independence Party) went into the May 2015 General Election with policies to end financial support for onshore wind.

An important conclusion from policy developments in Wales is that not all social concerns about wind energy can be mediated by strategic spatial steering. Social science research on wind energy has shown that the choice of sites is an important factor shaping public responses, but public attitudes are also entangled with other things: with attitudes to the technology, feeling about the places and landscapes affected, and the trust felt in the developers and decision-making processes. We now proceed therefore to unpack some of the key issues that underlay public (un)acceptability in relation to wind energy.

Public perspectives

As discussed in the introduction, McKenzie Hedger gave great attention to outlining the key groups and stakeholders who were, at the time, either for or against onshore wind energy in Wales, and to delineating their concerns (as summarized in table 13.1). Since 1994, research on societal responses to wind energy has burgeoned, but most of this has been focused less on groups than on an antecedent issue – to investigate reasons for public opposition, primarily by examining attitudes and perceptions.

It is not difficult to understand why the academic gaze has turned to unpacking the drivers of contestation. In the UK, as elsewhere in the world, opposition to wind energy has proven to be a major factor shaping developments rates, prompting significant attention to issues of 'social acceptability' (see, for example, Huber et al., 2012), and how changes to decision-making processes or the costs and benefits of wind power projects might improve local responses. Researchers have been animated by an apparent 'social gap' (Bell et al., 2005) between what

Table 13.1: Summary of the reasons for support and opposition outlined in McKenzie Hedger (1994)

Support	*Opposition*
Symbols of environmental awareness	Industrialization of the hills
Positive economic benefits (e.g. ecotourism), particularly in economically depressed areas.	Irreversible effects to the landscape
Landowner earnings	No economic benefit perceived
Little disruption to lives once completed	Negative impact on house prices
Not an eyesore	Noise from turbines
Flexibility	Disruption during construction
Cleaner (than fossil fuels)	Protectionist stance – need to protect unspoilt countryside
Does not emit effluence	(Negative) Landscape impacts outweigh the benefits of wind
	Not in my backyard.

Source: Adapted from McKenzie Hedger, 1994.

survey research reveals as generally positive attitudes towards wind and increasing local contestation often characterized as being Not In My Back Yard (although we note that subsequent research has begun to regard this 'social gap' not as an expression of NIMBYism – in which people generally support wind power but then resist it in their local backyard – but in part a methodological artefact (see Batel and Devine-Wright, 2015). McKenzie Hedger draws on early surveys in Wales, showing a majority of respondents displaying positive attitudes (CCW, 1994), and most subsequent survey research has charted continuing public support for renewable energy (including onshore wind) at the UK national level (see Demski et al., 2013a).

When drilling down into national survey data pertaining to Wales, it is clear that wind energy (onshore and offshore) is still seen in terms that are 'very' or 'mainly favourable' to a significant proportion of respondents (68 per cent), but offshore wind is deemed more likely to engender support than onshore (78 and 57 per cent respectively – see Demski et al., 2013b). When asked how likely they were to support or oppose the building of a new wind farm in their area, attitudes become more split, but overall there was still more support than opposition: 51 per cent strongly or tend to support; 20 per cent neither support nor oppose; 28 per cent strongly or tend to oppose (see Demski et al., 2013b).Whilst respondents were more positive towards other renewable energies (see table 13.2) than wind, it is still the case that wind has significant support at the Welsh national level and for new developments in people's local areas.

Local public perspectives – onshore wind

Warren et al. (2005) notes that supporters of onshore wind characterize the technology as being clean, renewable, helping with a shift away from fossil fuels, an inherently good thing facilitating global altruism, and a sustainable energy source that will help current generations meet their needs whilst safeguarding the needs of future generations. As McKenzie Hedger found, other work indicates that onshore wind is symbolically represented as society being in sync with nature (see Woods, 2003; Parkhill, 2007). Other positives include that the wind farm may add to what is perceived as a desolate landscape and help such areas to become more productive spaces (see Woods, 2003; Parkhill, 2007; Butler et al., 2013).

Table 13.2: Participant responses to the question 'How favourable or unfavourable are your overall opinions or impressions of the following energy sources for producing electricity currently?'

	Very favourable %	Mainly favourable %	Neither favourable nor unfavourable %	Mainly unfavourable %	Very unfavourable %	Never heard of %
Biomass, that is wood, energy crops, and human and animal waste	20	38	29	7	1	5
Coal	5	15	38	29	12	*
Gas	7	31	39	18	4	*
Hydroelectric power	41	35	16	2	*	5
Nuclear power	10	20	27	23	20	1
Oil	4	15	41	29	11	1
Sun/Solar power	47	41	10	2	1	0
Wind power	29	39	17	8	6	*
Marine power (tidal and wave power)	43	36	15	1	1	4

These results stem from a sub-analysis of Welsh-only responses (n=507) to a survey that was carried out online with Ipsos MORI panellist's aged 18+ years old living in Great Britain (total n=2441). *Source*: Demski et al., 2013b.

In contrast, those against onshore developments characterize it as, for example, spoiling the visual amenity, damaging tourism, causing negative environmental impacts, inhibiting sustainable development through damage to local landscapes, being noisy, causing tensions between rural and urban dwellers (due to most developments being in rural areas yet the energy produced being perceived as needed in urban areas), being developed in such a way where local communities are not engaged, and leading to the industrialization of rural spaces (see Woods, 2003; Warren et al., 2005; Parkhill, 2007). However, it has been observed that 'much of this opposition is aesthetic in character. It is grounded in a rather sharp separation between nature and technology, expressed in the thought that wind turbines and solar panels in the landscape are ugly' (Brittan, 2001 cited in Woods, 2003, p. 277).

Woods's (2003) analysis of opposition to the Cefn Croes project on the Cambrian Mountains in mid Wales focuses on how the landscape and nature were socially constructed by opponents to the wind farm. Opponents were found to socially construct the area as natural (particularly due to the absence of man-made features), unspoilt, peaceful and beautiful. The Cambrian Mountains were believed to be 'a rare surviving example of nature as wilderness', where visual contemplation was imbued with affective dimensions (Woods, 2003, p. 280). Nature was at once immense and powerful, whilst simultaneously being fragile, with wind turbines being constructed as unnatural entities, due in part to their size and scale. As such, for opponents, wind turbines would be 'incompatible' or 'out of place' in this area (Cresswell, 1996; Butler et al., 2013).

The work of Woods was pivotal in recognizing that opposition complaints about the unsightliness of a wind farm are far more powerful and layered than superficial assessments of the visual amenity. Social constructions and symbolism of landscape and nature were shown to be integral to the informal regulation of rural spaces (also see Parkhill, 2007). Indeed Woods (2003, p. 287) concluded that such social constructions of nature could be the 'tripping stone of the regulation of rural space, and its alluring power yet coy ambiguity will form the fissures of many conflicts as the quest for a sustainable countryside continues'.

More recent work by Butler et al. (2013) indicates that the perceived proliferation of onshore wind energy in Wales is indicative to some of the continued marginalization of the Welsh people by the English. Connecting with the earlier sections of this chapter on the governance of energy in Wales, this research suggests that '[a] key source of contention for participants in both Scotland and Wales is that many of the policy decisions appear to be taken by Westminster, rather than their devolved governments' (Butler et al., 2013, p. 36). The authors note that not only do such concerns connect with issues of environmental and social (in)justice, they may also have significant implications for the policy development and implementation of policies related to energy and onshore wind farms. As such the authors conclude that the devolved governments of Scotland and Wales perhaps 'need to do more to distinguish whether or not they support policies flowing out of Westminster, including delineating how they envision such policies might benefit their constituents' (Butler et al., 2013, p. 36). At the same time, the authors suggest that the UK government needs to 'make clearer how their energy strategy incorporates concerns of citizens living in devolved administrations' (Butler et al., 2013, p. 36).

Mason and Milbourne (2014), in their study examining public support and opposition of the Nant y Moch proposal in Ceredigion, take landscape as their organizing concept, tying it with constructions of justice. Their analysis of the views of opponents to the wind farm, similarly to Woods (2003), shows that opponents' discourses evoke 'a heady mix of values and affect in favour of the present [wind farm-free] landscape' (Mason and Milbourne, 2014, p. 109). The values associated with a wind farm-free landscape include 'beauty, peace, harmony, unity with nature ... freedom, independence, choosing own goals ... social order, sense of belonging, and tradition'. Affective aspects 'arise primarily from the solitude and tranquillity afforded by landscape' (Mason and Milbourne, 2014, p. 109). However, proponents characterize the same landscape as 'ugly and intimidating' (Mason and Milbourne, 2014, p. 110). Contrasting with their perceptions of a wind farm-free landscape, opponents construct 'a wind farm landscape as ugly, noisy and not protecting the environment' (Mason and Milbourne, 2014, p. 109). Proponents point to TAN8 as exacerbating some of these negative perceptions of a wind farm landscape, citing the exemption of national parks as reifying the notion that wind farms devalue the landscape.

In relation to justice, opponents view the proposal as representing spatial injustice, in numerous dimensions: local landscape being sacrificed for national interests; Wales being exploited by England under the mask of UK national interests; the needs of urban areas being prioritized above rural areas; rural values and lay knowledges being usurped by urban values and knowledges. Mason and Milbourne (2014) delve further into issues of (in)justice in relation to opponents' discourses, a key conclusion being that discourses of local injustice are embedded in opponents' narratives. This is juxtaposed with proponents' discourses that are imbued with notions of global justice, through for example, 'exploiting local landscape resources to protect the global environment' (Mason and Milbourne, 2014, p. 113). Mason and Milbourne (2014, p. 114) conclude that '[t]he development of wind energy ... demands a new ethic ... [which] must be mediated locally and have landscape/dwelling here and there in space and time at its heart'.

The body of work reviewed here is part of a much wider set of research that has sought to unpack the reasons underpinning attitudes (positive and negative) towards onshore wind. However, the insights highlighted here clearly show how research based on Welsh case studies has built upon the intuitions McKenzie Hedger outlines in her original article. Yet the story of wind does not end here: over the past two decades offshore wind has emerged as a potentially integral source of low carbon energy. We now turn our attention to attitudes towards offshore wind.

Local public perspectives – offshore wind

Although a relatively new and emergent sector compared to onshore wind, the UK has been a world leader in offshore wind since 2008, 'with as much capacity installed as the rest of the world combined' (RenewableUK, 2015). Such claims translate into an installed capacity of 4049MW, with a further 12.7GW either under construction or consented (RenewableUK, 2015). Additionally, 'many experts view this sector as the most likely vehicle for meeting climate change policy targets to reduce greenhouse gas emissions from electricity generation' (Devine-Wright and Howes, 2010, p. 271). In Wales there are currently three offshore wind projects, all located in the north of the country: Gwynt y Môr (160 turbines, under construction, 576MW capacity), North Hoyle (30 turbines, operational, 60MW capacity) and Rhyl Flats (25 turbines, operational, 90MW capacity).

Systematic research into public attitudes towards marine renewable energies, including offshore wind, has lagged behind analysis of onshore developments (Wiersma and Devine-Wright, 2014). However, the work of Haggett (2008) and Devine-Wright and Howes (2010) are notable exceptions, who, in separate studies, examined attitudes towards Gwynt y Môr. However, before focusing on this case study, it is worth summarizing what is known from the offshore wind farm literature more widely.

Evidence from attitudinal research indicates that many of the perceived advantages of offshore wind are similar to those for onshore wind (and indeed renewables more generally). This includes that the public perceives offshore wind as being clean, renewable, green and facilitating a shift from a perceived over-reliance on fossil fuels (see Parkhill et al., 2013). There is also preliminary evidence that the public perceive offshore wind, and marine renewables more widely, as representing an opportunity to boost the economy of Wales and UK through developing a turbine-manufacturing base within the UK (Butler et al., 2013).

Haggett (2008), in her critical comparative review of the onshore and offshore literature, also notes that many perceive offshore wind as a 'fix' to the numerous issues onshore wind is believed to have. However, she found that 'many of the issues that are relevant to siting turbines onshore are just as relevant offshore and that they merely manifest in slightly different ways' (Haggett, 2008, p. 290). Notable here is Haggett's (2008) findings that: public opposition to offshore wind certainly does exist; there remains a fractious relationship between distant global benefits and local risks; and offshore wind will likely be competing with different users of the space, for example, tourists and fishermen. Indeed, Haggett found that rather than being 'out of sight' and therefore 'out of mind', many offshore wind farms are near shore and as such are often visible to fairly large coastal populations.

Haggett uses a preliminary analysis of research carried out in and around Gwynt y Môr to further unpack public opinion. As with onshore wind, issues of ownership and control of the wind farm were key issues in that most people felt they had none, and efforts by the developer to engage local residents were perceived as vapid public relations exercises. Indeed, local people felt excluded from decision-making and that their concerns were being ignored, risking an erosion of social trust between the public and developer and thus exacerbating opposition (Haggett, 2008; also see Devine-Wright and Howes, 2010).

In Haggett's work, a key concern raised by residents against Gwynt y Môr was the importance of tourism to the local economy, particularly in the famed Victorian resort of Llandudno, with fears of potential negative effects on tourism arising from the development. Protestors asserted that 'the developer's application takes no account of the unique status and character and of the outstanding natural beauty of Llandudno and its bay' (cited in Haggett, 2008, p. 297). Devine-Wright and Howes (2010), in their study exploring attitudes towards Gwynt y Môr, also found that the symbolic meanings associated with the wind farm were integral to whether or not the wind farm was deemed to 'fit' with the place. In quantitative work, they found that Llandudno was predominantly associated with positive visual aesthetics, with residents emphasizing 'the place's scenic beauty linked to its coastal situation and environmental features, which provide distinctive qualities as a tourist resort' (Devine-Wright and Howes, 2010, p. 275).

Gwynt y Môr would also be visible to Colwyn Bay but, in contrast, Colwyn Bay residents represented their area as being run down, 'emphasising its former beauty linked to its coastal situation and its decline in part due to the influx of undesirable outsiders'. These associations with place were found to be integral to how the wind farm was perceived. Both Llandudno and Colwyn Bay participants emphasized the 'gigantic' size of the 'numerous' turbines '[g]oing everywhere round the coast' (Devine-Wright and Howes, 2010, p. 275). However, the perceived outcomes differed markedly. Llandudno participants characterized the wind farm proposal as industrial and presenting 'a significant threat to the town'. Colwyn Bay participants also saw the proposal as industry, but saw this as potentially being positive: 'boosting employment and prosperity locally' (Devine-Wright and Howes, 2010, p. 276).

Llandudno residents were seen to have a higher 'place attachment' (a positive emotional bond between individuals and/or groups and their local area) than Colwyn Bay residents. Devine-Wright and Howes (2010) conclude that there are links between place attachment and the responses of those who oppose such developments. Clearly, then, the socio-cultural context, social constructions of place and the turbines are just as critical for perceptions of offshore wind as they are for onshore developments (also see Haggett, 2008, 2011) and, as such, specific offshore wind developments can be just as contentious as their onshore cousins, in Wales and elsewhere.

In explaining social responses to wind energy, then, social constructions of place emerge more strongly than attachments, attitudes or identities based on notions of Welshness: McKenzie Hedger was justified in treating this issue with agnosticism in her account. Place also offers avenues for explaining divergent attitudes to wind energy and the implementation of TAN8.The vociferous opposition in mid Wales can be seen as an escalation of concerns identified by Woods (2003) about the Cefn Croes project, with protection of unspoilt upland countryside as the key driver. While wind farm schemes have attracted opposition in south Wales, many of the wind farms proposed for SSAs are situated within areas of industrial forestry from which local populations feel relatively alienated (Milbourne et al., 2008), and sustained organized opposition is harder to find. Issues of political allegiance warrant further exploration: would opponents to wind farms in the traditional Labour heartlands of the Welsh coalfields be as happy to offer expedient support to anti-wind Conservative politicians as we have seen with wind farm opponents in mid Wales? Ongoing wind farm conflicts thus shine an interesting light on social attitudes to Welsh-level governing institutions as the 'right level' at which to mediate these disputes.

Renewable energy and Welsh civic identity

In this section we examine how the wind energy debate has affected civic identification with Welsh institutions and devolution. This is an important issue, given the thinner majority support among the public for devolution in Wales compared to Scotland. Conflict around onshore wind in Wales regularly led Assembly politicians to argue that it would be better – for reasons of public accountability, institutional simplicity and more effective delivery – if the Welsh Government acquired more powers to determine energy projects within its territory. Westminster consistently rebuffed any such requests. However, the fact that Westminster rather than the Welsh Government issued consents for the largest energy projects, including the largest wind farms, became a key subject in two major inquiries: the 2011–12 National Assembly Environment and Sustainability Committee inquiry into Energy Policy and Planning in Wales (a process itself arising from growing political opposition to TAN8); the Commission on Devolution in Wales (often referred to as the Silk Commission).

The Silk Commission conducted its own opinion poll (Commission on Devolution in Wales, 2014), which found that 70 per cent of respondents were in favour of the National Assembly having control of renewable energy: in terms of consenting powers, 55 per cent supported the National Assembly dealing with large wind farms, 21 per cent by local authorities and 16 per cent the UK Government. As we have noted above, however, opinion polls can give simplistic views about what it is that the public feels (Ellis et al., 2007). Other forms of data, such as the written consultation responses and transcripts of evidence-gathering sessions across the two inquiries, provide illuminating insights into the state of social attitudes towards the prospect of further devolution in the energy field.[3]

The Welsh Government itself has been a major advocate for the devolution of consenting powers, and support has also come from major conservation bodies – statutory and non-governmental – who see devolution as offering better scope for territorially cohesive policy-making around energy. With the Welsh Government in control, wind farm proposals outside SSAs might be better regulated. The responses of major energy companies are remarkable for their apparent agnosticism to the allocation of powers, but they were firm and consistent on the qualities that governance processes should display. West Coast Energy (para. 2.1) captures a widely shared view: 'the decision making tier ... is possibly secondary to the issue of positive and consistent policy making'. The industry was critical of the 'slow and unpredictable' progress with wind energy in Wales, but held out a positive challenge for devolution: '[s]hould energy consenting powers be devolved to the Welsh Government, we believe that this should be viewed as an opportunity for the Welsh Government to demonstrate its commitment to delivering renewable energy in Wales' (Scottish Power, para. 9). The main political parties in Wales and organizations like the TUC also supported the devolution of consenting powers.

For many community groups, getting TAN8 reviewed was the main objective for participating in these inquiries, though some raised concerns about institutional arrangements between Cardiff and Westminster. Many used the inquiries to invoke narratives of environmental injustice discussed earlier: that 'the natural resources of Wales will be exploited once more by the Nation with the benefits of this investment being most realised in the distant manufacturing and wealthier economic centres' (Llanfechain Community Council; see also Volunteers for Abergorlech, Llansawel and Rhydcymerau; Montgomeryshire Against Pylons). However, for mid Wales groups, wind power represented this exploitation, for other environmental groups it was focused differently: devolution of consenting powers offered an opportunity to resist fossil energy developments encouraged by Westminster, and promote greener energy futures in Wales (FoE Cymru; see also Montgomeryshire Wildlife Trust, Eco Cymru).

Many organizations, especially those resisting development in mid Wales, did recognize institutional and procedural problems in the governance of energy, but rarely did this translate into a neat, linear case for greater Welsh autonomy. For some, since the energy systems of England and Wales were integrated, what was required was 'common planned policies ... on the basis of partnership, rather than master servant' (Volunteers for Abergorlech, Llansawel and Rhydcymerau). Groups like Montgomeryshire Against Pylons were critical of the current split of responsibilities, allowing '[t]he excuses of Westminster blaming Cardiff and *vice versa*' (see also Llansanffraid Action Group), causing 'despondency and cynicism amongst local constituents', yet had 'no position on where these decisions should be made but it is essential that the voices of local people are heard with regard to the future of their own communities'. For others, devolving the issues to the Welsh Government served the pragmatic purpose of ensuring that the review of TAN8 would 'ensure coordination and confidence to the electorate that all matters are considered comprehensively', but a greater role for local democracy was more central to the cure (Montgomeryshire Local Council Forum; Llandrinio and Arddleen Community Council; Llandysilio Community Council). In many respects, then, the bruising experiences of TAN8 and its stumbling implementation had shaped their views of devolution. This is equally true of people in the wind energy industry, many from Wales, for whom any personal preferences for devolution were matched with doubts that the Welsh Government would drive forward the delivery of their wind energy projects.

The Silk Commission recommended that the powers of the Welsh Government be extended, to grant it the executive authority to determine power station consents up to 350MW: an awkward compromise, reflective perhaps of how energy developments remain torn between strategic, national goals and accountability to the localities in which they are developed. It was in the manifestos of all main parties going into the May 2015 election that Silk be implemented; whatever the future implications, this may do little to change the balance of power over large wind farm projects already stuck in the planning system.

Conclusion

When McKenzie Hedger wrote 'Wind Energy: the Debate in Wales', the wind industry was an emerging sector in Wales and the UK more widely. Offshore wind was largely absent from public and policy discourses. What is startling from that original paper is the breadth of issues McKenzie Hedger prophetically outlines. What has emerged since then is a plethora of work focused on many different aspects of wind energy ranging from the technical, through to governance and public attitudes. This contemporary research, particularly that reviewed here, has sought to unpack the complexities underpinning the many dimensions of the debate about wind energy in Wales, which were perhaps only hinted at by McKenzie Hedger. In this final section, we wish to outline the key insights from our chapter, how they differ and/or build upon those by McKenzie Hedger and, finally, consider where next for the debate on wind in Wales.

McKenzie Hedger (1994, p. 132) prophetically stated that 'it is unlikely that a consensus viewpoint will emerge [on wind farms] in the short term'. Indeed, the stakes have increased in the intervening years and consensus over wind energy development seems as distant a prospect as ever. Arguably, the interventions that we have analysed in this chapter such as TAN8 fall short of the comprehensive, inclusive ideals alluded to in the early 1990s, though they have served to bring many more actors into the debate and for arguments to be refined. Moreover, they remind us that technical procedures (and emollient discourses like sustainable development) rarely straightforwardly engender consensus when the underlying issues are difficult to bridge. Such issues include divergent views on the appropriate future for landscapes, but also tensions around the scale and power relations of governance, both between the Welsh Government and UK Government but also between places and future, national energy pathways. Such tensions, clearly manifest in empirical research on public attitudes to wind energy in Wales, also connect with a wider academic focus on aspects of environmental and social justice.

In our analysis, it is clear that the rural landscapes and perceptions of nature and rurality are, as Woods (2003) suggested, key tripping points for the regulation of space, and that devolution has altered the arenas but not wholly shifted the arguments. Our discussion of attitudes towards offshore wind suggested that abandoning onshore projects in favour of developing wind in marine environments would not wholly resolve the issue and would, for some sites at least, transpose the contestation to a new arena. With the coming on stream of the 228MW Pen-y-Cymoedd wind farm in 2015, and the 576MW Gwynt y Môr in 2016, we will see a doubling of wind capacity in Wales, transforming

figure 13.1. However, it is significant that most major new developments of wind are located outside mid Wales, avoiding areas where contestation has been particularly vociferous.

In the aftermath of the May 2015 General Election, the future of wind energy in Wales, and indeed the UK, is clouded in uncertainty. The Conservative Party was elected into government and quickly announced their intentions to end new public subsidy for onshore wind farms, threatening the flow of financial support to wind farms in Wales. In party political terms, we see Welsh Government strategic policy, as represented by TAN8 and Welsh Government energy strategies, supported by successive Labour-led Welsh governments and the Liberal Democrats, undermined by actions in Westminster that have been advocated inter alia by opposition action groups in mid Wales, acting through politicians and the Conservative Party at multiple levels of government. If wind energy is testimony to the enduring nature of land-use-development conflicts, it also shows the uncertain status of devolved government in Wales as an arena of conflict resolution.

Notes

[1] Interviews with wind energy developers, 22 September 2011, 28 September 2011.

[2] Interview with local protest group, 12 September 2012.

[3] The analysis in the following section draws on written consultation responses submitted to the 2011–12 National Assembly Inquiry and to the Silk Commission. A full set of consultation responses for each inquiry, respectively, can be obtained as follows: *www.senedd.assembly.wales/mgIssueHistoryHome.aspx?IId=1336* (accessed 26 November 2015); *http://webarchive.nationalarchives.gov.uk/20140605075122/http://commission-ondevolutioninwales.independent.gov.uk/search/doc-type/evidence/* (accessed 26 November 2015). All of the quoted material comes from submissions to the National Assembly for Wales inquiry.

References

Batel, S. and Devine-Wright P., 'A Critical and Empirical Analysis of the National-local Gap in Public Responses to Large-scale Energy Infrastructures', *Journal of Environmental Planning and Management*, 58/6 (2015), 1076–95.

Bell, D., Gray, T. and Haggett, C., 'The "Social Gap" in Wind Farm Siting Decisions: Explanations and Policy Responses', *Environmental Politics*, 14/4 (2005), 460–77.

Butler, C., Parkhill K. A. and Pidgeon, N., *Deliberating Energy System Transitions in the UK – Transforming the UK Energy System: Public Values, Attitudes and Acceptability* (London: UKERC, 2013).

Commission on Devolution in Wales, *Empowerment and Responsibility: Legislative Powers to Strengthen Wales* (Cardiff: Commission on Devolution in Wales, 2014).

Countryside Council for Wales (CCW), *Wind Turbine Power Station Construction Monitoring Study* (Bangor: Chris Blandford Associates in association with University of Wales, 1994).

Cowell, R., 'Wind Power and "the Planning Problem": the Experience of Wales', *European Environment*, 17/5 (2007), 291–306.

——, 'Wind Power, Landscape and Strategic Spatial Planning – the Construction of "Acceptable Locations" in Wales', *Land Use Policy*, 27/2 (2010), 222–32.

——, Bristow, G. and Munday, M., *Wind Energy and Justice for Disadvantaged Communities*, Viewpoint produced for the Joseph Rowntree Foundation (York: Joseph Rowntree Foundation, 2012), p. 44.

——, Ellis, G., Sherry-Brennan, F., Strachan, P. and Toke, D., 'Re-scaling the Governance of Renewable Energy: Lessons from the UK Devolution Experience', *Journal of Environmental Policy and Planning* (2015).

Cresswell, T., *In Place/Out of Place: Geography, Ideology, and Transgression* (Minnesota: University of Minnesota Press, 1996).

Department of Energy and Climate Change (DECC), *National Policy Statement for Renewable Energy Infrastructure (EN-3)*, July (London: The Stationery Office, 2011).

——, *Renewable Energy in Scotland, Wales, Northern Ireland and the Regions of England* (London: Crown Copyright, 2014).

Demski, C., Spence, A. and Pidgeon, N., *Summary Findings of a Survey Conducted August 2012 – Transforming the UK Energy System: Public Values, Attitudes and Acceptability* (London: UKERC, 2013a).

——, —— and ——, *Transforming the UK Energy System: Public Values, Attitudes and Acceptability – Wales Survey Results* (Cardiff: Cardiff University, 2013b).

Devine-Wright, P., 'Rethinking Nimbyism: The Role of Place Attachment and Place Identity in Explaining Place Protective Action', *Journal of Community and Applied Social Psychology*, 19/6 (2009), 426–41.

—— and Howes, Y., 'Disruption to Place Attachment and the Protection of Restorative Environments: A Wind Energy Case Study', *Journal of Environmental Psychology*, 20 (2010), 271–80.

Ellis, G., Barry, J. and Robinson, C., 'Many Ways to Say "No", Different Ways to Say "Yes": Applying Q-methodology to Understand Public Acceptance of Wind Farm Proposal', *Environmental Planning and Management*, 50/4 (2007), 517–51.

ENDS, *Unambitious English regions place onus on Scottish renewables*, *ENDS Report*, 325 (2002), 8–9.

Freeden, M., 'Is Nationalism a Distinct Ideology?', *Political Studies*, 46/4 (1998), 748–65.

Haggett, C., 'Over the Sea and Far Away? A Consideration of the Planning, Politics and Public Perception of Offshore Wind Farms', *Journal of Environmental Policy & Planning*, 10/3 (2008), 289–306.

——, 'Understanding Public Responses to Offshore Wind', *Energy Policy*, 39 (2011), 503–10.

Hamilton, P., 'The Greening of Nationalism: Nationalising Nature in Europe', *Environmental Politics*, 11/2 (2002), 27–48.

Huber, S., Horbarty, R. and Ellis, G., 'Social Acceptance of Wind Power Projects: Learning from Trans-National Experience', in J. Szarka, R. Cowell, G. Ellis, P. Strachan and C. Warren (eds), *Learning from Wind Power: Governance and Societal Perspectives on Sustainable Energy* (London: Palgrave Macmillan, 2012), pp. 215–34.

Irwin, A., 'The Politics of Talk: Coming to Terms with the "New" Scientific Governance', *Social Studies of Science*, 36/2 (2006), 299–320.

McKenzie Hedger, M., 'Wind Energy: the Debate in Wales', *Contemporary Wales*, 7 (1994), 117–34.

Mason, K. and Milbourne, P., 'Constructing a "Landscape Justice" for Windfarm Development: The Case of Nat Y Moch, Wales', *Geoforum*, 53 (2014), 104–15.

Milbourne, P., Marsden, T. and Kitchen, L., 'Scaling Post-Industrial Forestry: The Complex Implementation of National Forestry Regimes in the Southern Valleys of Wales', *Antipode*, 40/4 (2008), 612–31.

Nadai, A., '"Planning", "siting" and the local acceptance of wind power: Some lessons from the French Case', *Energy Policy*, 35 (2007), 2715–26.

Parkhill, K., 'Tensions between Scottish National Policies for Onshore Wind Energy and Local Dissatisfaction – Insights from Regulation Theory', *European Environment*, 17/5 (2007), 307–20.

——, Demski, C., Butler, C., Spence, A. and Pidgeon, N., *Transforming the UK Energy System: Public Values, Attitudes and Acceptability – A Synthesis Report* (London: UKERC, 2013).

Power, S, and Cowell, R., 'Wind power and spatial planning in the UK', in J. Szarka, R. Cowell, G. Ellis, P. A. Strachan and C. Warren (eds), *Learning from Wind Power. Governance, Societal and Policy Perspectives on Sustainable Energy* (Basingstoke, Hants: Palgrave, 2012), pp. 61–84.

RenewableUK, *UK Wind Energy Database (UKWED)* (2015), *www.renewableuk. com/en/renewable-energy/wind-energy/uk-wind-energy-database/index.cfm* (accessed 13 May 2015).

Scott J. C., *Seeing Like a State. How Certain Schemes to Improve the Human Condition Have Failed* (Yale: Yale University Press, 1998).

Stevenson, R., 'Discourse, Power, and Energy Conflicts: Understanding Welsh Renewable Energy Planning Policy', *Environment and Planning C: Government and Policy*, 27/3 (2009), 512–26.

Strachan, P., Cowell, R., Ellis, G., Sherry-Brennan, F. and Toke, D., 'Promoting Community Renewable Energy in a Corporate Energy World', *Sustainable Development* (2015).

Warren, C. R., Lumsden, C., O'Dawd, S. and Birnie, R. V., '"Green on green": Public Perceptions of Wind Power in Scotland and Ireland', *Journal of Environmental Planning & Management*, 48/6 (2005), 853–75.

Welsh Assembly Government (WAG), *Technical Advice Note 8: Renewable Energy* (Cardiff: WAG, 2005).

——, *A Low Carbon Revolution: The Welsh Assembly Government Energy Policy Statement* (Cardiff: WAG, 2010).

Wiersma, B. and Devine-Wright, P., 'Public Engagement with Offshore Renewable Energy: A Critical Review', *WIREs Climate Change*, 5/4 (2014), 493–507.

Woodman, B. and Mitchell, C., 'Learning from Experience? The Development of the Renewable Obligation in England and Wales, 2002–2010', *Energy Policy*, 39/7 (2011), 3914–21.

Woods, M., 'Conflicting Environmental Visions of the Rural: Windfarm Development in Mid Wales', *Sociologia Ruralis*, 34/4 (2003), 271–88.

14

Conclusion

DAWN MANNAY

Introduction

This concluding chapter has the difficult task of revisiting and consolidating the intervening chapters, which dealt with diverse but connecting themes about Wales and contemporary Welsh life. Each chapter in the collection has reflected on the changes and continuities since the publication of key works in *Our Sisters' Land* and the seminal papers revisited from the journal *Contemporary Wales*. Therefore, the topics revisited have been selected from an expansive set of contributions. Consequently, there are omissions such as the contemporary experiences of women in rural Wales (Ashton, 1994; Wenger, 1994), material culture (Vincentelli, 1994), sexuality (Crwydren, 1994) and religion (Morgan, 1994): these are important topics that call for further consideration. Nevertheless, the chapters have explored the role of men and women in Wales and Wales itself as a nation, a culture, an economy and a centre of partially devolved governance, and raised questions related to gender, equality and identity.

In summarizing the key arguments of the collection, the chapter takes a thematic approach, dealing with each section of the book in turn but also making reference to the ways in which the discussions connect and overlap. As well as reflecting on what the chapter authors can tell us, importantly the conclusion engages with the musical and photographic contributions, developed with Ministry of Life, and explores what can be learnt from the voices of young people living in Wales. In many ways, the chapters were constrained by their revisiting; however, the open nature of the arts-based contributions has engendered new viewpoints and an opportunity to explore issues of ethnicity, body image, bullying and the active political voice of young people beyond discourses of apathy and disengagement.

Accordingly, the collection has worked to engage with marginalized young people in Wales and provide the opportunity for their conceptualizations of nation, identity, Welsh culture and social issues to have a voice in the publication and the associated audio and visual outputs. These creative outputs were not simply a reflection of the content of the chapters; rather the young people involved took the themes and came back with issues that had not necessarily been considered by the academic authors, issues that were nonetheless of central importance to them. Considering the breadth of these diverse inputs, as well as looking back, the chapter also looks forward to the next decades of changing identities, gender relations and discourses of class, suggesting future academic research and emerging agendas from the volume, and considering the future of *Our Changing Land.*

Revisiting Wales, Welshness, language and identity

Jane Aaron opened this section of the book with her insightful reflections on Welsh women authors' work, in all its various genres, since devolution, and suggested that in the changing land of present-day Wales, gender equality in the literary field is no longer a distant prospect. However, given the declining gender parity in Welsh governance and the instability of women in public life and employment more widely (see Chaney, Rees and Lloyd this volume), Aaron is cautious in celebrating this victory, hoping that the current luminosity of Welsh female creativity will be sustainable and not a time that will be regarded in retrospect as 'but a bright flash in the pan'.

For Aaron, Gwyneth Lewis's bilingual lines emblazoned on the forehead of the Millennium Centre, which are featured in Ian Homer's photograph, serve as an inspiration for women writers and the works visited in her chapter illustrate the vibrancy and value of their writing. However, despite this revolution of female creativity the subject matter discussed by the authors still raises questions about the pervasive nature of systems of patriarchy, unemployment in the post-industrial landscape, environmental depletion and scarring, health inequalities, migration and ethnic differences. Therefore, although freedoms now exist for Welsh women to write, their creativity remains encased in the complex and divided land of the Welsh nation, which is reflected and represented in their literary forms.

A further characteristic of Welsh 'differences and divisions' is linguistic difference and Aaron charts the rise of Welsh speakers through Welsh-medium schooling, but also notes the limited opportunities for students to engage with the language outside the educational arena. Drawing on Catrin Dafydd's (2007, 2015) popular fictions, Aaron reflected on how Dafydd's character, Samantha Jones, attempted to keep up her Welsh-speaking skills after leaving school, aided only by an ailing Welsh-speaking grandmother and the television series *Pobol y Cwm*. This idea of a paucity of spaces for the social use of Welsh is taken up by Non Geraint in the following chapter, where she revisits Heini Gruffudd's (1997) article from *Contemporary Wales*, 'Young People's Use of Welsh: The Influence of Home and Community'.

Geraint sensitively charts the struggle and conflict that has dominated the linguistic history of Wales, detailing *Brad y Llyfrau Gleision* ('The Treachery of the Blue Books') and the political, social and economic impacts, which worked together to marginalize the Welsh language, before charting the recent resurgence of the language, primarily driven through the growing provision of Welsh-medium schooling. In her empirical work with secondary schoolchildren, Geraint found a strong identification with Wales in terms of national identity and, echoing Gruffudd's (1997) study, participants held consistent positive views towards the Welsh language and its importance as a national and cultural symbol of Welshness; however, English dominated as the language of social relationships in the school setting.

Geraint argued that it is crucial that the Welsh language is developed as a social language beyond the opportunities provided within education and the workplace, if Welsh is to survive as an active, thriving and vibrant language. The photograph created for Geraint's chapter represents the lack of opportunity for young people to access 'fashionable' media in the Welsh language, and the dominance of English forms of print media, but as Mackay argued in chapter 12, this English-language dominance can be extended to other mediated forms. Geraint's chapter suggests that for the Welsh language to become sustainable as a first language the extension of social, cultural and media-based Welsh opportunities for young people should be a Welsh Government priority.

My own chapter was concerned with the tension between post-feminist discourses of freedom and the everyday negotiation of feminized identities in the private space of the home for mothers residing in a marginalized locale in urban south Wales. In exploring the everyday realities of lived Welsh working-class femininities, with a focus on housework, the chapter argued that women are caught in an untenable position between the ideologies of the 'Welsh Mam' and competing neo-liberal discourses that expect women to contribute economically and attain acceptable forms of motherhood and mothering. Despite evidence of personal agency, women's accounts spoke of the impossibility of achieving feminist and egalitarian ideologies for mothers and daughters on the margins of contemporary Wales.

This positioning between impossible expectations and the emotional cost of maintaining acceptable forms of motherhood, domesticity, paid work and working-class femininity are echoed in the later chapters by Morgan and Salisbury, suggesting that the last two decades have resulted in more complex and difficult negotiations between public and private life for women in Wales. However, the photograph for the chapter, whose frame was selected by young people in the workshops reflecting on their own experiences, presents a more positive visual trope for the future as a father washing the dishes is watched by his young daughter. Personal history, subjectivity and practices are formed in social relations and the affective routines of everyday family life (Wetherell, 2012), and this image suggests that as working patterns change a more equitable sharing of the domestic sphere could emerge. In this way, the question of 'who should do the dishes?' in future generations in Wales may engender responses that are not fixed in traditional, outdated gendered discourses.

Gendered identities were also explored by Ward, who refocused the discussion to examine the lives of young men in south Wales. Again, there were tensions between traditional ideologies of being a 'real man' in Wales and the context of the post-industrial employment landscape. Ward explored the ways in which young men in Wales construct an acceptable form of working-class masculinity by drawing on their family backgrounds and the industrial heritage of place. For many young men, an archetype of masculinity associated with an older world of industrial work was outwardly performed through 'masculine' affirming practices within the school and 'risky' leisure pleasures outside it. Although some of these young men aimed for traditional apprenticeships in the space of physical work, this is problemetized by deindustrialization and the loss of heavy industry, as discussed by Adamson in chapter 10 and represented by Ian Homer's photograph, communicating the physical landscape of a post-industrial Welsh valley.

Ward also discussed alternative forms of masculinity based around music, different leisure pursuits and academic identities, the latter being potentially advantageous in relation to the shift to a knowledge economy (see Ward, 2014). However, these routes to escape from the de-industrial community produced a troubled and risky subject position, whereby young men following alternative pathways were often subject to peer bullying, a subject that resonated with the song produced for the Education, Labour Markets and Gender in Wales theme, which I return to later in this chapter. Ward argues that a particularly 'hard' form of working-class masculinity in this de-industrial community is still the default reference point. Following, or working against, these default historical legacies, about what it means to be a 'real' Welsh man, or woman, impact on individuals' educational and employment possibilities, and also the everyday gendered experiences, of both young people and adults in contemporary Wales.

In exploring Welsh identities this section has focused on gender and linguistic differences within the nation; however, in revisiting previous works there was little space to explore the array of possible ethnicities within the boundaries of Wales. Aaron reflected on the representation of multiple ethnicities in literature, for example, considering Charlotte Williams's *Sugar and Slate* (2002), and the Afro-Caribbean and north Wales slate-quarrying heritage, which meant that Williams opted for the ethnicity of Welshness because Wales is so diverse, 'mixed up ... fragmented, because there is a loud bawling row raging, because its inner pain is coming to terms with its differences and its divisions, because it realises it can't hold on to the myth of sameness, past or present' (Williams, 2002, pp. 169 and 191).

The song created for the first section theme, Wales, Welshness, Language and Identity, celebrates the idea and value of hybrid identities within Wales. The song, *Hybrid Identity*, written and performed by KAOS, expresses pride associated with a diverse heritage, which can allow space for simultaneous associations with Wales and Welshness, 'I'm at Cardiff City games saying I'm proud to be Welsh', however, the lyrics also demonstrate the pervasiveness of prejudice and discrimination. As a nation that has been historically marginalized, there is an argument that the Welsh have developed a different articulation of racial superiority and inferiority, a claim that the Welsh nation is welcoming, in relation to the narrow xenophobia and overt racism of English nationalism, but it is a claim that is and should be challenged (Williams, 1999).

The silencing of 'race' in Wales is supported by an investment in discourses of empathy with oppressed people and the imagining of Wales as a tolerant nation, where any ideas of xenophobia are defined through the Welsh/English dichotomy. This culture of disbelief refuses to acknowledge the significant levels of mistreatment experienced by ethnic minority groups inside and outside the workplace, including racial harassment, physical attacks and job discrimination (Wooding, 1998; Robinson and Gardner, 2004). A recent report argues that the economic downturn has contributed to a climate of blame where everyday racism takes the form of spitting, verbal abuse, threatening gestures and throwing objects, directed at black and ethnic minority communities (Crawley, 2012). Importantly, white residents in Wales from other parts of the UK report incidents of xenophobia, and in contemporary Wales historical discourses of English oppression are evoked to excuse the persecution of individuals who become a convenient target of ridicule and aggression.

In considering Wales, Welshness, language and identity there is much in the big history of a small nation that provides a secure sense of self; however, history, by its very nature, will always be an eclectic of fact, perspective and interpretation. For example, the eighteenth-century writer Iolo Morganwg succumbed to the temptation of creating the past, and his forgeries earned him the title 'rogue elephant of the literary tradition' among historians; but his embellishments still inform contemporary understandings of Wales (Barlow, 2009). Custom and tradition, real and imagined, are seen to engender nationalism and the Welsh language is also a vehicle for forging and maintaining connection within Wales. These themes are drawn upon to separate Wales from England, maintain a sense of nationhood and inform ideologies of acceptable masculinities, femininities and ethnicities. However, it is important that these symbolic, cultural and narrative forms are drawn upon with caution and act as a base to form new, inclusive and progressive forms and articulations of Wales, Welshness and identity, rather than constraining and shadowing the opportunities for both the nation and its diverse citizens.

Revisiting education, labour markets and gender in Wales

Melanie Morgan opened this section with 'Re-Educating Rhian: Experiences of Working-class Mature Student Mothers', that revisited Pam Garland's (1994) contribution to *Our Sisters' Land*, which charted the experiences of mature women students in higher education. In revisiting and updating this earlier study, Morgan found many continuities across the decades and the idea of the pressures of combining studies with the domestic life emerged as a dominant trope, where women were caught between the 'greedy' institutions of family and university (Edwards, 1993, p. 62; Currie et al., 2000). Resonating with my earlier chapter, Morgan explored how neo-liberal shifts have exerted an increasing pressure on mothers to be both effective care givers and economically active providers.

This key shift was made visible through the mature student mothers' earlier journeys back into higher education, as where in Garland's study women had waited until their children were older and more independent, in Morgan's sample women were embarking on higher education while their children were still very young. Morgan argued that returning to learn within such a demanding stage of the family life cycle, although achievable, is not without practical, emotional and psychological costs for mature student mothers in Wales. This is reflected visually with the chapter photograph, designed in workshops with young people who suggested the struggle of this positioning be reflected with a mother and young child negotiating the steps to Cardiff University, laden with books, communicating the physical sense of balancing child care and study within projects of educational and social mobility.

Jane Salisbury moved from a focus on students to those who teach, but also continue to seek credentialization, in her chapter 'Private Lives Used for Public Work: Women Further Education Teachers in Wales'. The emotional and psychological costs of caring for families discussed earlier in the book (see Mannay and Morgan this volume) transfers to the educational setting where the 'capacity to care' (Hollway, 2006) is translated into teachers' pastoral relationships with students. Salisbury argues that women teachers are caught in a system of increased scrutiny, overburdening administrative duties and target setting, which means that their emotional labour becomes commodified, as they work outside their paid hours to meet the occupational challenges of contemporary further education.

As well as negotiating the neoliberal managerialism of an educational sector that has been subject to extensive funding cuts, to be and remain effective teachers, the women featured in the chapter were also involved in 'chasing credentials'. Their engagement, again, was connected to the altruistic goals of being a more effective teacher and also wider projects of self-improvement and employability, an important aspect because women continue to be under-represented in the higher ranks of all educational sectors in Wales. Like the additional work that these women contribute, their positioning in educational systems is often made invisible; Salisbury ends her chapter by concluding that the Education Workforce Register for Wales will hopefully improve the visibility of important teacher characteristics – not least that of gender. The invisibility of women teachers' pastoral work and their gendered marginalization in educational institutions is symbolized in the chapter photograph featuring a panther chameleon. Well known for its ability to adapt to changing environments and in doing so becoming less visible, the chameleon is pictured among certificates of credentialization.

Focusing on a different employment sector, low-wage manufacturing industries and the low-wage service sector work, Caroline Lloyd argued that in Wales, improvement in the quality of this type of work remains bleak. The photograph for the chapter, women working at sewing machines, represents the clothing industry, which was a major employer for women when Lloyd was writing in the 1990s. However, the industry has since gone into serious decline and workers have been displaced into the fragile economy of the service sector. Wales had already suffered disproportionately during the 1980s recession, reinforced by long-term decline in the coal and steel industries, and therefore the loss of manufacturing and the clothing industry was felt even more keenly in the labour market.

Lloyd resists the temptation to gloss the experience of working in the clothing industry in terms of nostalgic references to camaraderie on the shop floor and she is careful to stress that these manufacturing jobs were typically low paid and consisted of routine and repetitive forms of work. However, although conditions were far from perfect, in relation to the current opportunities in the service sector they did at least offer some form of security with predictable working hours and secure contracts. In reflecting on low-waged work in contemporary Wales, Lloyd centralizes the rise of zero-hours contracts, which provide no guaranteed hours and leave the worker facing variations in both working time and pay on a weekly basis. In this way, the problematic nature of low-paid work, for both men and women, has intensified, leaving them in a vulnerable and insecure position, which current policies in Wales, and the UK more widely, are unable and ill-equipped to alleviate.

These issues were also explored by Alison Parken in her chapter, which examined the present picture for women in paid work in Wales across a wide base of employment and pay parameters. Revisiting earlier work conducted by Teresa Rees (1994), Parken argued that at the top end of the occupational structure, there is now gender balance in the professional occupations overall; however, women professionals in Wales are mainly restricted to the sectors of education, health and social care. At the bottom of the labour market hierarchy, elementary occupations are also gender balanced overall but men and women have starkly opposing working patterns in terms of full- and part-time work; they also work in highly gender segregated jobs. The last two decades have seen some improvements in relation to gender equality, and Parken discusses how Welsh Government policy has evolved to recognize the need to support the implementation of equality duties, such as the 'equal pay duty'. She cites the Women Adding Value to the Economy (WAVE) programme as an example of movement from declaratory intent (Chaney, 2009, and this volume), to evidence-based action. However, in line with Lloyd, Parken argues that the Welsh Government must work to address low-skilled, low-hours jobs as the default form of flexible working.

The photograph produced by Ian Homer for Parken's chapter features Paula, a cleaner at Eastmoors Youth Centre. Paula's picture could be seen to represent the highly gender-segregated jobs in elementary occupations; however, the picture also represents Paula's personal experience of paid work. Paula was nominated for a Local Hero Award for her work at Eastmoors, where she not only takes pride in the task of maintaining the physical space but also befriends, supports and encourages the staff and young people that use the centre. This emotional labour and capacity to care is beyond the remit of Paula's employment, but like the teachers in Salisbury's study, Paula builds relationships within her community. However, Paula can only do this as her contract offers her fixed, regular hours, based in the same youth centre; a zero-hours contract, spread out insecurely across different venues with unpredictable hours, would not allow this form of secure work. In this way, zero-hours contracts not only engender insecurity, poverty and vulnerability but they also close down the opportunities for workers like Paula to build relationships and contribute to sustainable communities.

Tasha Harvey's song for this chapter also moves away from and beyond the themes revisited in this section, as her interpretation of education in Wales seeks to illustrate the everyday educational experiences of young people from an alternative perspective. The title of the song, *Beautiful*, captures the essence of the vocal arrangement and Tasha's performance of the song but the message speaks of the destruction of beauty, youth and family and the ultimate loss of an untimely death. The song offers an insight into the lived experience of bullying 'This beautiful girl I knew just started high school, Bullied just because she walked into the classroom', and its pervasive effects 'Being anorexic and skinny to the bone, Still people picked on her because she was alone'. The accompanying video also communicates a sense of isolation as Tasha performs the song within a busy city yet communicates a sense of being alone.

The chapters in this section have focused on the inequalities of the gendered educational landscape and labour market that have to be continually negotiated by adults in Wales, while Tasha Harvey asks us to consider the barriers faced by young people. The inclusion of this song offered an opportunity to raise important questions about bullying, pressures around body image and the commodification of young bodies in a consumer society. These issues link with the performance of acceptable (and unacceptable) masculinities in the school, discussed earlier in the book (see Ward), but beyond education spaces young people are enmeshed in a postmodern, mediated world of flux, change and uncertainty where they also need to deal with the bullying of a digital age, where they are surrounded by portals to the virtual world. The documentary *Bridgend* (2013) and the film *A Bridgend Story* (2015) explore the impact of young people and suicide in south Wales but beyond these dramatized representations important work has been done in Wales to gain a more nuanced insight into the everyday gendered experiences of young people in educational and online settings (Ivinson and Renold, 2013; Renold and Ringrose, 2011; Ringrose 2013; Ringrose and Renold, 2010), which is worth pursuing to gain an understanding of this important area.

Revisiting Welsh public life, social policy, class and inequality

The final section of this collection began with Dave Adamson's poign-ant reflection on his work on class relations in the 1990s. At this time, the poverty of the marginalized working class was expected to be a short-lived effect of industrial restructuring that would be resolved by government policies, which would act to regenerate employment in post-industrial areas. However, these hopes were not actualized and reflecting on the situation in contemporary Wales, Adamson argues that rather than being alleviated, poverty has become a normalized, pervasive, intergenerational feature of Welsh life in marginalized locales. Moreover, the restricted nature of devolved power means that Welsh Government has only been able to offer ameliorative policies that seek to make the lived experience of poverty more manageable, but these policies cannot tackle the fundamental causes of poverty in Wales.

The photograph for the chapter represents the loss of industry in Wales, featuring Merthyr Tydfil's Hoover factory. When Adamson was exploring the 'new poverty' of the 1990s, the prospect of job cuts was already on the horizon for the workers at Hoover and, in 2009, 337 staff clocked off for the last time joining the ranks of the unemployed in the increasingly marginalized town (WalesOnline, 2009). The photograph is symbolic of the high levels of employment and poverty, which have become established as a permanent feature of Welsh society. In this post-industrial landscape, towns like Merthyr Tydfil, which were once productive centres of industry, become marginalized and stigmatized in a popular and political culture that has little empathy with the poorest Welsh communities.

In the following chapter, Paul Chaney shifted the lens of analysis to explore devolution, civil society and political representation with a particular focus on gender. The emergence of the National Assembly, with its highly visible display of women Assembly members, acted as a symbol of hope and inspiration for new forms of governance and public life; and, to some extent, this has been supported by empirical evidence charting advances in the substantive representation of women and the promotion of gender equality. However, for Chaney, despite these gains the record of devolved governance in terms of its ability to claim gender parity has been disappointing in three key respects – depth, breadth and permanency – not only in terms of the reversibility in the number of women holding key political seats but also in relation to policy making and its inability to fully address key gendered barriers in a climate of austerity and cuts, which disproportionally affect the social and economic aspects of Welsh women's lives.

The idea of women in public life was represented in Ian Homer's image of young women protesting against the war in Iraq, representing their commitment to change through direct action. In picturing political engagement within the hands of a general public, the image speaks of the power, ability and commitment of people in Wales to effect change and to speak out against the decisions of wider governance. This participatory model of engagement in public life, through many forms, not simply that of direct action, resonates with the aims of many of the civil society organizations interviewed by Chaney in his research. For example, the flagship programme Women Making a Difference has been central in providing women with opportunities to engage with public life by offering a range of courses, mentoring and role shadowing, which has led to positions for women such as community councillors and public appointments. However, while these measures are invaluable, a far wider scale of structural and cultural transformation will be required too if Wales is to achieve an equal and inclusive governance structure.

The following chapter opened with Nathan Bond's artistic interpretation of *Dr Who*. Along with other high-profile programmes such as *Gavin and Stacey* and *Torchwood*, *Dr Who* has been filmed in Wales and the new *Dr Who Experience* visitor centre has mapped Cardiff as the contemporary home of this science fiction classic. This mediated attachment to place has affected the ways in which Wales can be seen both inside and beyond its borders; however, arguably, although these programmes are filmed in Wales, they do not necessarily reflect 'Welsh life or communicate any sense of Welsh identity to a wider audience' (Blandford, 2010, p. 293). Furthermore, the geographical focus on a narrow range of predominantly urban centres means that these programmes only represent certain dimensions of Welsh life, to the exclusion of others. Hugh Mackay explored these issues of nation and representation in charting the transformation of the media in Wales.

Mackay revisited a sector that has seen huge changes over the past two decades. The print press in Wales, as in the UK more widely, has experienced a considerable demise, which has had significant impacts for those working in the media. However, Mackay found that the Welsh-language sector of the press has managed to negotiate some sustainability in its transition to online formats. In radio, Welsh-language programming has faced difficulties and the space for young people to engage with what they consider 'relevant' media is an ongoing concern (see Geraint, this volume). In television, despite cuts to funding, the move from analogue television to digital forms allows viewers outside Wales to enjoy Welsh programming, serving the demand of the Welsh-speaking diaspora. Most striking has been the expansion of the Internet that has allowed a multiplicity of voices, many of them in the Welsh language, which are able to connect with audiences through blogs and social media. It is then, perhaps, this form of media that has the greatest potential for communicating the multiplicity of Welsh identities within the nation and allowing a space for more nuanced and meaningful representations of Welsh life, values, art and creativity.

In the final chapter, Karen Parkhill and Richard Cowell revisited Merylyn McKenzie Hedger's (1994) article, 'Wind Energy: the Debate in Wales'. The chapter highlighted many continuities with this earlier work, not least the persistence of public opposition to wind energy development in Wales. Resonating with the image of activism that represented Chaney's chapter, the photograph for this chapter illustrates an event held in Cardiff in 2011 to protest against proposals to build numerous large wind farms and high-voltage grid lines across tracts of rural Wales. The central placard 'No Way to Powys Pylons' sends a clear message to the Welsh Government housed within the Senedd. However, there have been differential responses in Wales with some communities challenging plans for wind farms because they compromise the scenic beauty, while others welcome the potential opportunity for local employment and prosperity. Reflecting on Adamson's chapter, the desire for employment in marginalized areas can be seen to set up further inequalities in that residents may still have concerns about the long-term environmental impacts of large energy facilities but feel that this is the only available option for regenerating their locality and addressing long-term worklessness and poverty.

The Welsh Government has only enjoyed limited and restrictive powers in relation to the implementation of wind farm projects; consequently their plans and policies remain vulnerable to actions in Westminster. The Silk Commission recommended that the powers of the Welsh Government be extended, and the manifestos of all main parties going into the May 2015 election suggested that Silk be implemented. However, these additional powers to control the development of new energy infrastructure will not necessarily reduce conflict on the appropriate future for Wales's landscapes or tensions around the scale of wind energy developments. McKenzie Hedger's (1994, p. 132) prediction that 'it is unlikely that a consensus viewpoint will emerge [on wind farms] in the short term' has been born out in Parkhill and Cowell's revisiting, and their prognosis reaches a similar conclusion that the landscape of clean energy will continue to be a difficult and complex space to negotiate in Wales.

Jamie Feeney, aka Sapien, wrote the music and words for the final song of the collection, *Politricks*, and the video, produced by Magnus Oboh-Leonard of TAB Media, acts to powerfully reinforce the central messages with captions and a storyboard touching on austerity, government cuts and poverty. The song chimes with Adamson's discussion of poverty, 'To the gap between rich and poor, Contrast from a tramp to an entrepreneur', emphasizing the growing inequalities in Wales in terms of income and place. It also resonates with questions raised by Chaney, Parkhill and Cowell about the limitations on the Welsh Government to deliver change within their restricted political powers and how this generates apathy among young people – 'No surprise it's a low turnout at the polls'. In relation to Mackay's reference to the Internet as a dominant form of communication, information and voice, Sapien also explores the ways in which young people are searching for answers beyond the discourses of national politics: 'So we're looking at the global news, Conspiracy theories make more sense than the truth, That's why they're so popular with the youth.' In revisiting Welsh public life, social policy, class and inequality the chapters in this section, and the lyrics of *Politricks*, have much to tell us about how far Wales has come in the last twenty years and the changes necessary to move forward to attain a more equal, inclusive and sustainable Wales.

Conclusion

In reflecting on the collection as a whole there is much to celebrate in post-devolution Wales and there have been significant changes for the better where the Welsh Government has governed in a distinctly 'Welsh way', committed to communitarian and collective policies that embrace bilingualism, civic nationalism and a more inclusive political system. However, there are also substantial concerns about marginalization, in-work poverty and sustainability, which need to be addressed urgently. Furthermore, the everyday lives of people in Wales are complicated by historical gendered and racialized discourses that compete against the contemporary requirements of the knowledge economy, create additional burdens for dual-earner households and allow the continuance of discrimination and xenophobia.

The photographs, audios and videos created for this collection offered the opportunity for new voices to be heard and for their messages to be communicated at the level of affect (Mannay, 2016). The young people involved have generously shared their ideas about Wales as a nation and raised important issues to place on the agenda. In looking forward to the evolving future of the nation it is clear that issues of bullying and racism need attention, and that the new programme of government cuts are a threat to ideologies of equality and community. Austerity has already disproportionality impacted on the most marginalized communities in Wales, and the Welsh Government will need to carefully consider how this trend can be reversed if it is to both stand for and serve the people of Wales. In reaching the end of the book, I would encourage the reader to go back and listen to the audios or watch the videos for each of the themes again, engaging with and reflecting on the lyrics created by KAOS, Tasha Harvey and Jamie Feeney, aka Sapien. At the end of the *Politricks* video we see the presentation of a set of flash cards, reading 'Say No to the Cuts', 'Focus on Local Views' and 'Promote Equality' – these are the messages that bring the collection, *Our Changing Land*, to an end, and for the last word and take-home message, I offer the hopes and fears presented in the final lines of *Politricks*:

> And I, dream of a future where the government try
> To do right by the people, just living their lives
> But we're stuck in the system, funding's cut by the knife.

References

Ashton, S., 'The farmer needs a wife: women in rural Wales', in J. Aaron, T. Rees, S. Betts and M. Vincentelli (eds), *Our Sisters' Land: The Changing Identities of Women in Wales* (Cardiff: University of Wales Press, 1994), pp. 122–39.

Barlow, H., *Small Country, Big History: Themes in the History of Wales – The Reader* (Milton Keynes: The Open University, 2009).

Blandford, S., 'Cultural representation', in H. Mackay (ed.), *Understanding Contemporary Wales* (Cardiff: University of Wales Press and The Open University, 2010), pp. 268–99.

Chaney, P., *Equal Opportunities and Human Rights: The First Decade of Devolution* (Manchester: Equality and Human Rights Commission, 2009).

Crawley, H., *Race and Racism in Wales: An Exploratory Study* (Swansea: Race Council Cymru, 2012).

Crwydren, R., 'Welsh lesbian feminist: a contradiction in terms?', in J. Aaron, T. Rees, S. Betts and M. Vincentelli (eds), *Our Sisters' Land: The Changing Identities of Women in Wales* (Cardiff: University of Wales Press, 1994), pp. 294–300.

Currie, J., Harris, P. and Thiele, B., 'Sacrifices in Greedy Universities: Are They Gendered?', *Gender and Education*, 12/3 (2000), 269–91.

Dafydd, C., *Random Deaths and Custard* (Llandysul: Gwasg Gomer, 2007).

——, *Random Births and Love Hearts* (Llandysul: Gwasg Gomer, 2015).

Edwards, R., *Mature Women Students: Separating or Connecting Family and Education* (London: Taylor Francis, 1993).

Garland, P., 'Educating Rhian: experiences of mature women students', in J. Aaron, T. Rees, S. Betts and M. Vincentelli (eds), *Our Sisters' Land: The Changing Identities of Women in Wales* (Cardiff: University of Wales Press, 1994), pp. 107–21.

Gruffudd, H., 'Young People's Use of Welsh: The Influence of Home and Community', *Contemporary Wales*, 10 (1997), 200–18.

Hollway, W., *The Capacity to Care: Gender and Ethical Subjectivity* (London: Routledge, 2006).

Ivinson, G. M. and Renold, E., 'Valleys' Girls: Re-theorising Bodies and Agency in a Semi-rural Post-industrial Locale', *Gender and Education*, 25/6 (2013), 704–21.

McKenzie Hedger, M., 'Wind Energy: the Debate in Wales', *Contemporary Wales*, 7 (1994), 117–34.

Mannay, D., *Visual, Narrative and Creative Research Methods: Application, Reflection and Ethics* (London: Routledge, 2016).

Morgan, E., 'Identity and religion', in J. Aaron, T. Rees, S. Betts and M. Vincentelli (eds), *Our Sisters' Land: The Changing Identities of Women in Wales* (Cardiff: University of Wales Press, 1994), pp. 267–72.

Rees, T., 'Women and paid work in Wales', in J. Aaron, T. Rees, S. Betts and M. Vincentelli (eds), *Our Sisters' Land: The Changing Identities of Women in Wales* (Cardiff: University of Wales Press, 1994).

Renold, E. and Ringrose, J., 'Schizoid Subjectivities? Re-theorizing Teen Girls' Sexual Cultures in an Era of "Sexualization"', *Journal of Sociology*, 47/4 (2011), 389–409.

Ringrose, J., *Postfeminist Education: Girls and the Sexual Politics of Schooling* (Abington: Routledge, 2013).

—— and Renold, E., 'Normative Cruelties and Gender Deviants: The Performative Effects of Bully Discourses for Girls and Boys in School', *British Educational Research Journal*, 36/4 (2010), 573–96.

Robinson, V. and Gardner, H., 'Unravelling a stereotype: the lived experience of black and minority ethnic people in rural Wales', in N. Chakraborti and J. Garland (eds), *Rural Racism* (Abington: Routledge, 2004), pp. 85–107.

Vincentelli, M., 'Artefact and identity: the Welsh dresser as a domestic display and cultural symbol', in J. Aaron, T. Rees, S. Betts and M. Vincentelli (eds),

Our Sisters' Land: The Changing Identities of Women in Wales (Cardiff: University of Wales Press, 1994), pp. 228–41.

WalesOnline, *Merthyr Tydfil Bids Farewell to Hoover Factory*, 13 March (2009), *www.walesonline.co.uk/news/wales-news/merthyr-tydfil-bids-farewell-hoover-2117675* (accessed 22 November 2015).

Ward, M. R. M., '"I'm a geek I am": Academic Achievement and the Performance of a Studious Working-Class Masculinity', *Gender and Education*, 26/7 (2014), 709–25.

Wenger, G. C., 'Old women in rural Wales: variations in adaption', in J. Aaron, T. Rees, S. Betts and M. Vincentelli (eds), *Our Sisters' Land: The Changing Identities of Women in Wales* (Cardiff: University of Wales Press, 1994), pp. 61–88.

Wetherell, M., *Affect and Emotion: A New Social Science Understanding* (London: Sage, 2012).

Williams, C., '"Race" and racism: What's special about Wales?', in D. Dunkerley and A. Thompson (eds), *Wales Today* (Cardiff: University of Wales Press, 1999), pp. 269–86.

——, *Sugar and Slate* (Aberystwyth: Planet, 2002).

Wooding, N., 'Equal opportunities', in J. Osmond (ed.), *The National Assembly Agenda: A Handbook for the First Four Years* (Cardiff: Institute of Welsh Affairs, 1998), pp. 94–100.

Index

Gender Pay Gap xiv, 11, 184, 186,
187, 188, 189, 191, 226, 233
Generation xiii, xvii, 2, 7, 12, 17, 26,
27, 29, 30, 34, 37, 39, 65, 67, 68,
72, 73, 74, 75, 79, 81, 82, 85,
113, 122, 205, 207, 208, 214,
262, 272, 276, 290, 297
Gething, Vaughan 167, 170
Gheradi, Silvia 174, 193
Gibbs, Sara 63
Giddens, Anthony 113, 126
Giles, Howard 50, 55, 56, 62, 63
Giles, Mary 14
Gleeson, Dennis 131, 148
Global warming 38
Goffman, Erving 89, 90, 95, 97, 100,
105
Goldethorpe, John 202, 217
Gornall, Lynne 139, 147, 148, 149
Gough, Lucy 30, 31, 40
Government of Wales Act 1998, 2006
176, 188
Gramich, Katie ii, 30, 40
Gray, Anne 140, 148
Gray, Tim 283
Green, Anne 164, 171
Griffin, Christine 67, 84
Grimshaw, Damian 185, 187, 195
Gross Value Added 180, 191, 201,
217, 218
Gruffudd, Heini 6, 7, 16, 43, 44, 46,
47, 48, 54, 55, 56, 57, 60, 61, 62,
289, 302
Gurner, Richard 243, 258
Gwanas, Bethan 27, 28, 40

Habermas, Jürgen 241, 258
Hadley, Tessa 26, 40
Haggett, Claire 264, 276, 277, 278,
283, 285
Haggett, Michael 244, 258
Hague, Douglas 153, 161, 170
Hakim, Catherine 177, 193
Hall, Tom 16, 220, 235, 236
Hamilton, Paul 285
Hammer, Nik 157, 170
Harbottle, Lynnette 139, 142, 147
Hargreaves, Andy 138, 148

Harris, Anita 143, 148
Harris, John 91, 105
Harris, Keith 99, 105
Harris, Patricia 126
Harvey, Tasha v, xi, xiv, xix, 14, 109,
296, 301
Hatt, Susan 115, 127
Hayes, Steven 157, 171
Hegemonic masculinity 78
Heller, Monica 58, 59, 62
Henriques, Julian 83, 84
Henry, Leo 53, 62
Hermann, Claudine 194
Higher education xiii, xiv, xv, 9, 93,
98, 112, 113, 114, 115, 116, 117,
119, 122, 123, 124, 125, 126,
127, 128, 143, 145, 162, 181,
190, 293
Higher Education Funding Council
for Wales (HEFCW) 115, 127
Hilden, Jytte 194
Hill, Michael 115, 127
Hills, John 175, 193
Hindess, Barry 201, 217
Hjellbrekke, Johs 217
Hochschild, Arlie 138, 148
Hodges, Rhian 48, 59, 62
Hodgson, Ann 130, 148
Hodkinson, Paul 99, 100, 105
Holland, Sally 91, 105
Hollway, Wendy 76, 80, 84, 121, 127,
135, 148, 293, 302
Homebirds 133
Homer, Ian vii, xi, xiii, xix, 15, 21,
42, 64, 87, 111, 129, 151, 173,
199, 219, 260, 288, 290, 295,
297
Honno Press ix, 24
Hopkins, Peter 89, 105
Hopwood, Mererid 23
Horbarty, Robert 285
House of Commons Library 165, 170
Housework v, 7, 17, 65, 67, 68, 73,
74, 75, 76, 77, 79, 81, 84, 85,
147, 290
Howe, P. David 91, 105
Howes, Yuko 264, 276, 277, 278, 284
Hoyle, Eric 142, 148

309